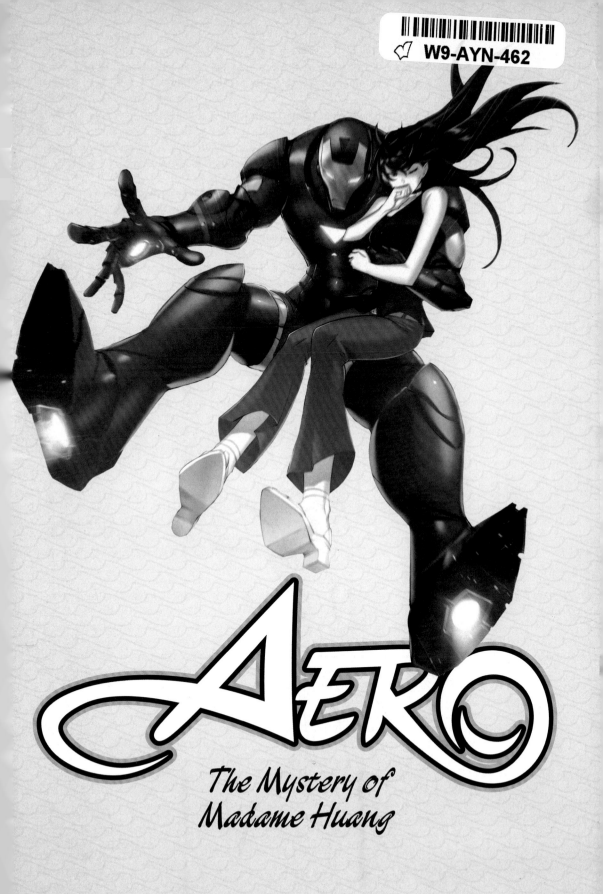

AERO

The Mystery of Madame Huang

Lei Ling is a brilliant architect in Shanghai who leads a secret double life as the wind-manipulating super hero Aero. Having a successful career while protecting her beloved city isn't easy, nor is balancing it all with her relationship with her boyfriend, Zou Yu.

As Aero, Ling has been dealing with series of attacks by mysterious, white-jade monsters who have appeared alongside strange spires throughout the city. She also had to deflect Zou Yu's suspicions about her secret identity, further straining their relationship. But Zou Yu isn't the only one closing in on the truth about Aero...Enter the mysterious Madame Huang!

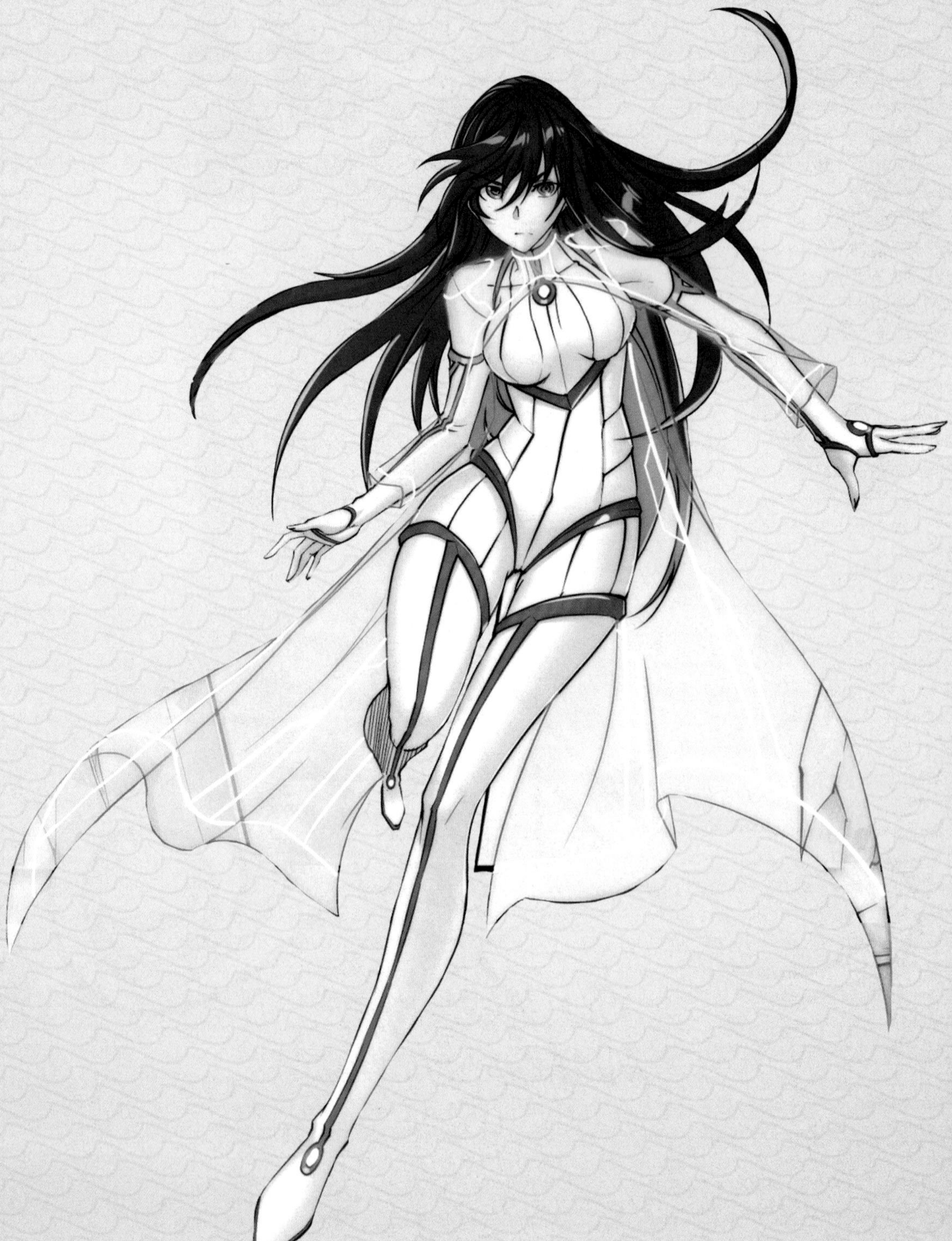

With the power of the wind at her command, Lei Ling is the master of the sky! She is the astonishing, awe-inspiring...

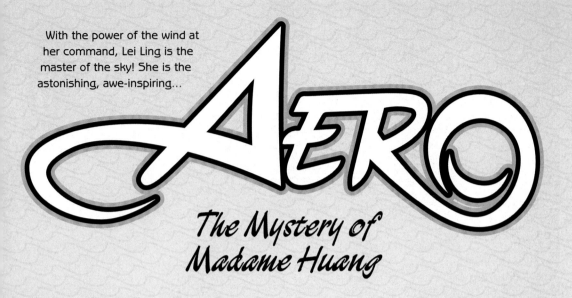

AERO

The Mystery of Madame Huang

Zhou Liefen
Writer

Keng
Artist

Amy Chu
Adaptation

VC's Joe Caramagna with **Joe Sabino** (#9)
Letterers

Keng
Cover Art

Carlos Lao
Logo Design

Martin Biro & **Tom Groneman**
Assistant Editors

Mark Paniccia
Editor

Special Thanks to
Winni Woo, Yifan Jiang & **Alexander Chang**

Collection Editor **Jennifer Grünwald**
Assistant Managing Editor **Maia Loy**
Assistant Managing Editor **Lisa Montalbano**
VP Production & Special Projects **Jeff Youngquist**
Book Designers **Stacie Zucker** with **Adam Del Re**
SVP Print, Sales & Marketing **David Gabriel**
Editor in Chief **C.B. Cebulski**

AERO VOL. 2: THE MYSTERY OF MADAME HUANG. Contains material originally published in magazine form as AERO (2019) #7-12. First printing 2020. ISBN 978-1-302-91945-0. Published by MARVEL WORLDWIDE, INC., a subsidiary of MARVEL ENTERTAINMENT, LLC. OFFICE OF PUBLICATION: 1290 Avenue of the Americas, New York, NY 10104. © 2020 MARVEL No similarity between any of the names, characters, persons, and/or institutions in this magazine with those of any living or dead person or institution is intended, and any such similarity which may exist is purely coincidental. **Printed in Canada.** KEVIN FEIGE, Chief Creative Officer; DAN BUCKLEY, President, Marvel Entertainment; JOHN NEE, Publisher; JOE QUESADA, EVP & Creative Director; TOM BREVOORT, SVP of Publishing; DAVID BOGART, Associate Publisher & SVP of Talent Affairs; Publishing & Partnership; DAVID GABRIEL, VP of Print & Digital Publishing; JEFF YOUNGQUIST, VP of Production & Special Projects; DAN CARR, Executive Director of Publishing Technology; ALEX MORALES, Director of Publishing Operations; DAN EDINGTON, Managing Editor; RICKEY PURDIN, Director of Talent Relations; SUSAN CRESPI, Production Manager; STAN LEE, Chairman Emeritus. For information regarding advertising in Marvel Comics or on Marvel.com, please contact Vit DeBellis, Custom Solutions & Integrated Advertising Manager, at vdebellis@marvel.com. For Marvel subscription inquiries, please call 888-511-5480. **Manufactured between 10/30/2020 and 12/1/2020 by SOLISCO PRINTERS, SCOTT, QC, CANADA.**

10 9 8 7 6 5 4 3 2 1

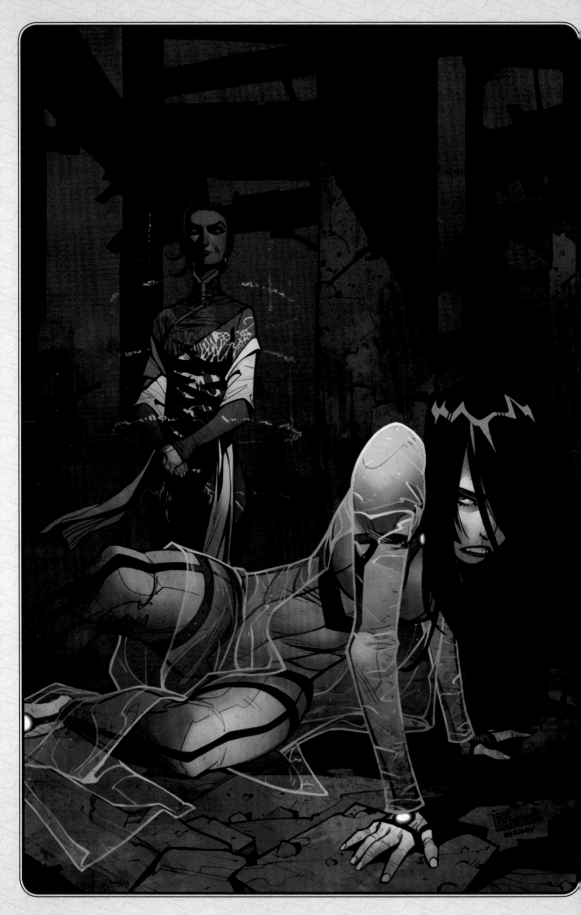

7 Beginnings

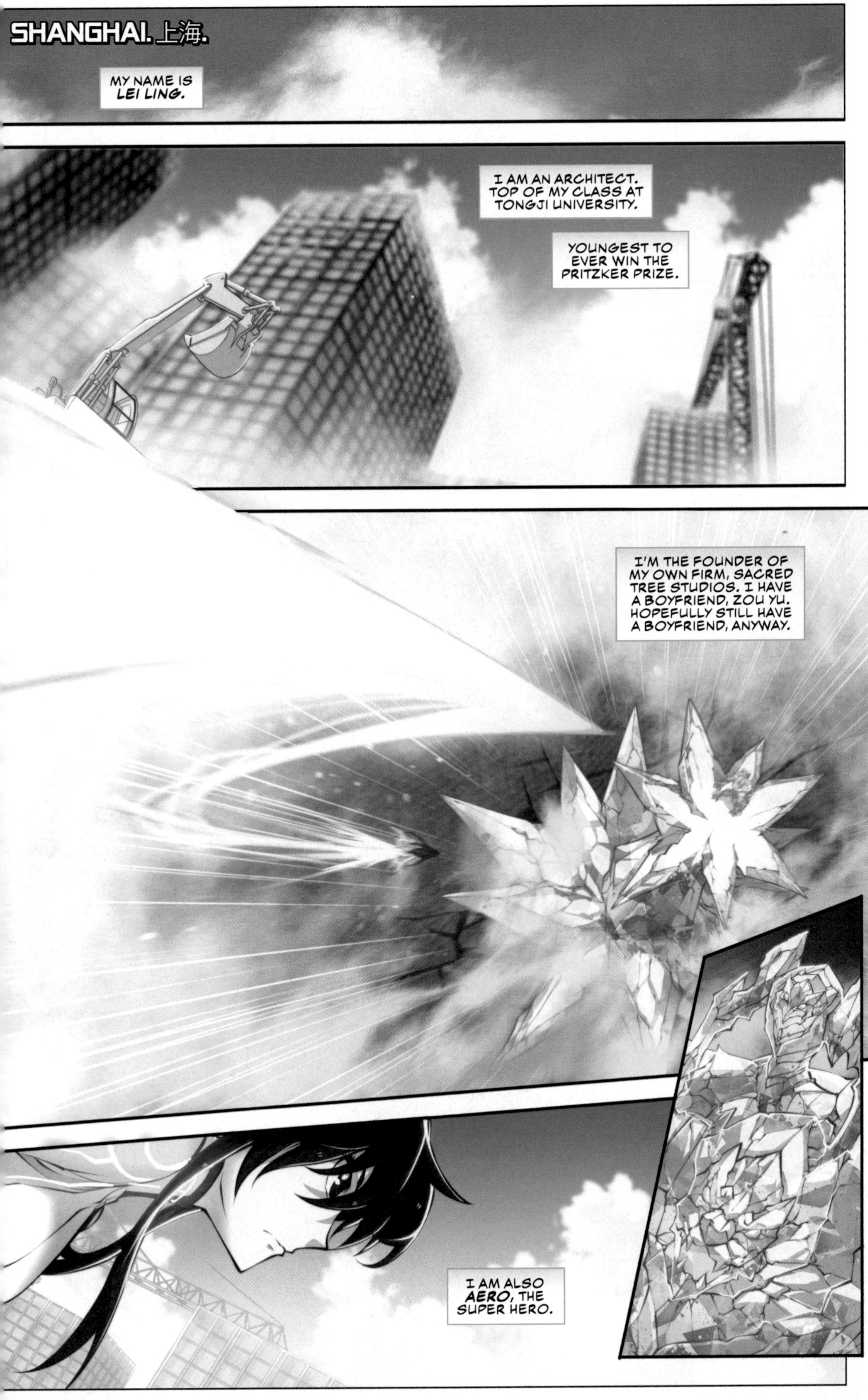

SHANGHAI. 上海.
MY NAME IS LEI LING.
I AM AN ARCHITECT. TOP OF MY CLASS AT TONGJI UNIVERSITY.
YOUNGEST TO EVER WIN THE PRITZKER PRIZE.
I'M THE FOUNDER OF MY OWN FIRM, SACRED TREE STUDIOS. I HAVE A BOYFRIEND, ZOU YU. HOPEFULLY STILL HAVE A BOYFRIEND, ANYWAY.
I AM ALSO AERO, THE SUPER HERO.

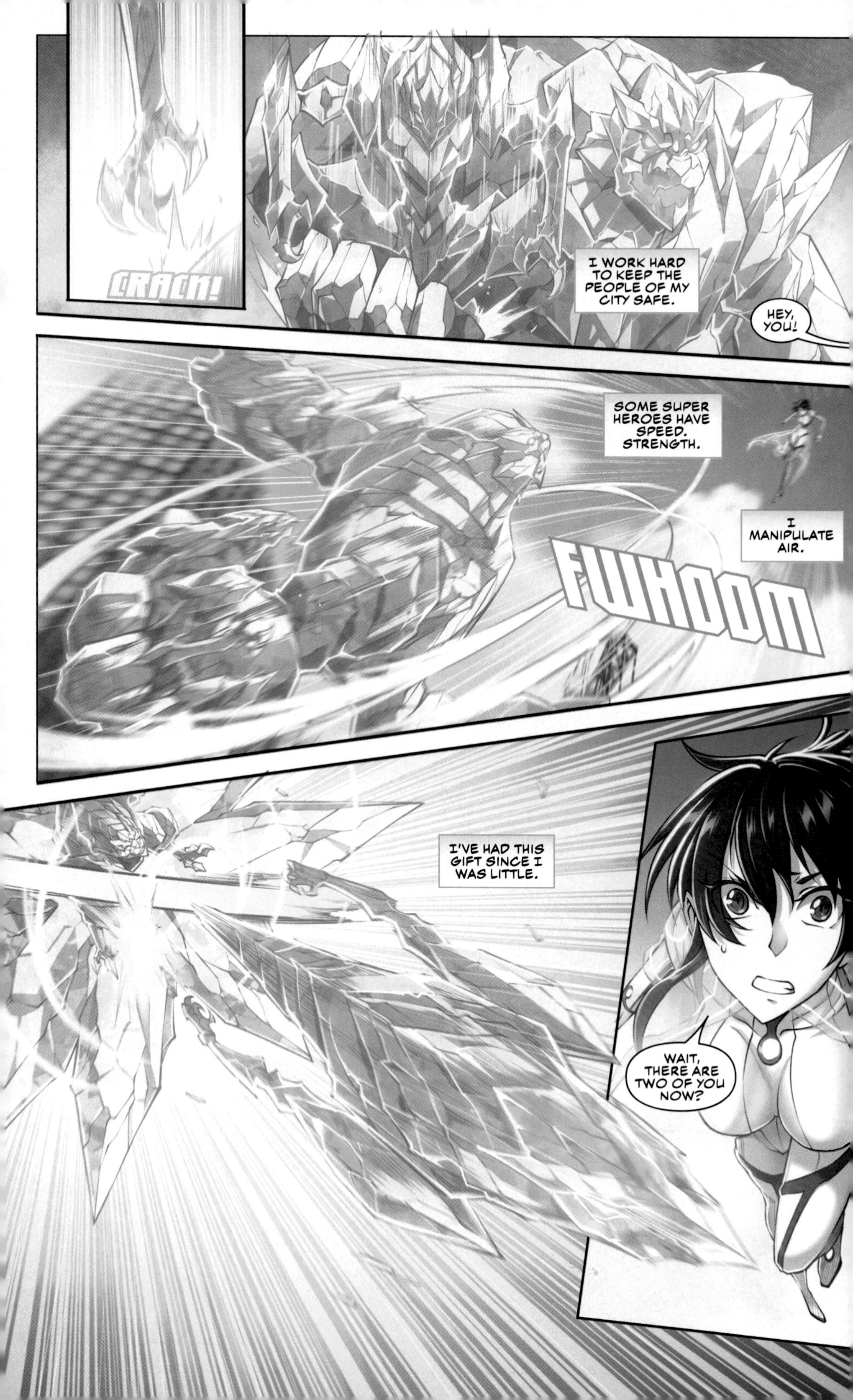
CRACK!
I WORK HARD TO KEEP THE PEOPLE OF MY CITY SAFE.
HEY, YOU!
SOME SUPER HEROES HAVE SPEED. STRENGTH.
I MANIPULATE AIR.
FWHOOM
I'VE HAD THIS GIFT SINCE I WAS LITTLE.
WAIT, THERE ARE TWO OF YOU NOW?

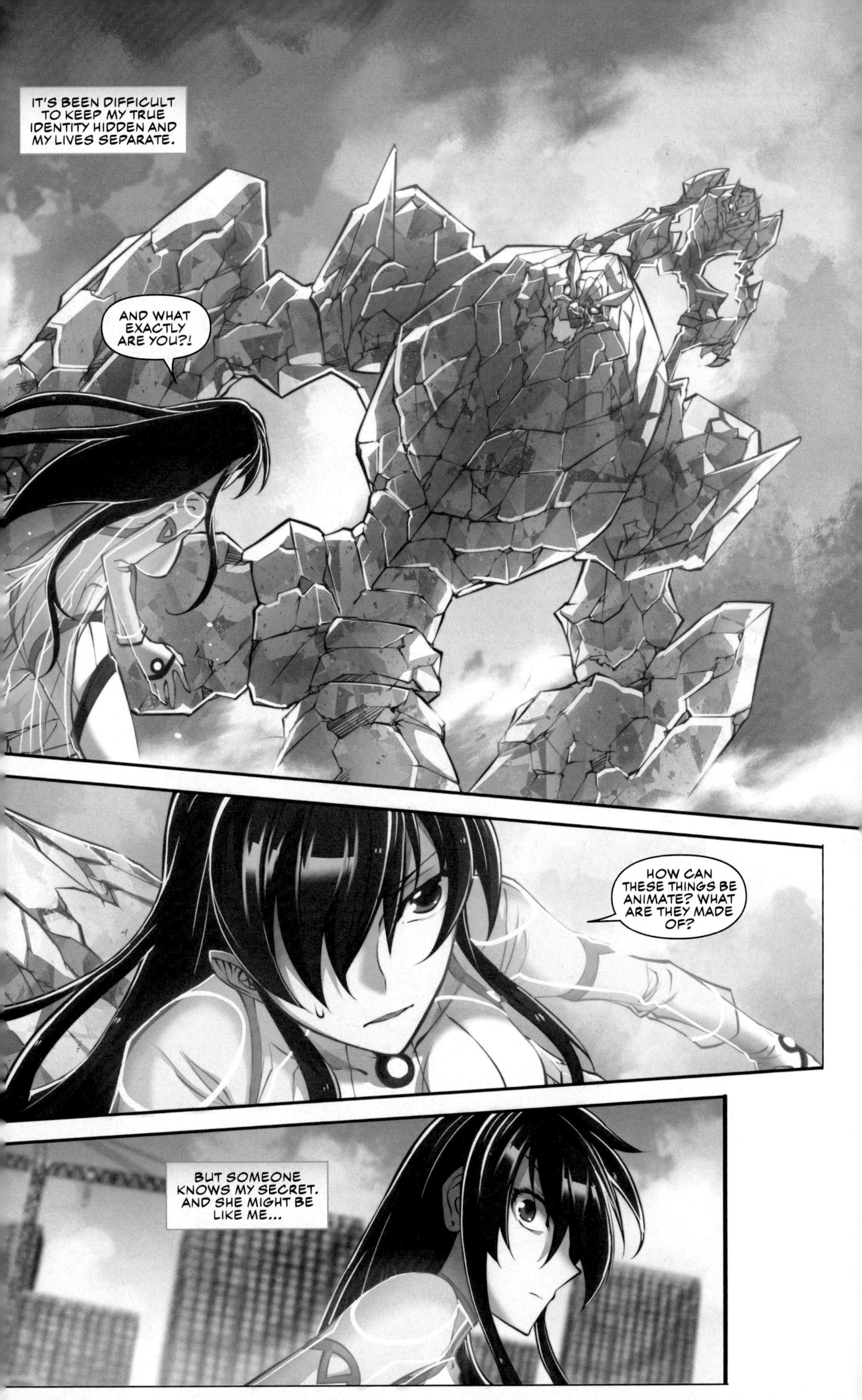
IT'S BEEN DIFFICULT TO KEEP MY TRUE IDENTITY HIDDEN AND MY LIVES SEPARATE.
AND WHAT EXACTLY ARE YOU?!
HOW CAN THESE THINGS BE ANIMATE? WHAT ARE THEY MADE OF?
BUT SOMEONE KNOWS MY SECRET. AND SHE MIGHT BE LIKE ME...

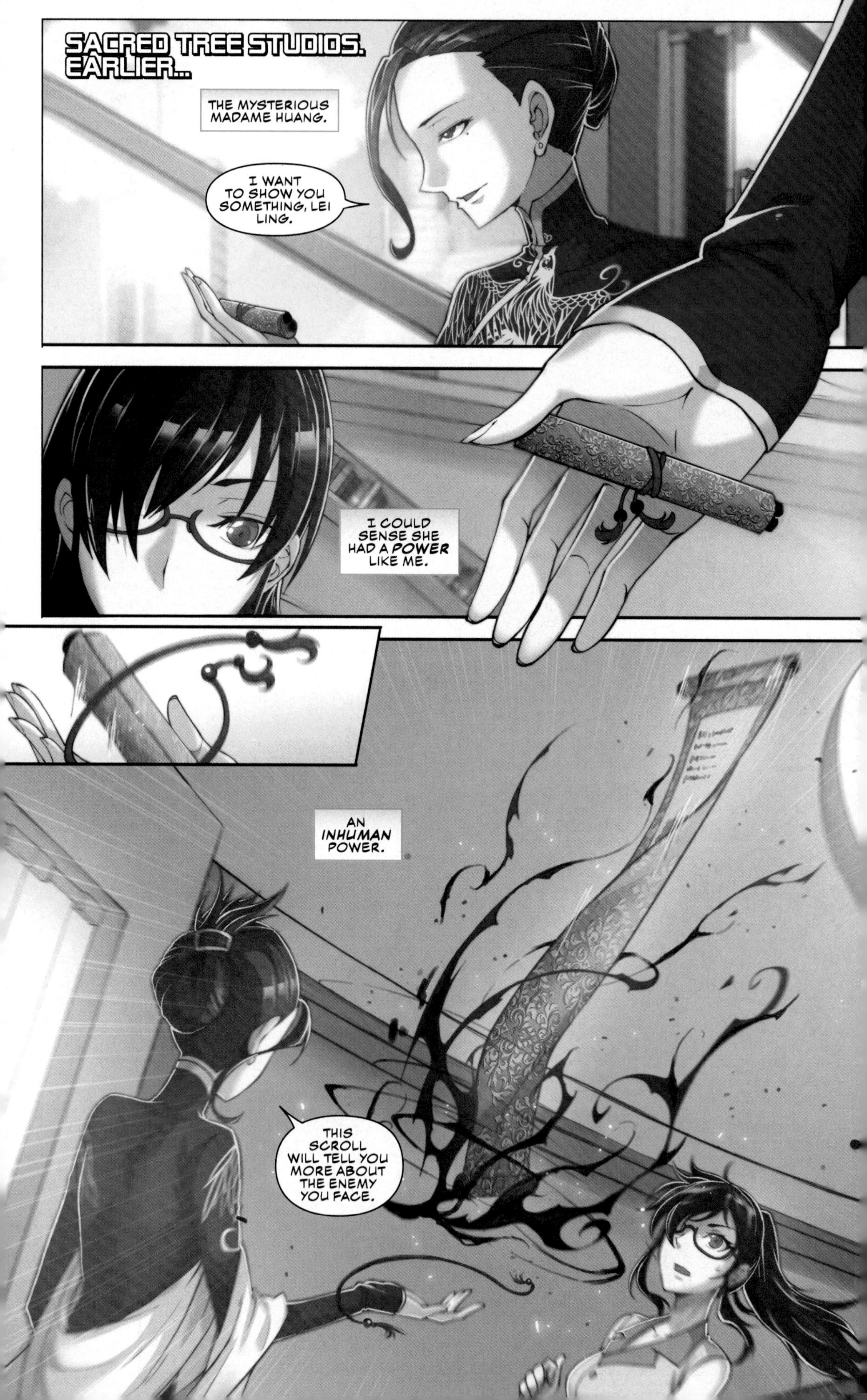
SACRED TREE STUDIOS. EARLIER...
THE MYSTERIOUS MADAME HUANG.
I WANT TO SHOW YOU SOMETHING, LEI LING.
I COULD SENSE SHE HAD A POWER LIKE ME.
AN INHUMAN POWER.
THIS SCROLL WILL TELL YOU MORE ABOUT THE ENEMY YOU FACE.

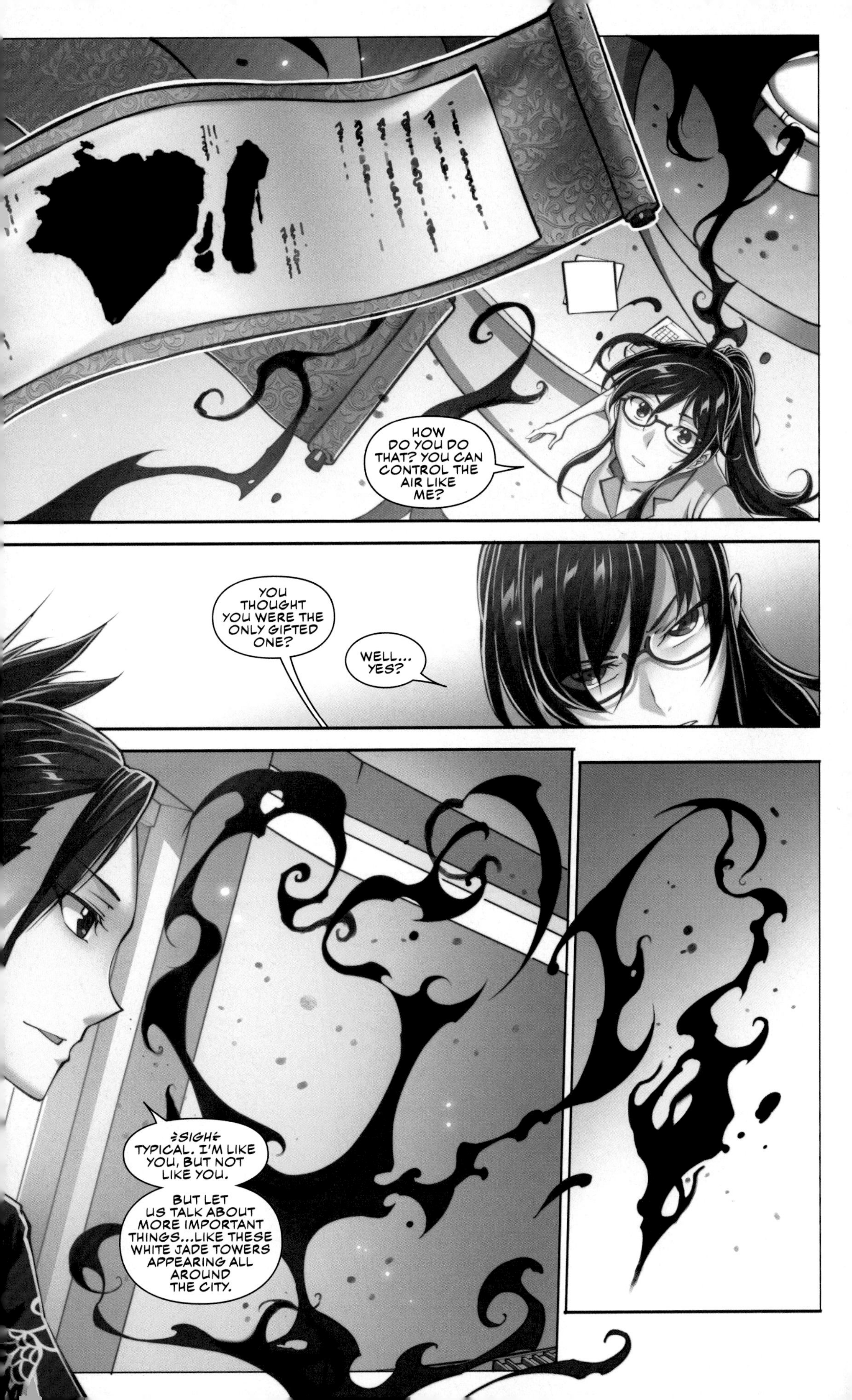
HOW DO YOU DO THAT? YOU CAN CONTROL THE AIR LIKE ME?
YOU THOUGHT YOU WERE THE ONLY GIFTED ONE?
WELL... YES?
SIGH
TYPICAL. I'M LIKE YOU, BUT NOT LIKE YOU.
BUT LET US TALK ABOUT MORE IMPORTANT THINGS...LIKE THESE WHITE JADE TOWERS APPEARING ALL AROUND THE CITY.

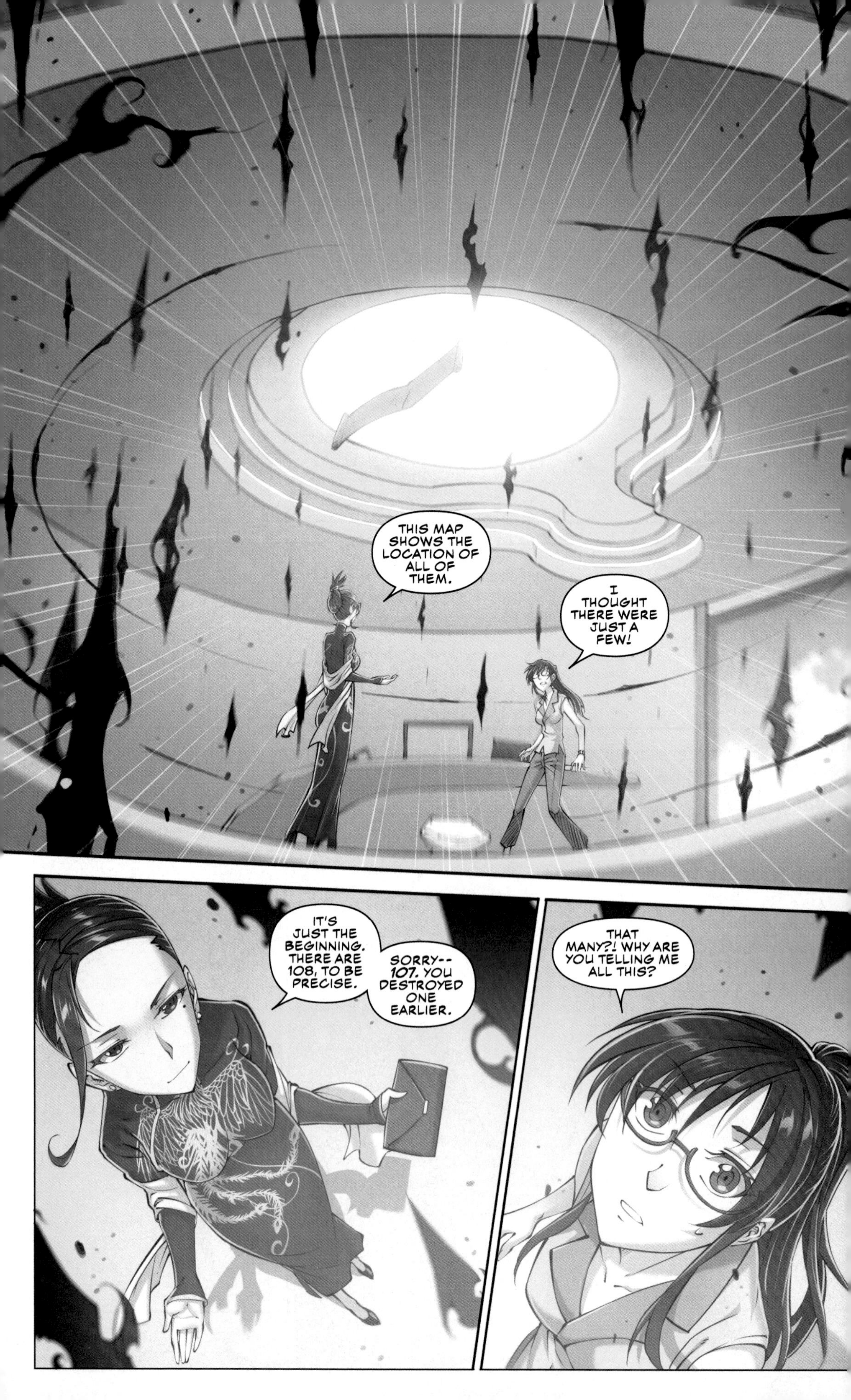
THIS MAP SHOWS THE LOCATION OF ALL OF THEM.
I THOUGHT THERE WERE JUST A FEW!
IT'S JUST THE BEGINNING. THERE ARE 108, TO BE PRECISE.
SORRY-- 107. YOU DESTROYED ONE EARLIER.
THAT MANY?! WHY ARE YOU TELLING ME ALL THIS?

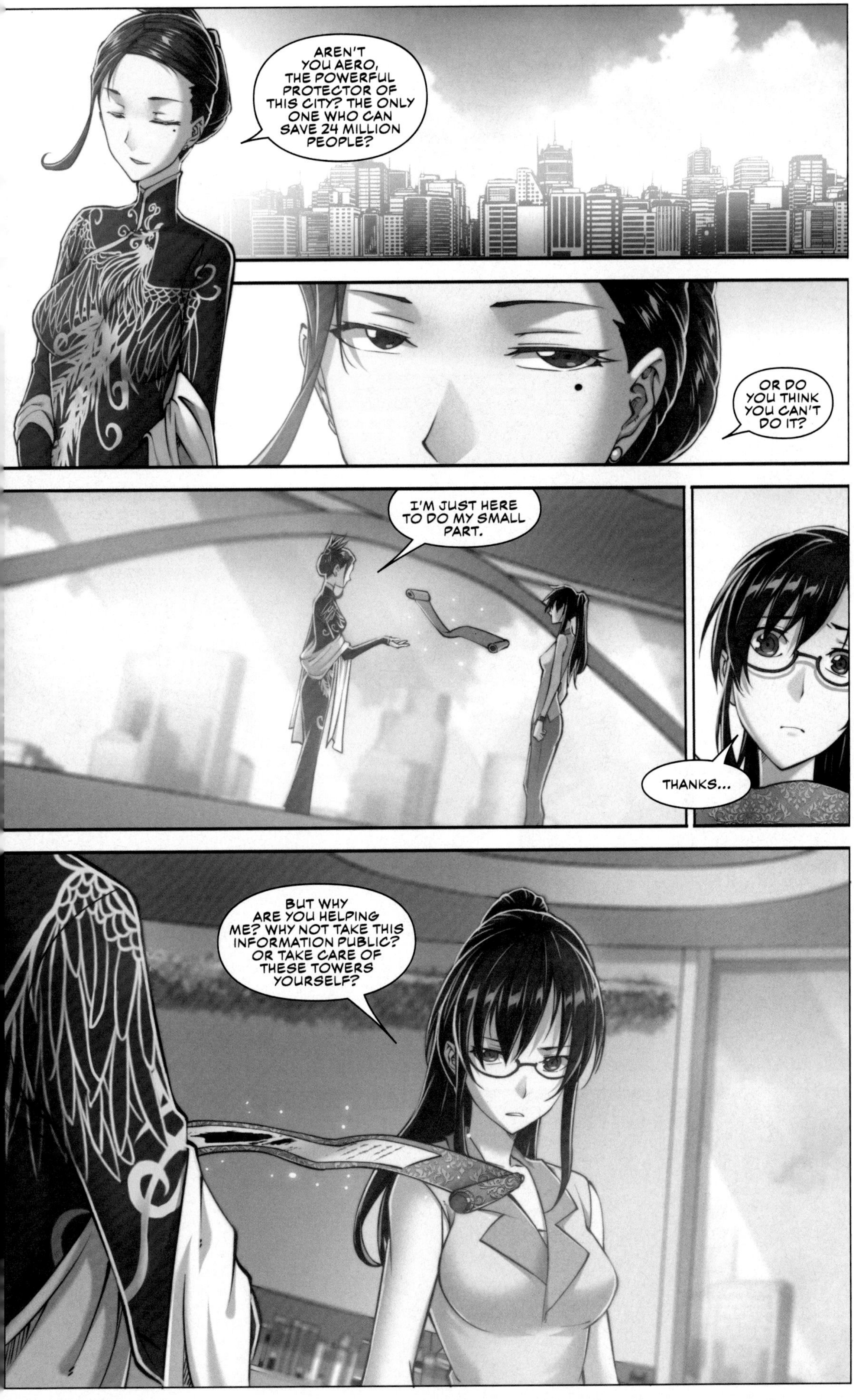
AREN'T YOU AERO, THE POWERFUL PROTECTOR OF THIS CITY? THE ONLY ONE WHO CAN SAVE 24 MILLION PEOPLE?
OR DO YOU THINK YOU CAN'T DO IT?
I'M JUST HERE TO DO MY SMALL PART.
THANKS...
BUT WHY ARE YOU HELPING ME? WHY NOT TAKE THIS INFORMATION PUBLIC? OR TAKE CARE OF THESE TOWERS YOURSELF?

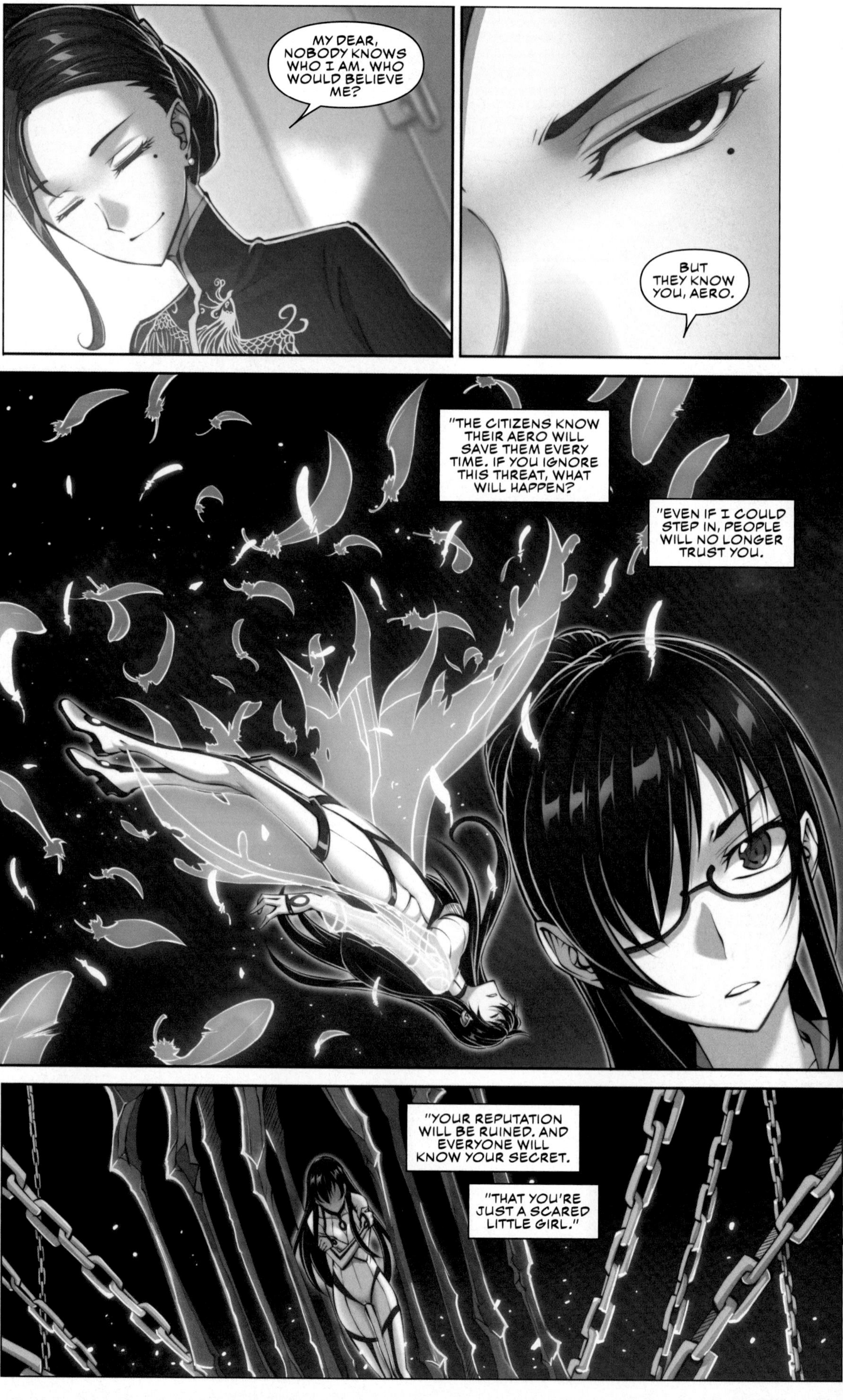
MY DEAR, NOBODY KNOWS WHO I AM. WHO WOULD BELIEVE ME?
BUT THEY KNOW YOU, AERO.
"THE CITIZENS KNOW THEIR AERO WILL SAVE THEM EVERY TIME. IF YOU IGNORE THIS THREAT, WHAT WILL HAPPEN?
"EVEN IF I COULD STEP IN, PEOPLE WILL NO LONGER TRUST YOU.
"YOUR REPUTATION WILL BE RUINED. AND EVERYONE WILL KNOW YOUR SECRET.
"THAT YOU'RE JUST A SCARED LITTLE GIRL."

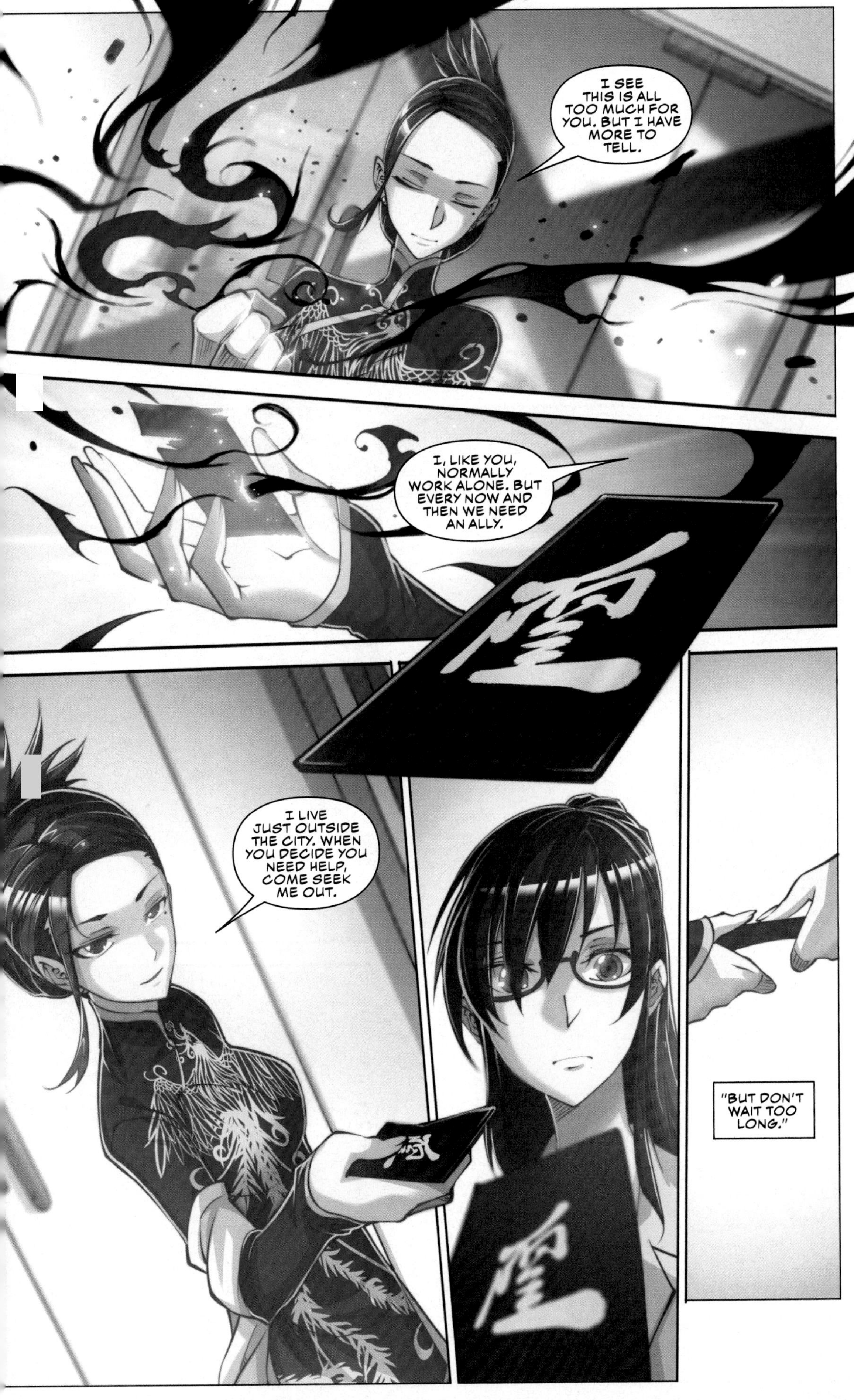
I SEE THIS IS ALL TOO MUCH FOR YOU. BUT I HAVE MORE TO TELL.
I, LIKE YOU, NORMALLY WORK ALONE. BUT EVERY NOW AND THEN WE NEED AN ALLY.
I LIVE JUST OUTSIDE THE CITY. WHEN YOU DECIDE YOU NEED HELP, COME SEEK ME OUT.
"BUT DON'T WAIT TOO LONG."

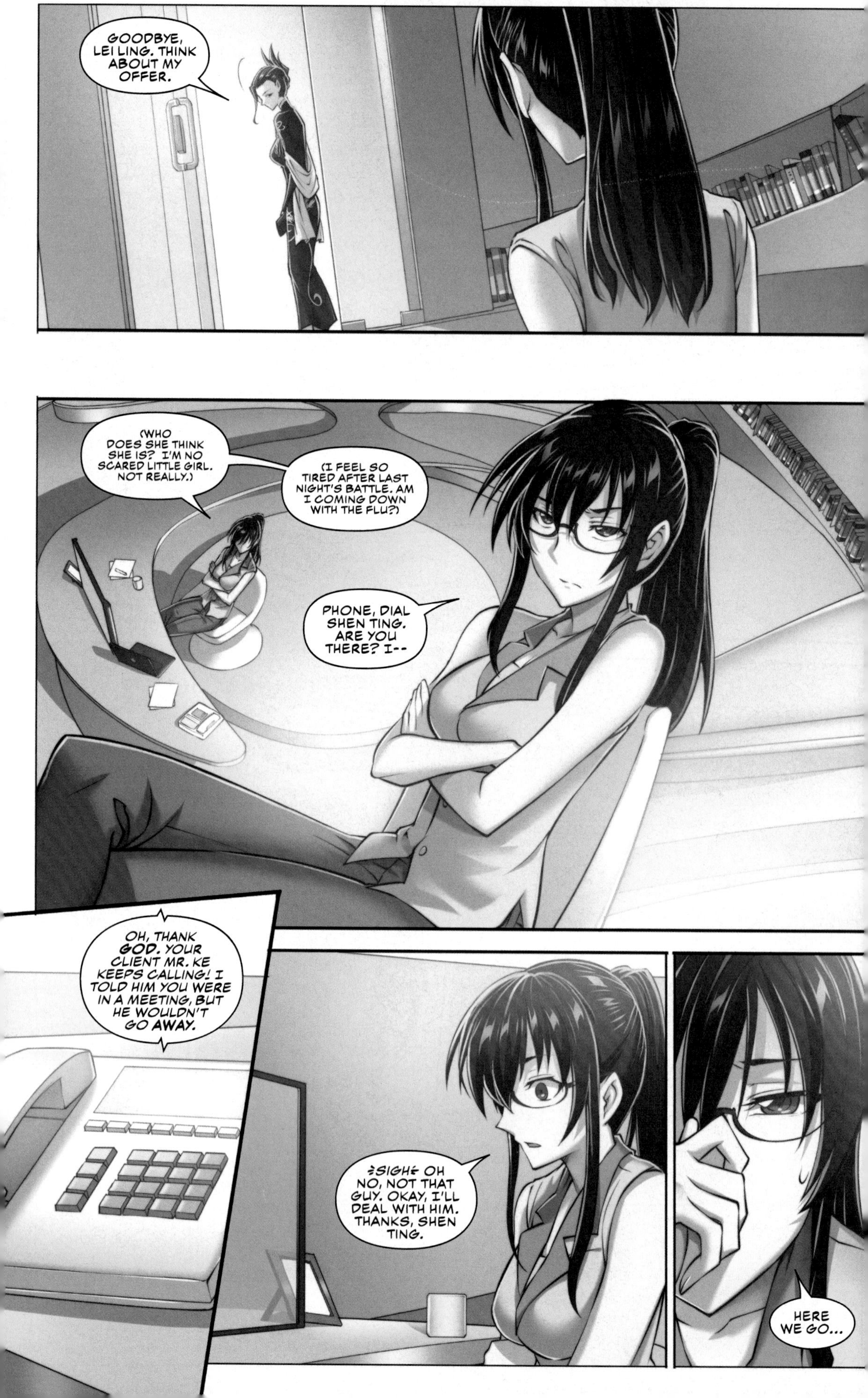
GOODBYE, LEI LING. THINK ABOUT MY OFFER.
(WHO DOES SHE THINK SHE IS? I'M NO SCARED LITTLE GIRL. NOT REALLY.)
(I FEEL SO TIRED AFTER LAST NIGHT'S BATTLE. AM I COMING DOWN WITH THE FLU?)
PHONE, DIAL SHEN TING. ARE YOU THERE? I--
OH, THANK GOD. YOUR CLIENT MR. KE KEEPS CALLING! I TOLD HIM YOU WERE IN A MEETING, BUT HE WOULDN'T GO AWAY.
SIGH OH NO, NOT THAT GUY. OKAY, I'LL DEAL WITH HIM. THANKS, SHEN TING.
HERE WE GO...

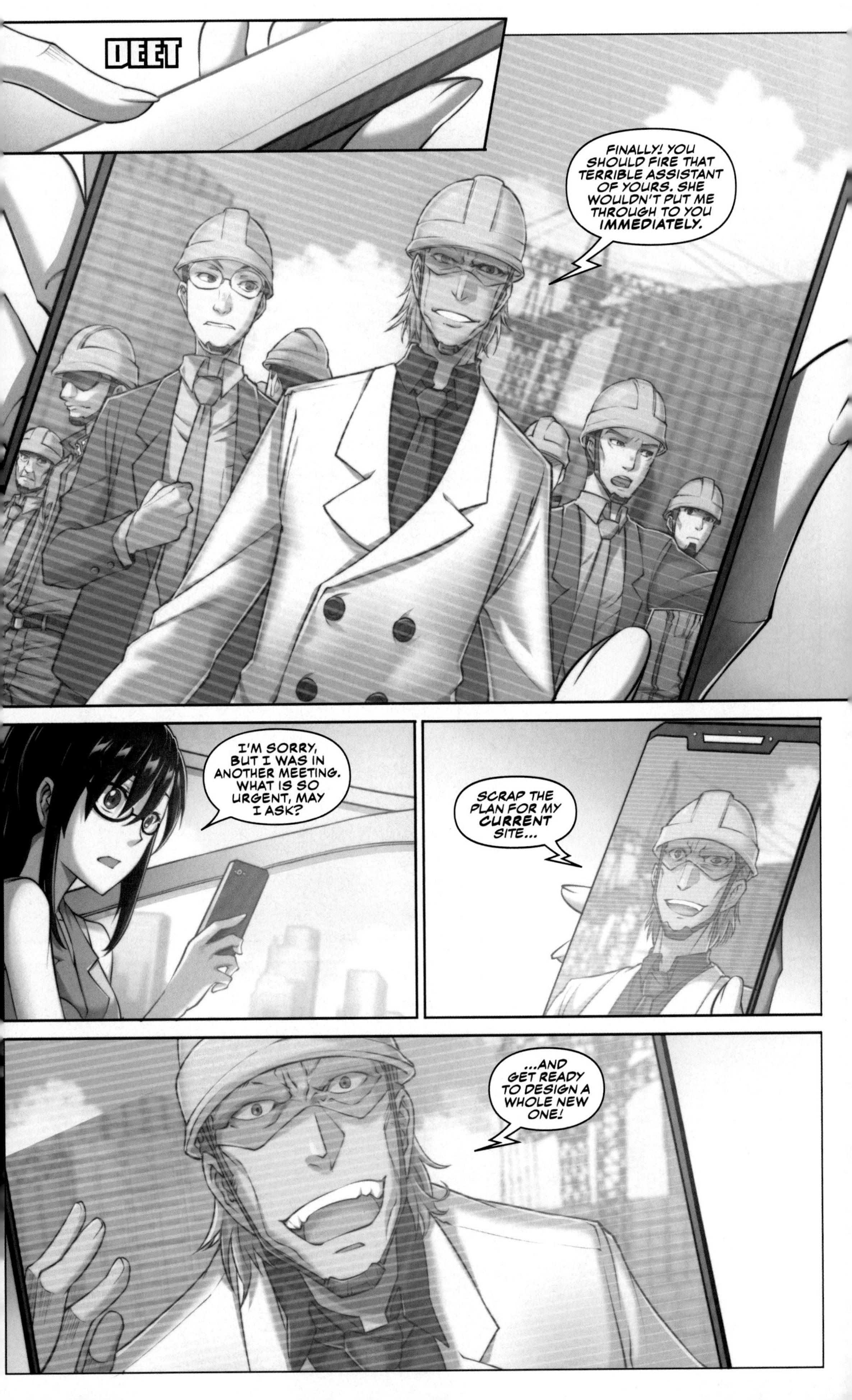
DEET
FINALLY! YOU SHOULD FIRE THAT TERRIBLE ASSISTANT OF YOURS. SHE WOULDN'T PUT ME THROUGH TO YOU IMMEDIATELY.
I'M SORRY, BUT I WAS IN ANOTHER MEETING. WHAT IS SO URGENT, MAY I ASK?
SCRAP THE PLAN FOR MY CURRENT SITE...
...AND GET READY TO DESIGN A WHOLE NEW ONE!

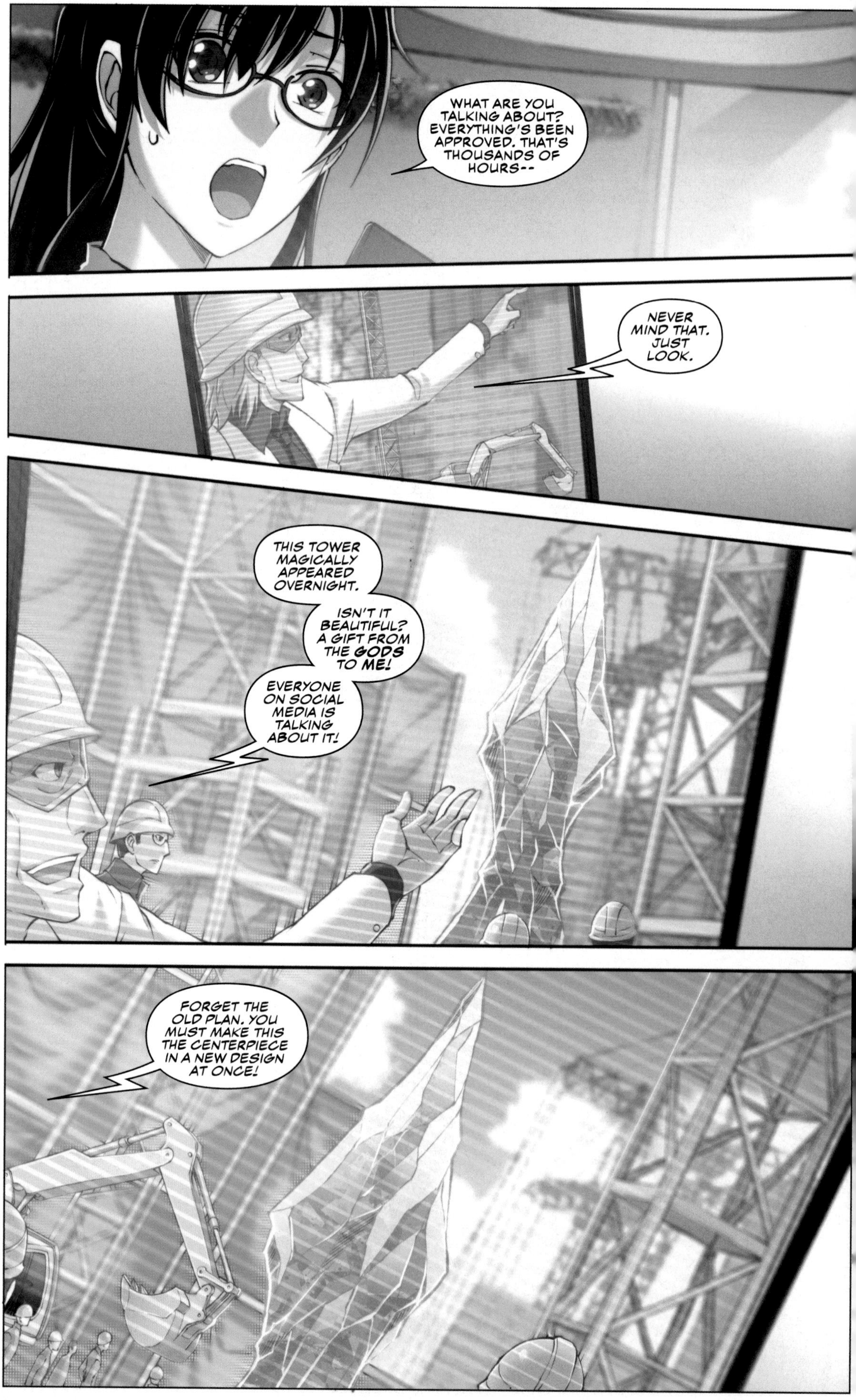
WHAT ARE YOU TALKING ABOUT? EVERYTHING'S BEEN APPROVED. THAT'S THOUSANDS OF HOURS--
NEVER MIND THAT. JUST LOOK.
THIS TOWER MAGICALLY APPEARED OVERNIGHT.
ISN'T IT BEAUTIFUL? A GIFT FROM THE GODS TO ME!
EVERYONE ON SOCIAL MEDIA IS TALKING ABOUT IT!
FORGET THE OLD PLAN. YOU MUST MAKE THIS THE CENTERPIECE IN A NEW DESIGN AT ONCE!

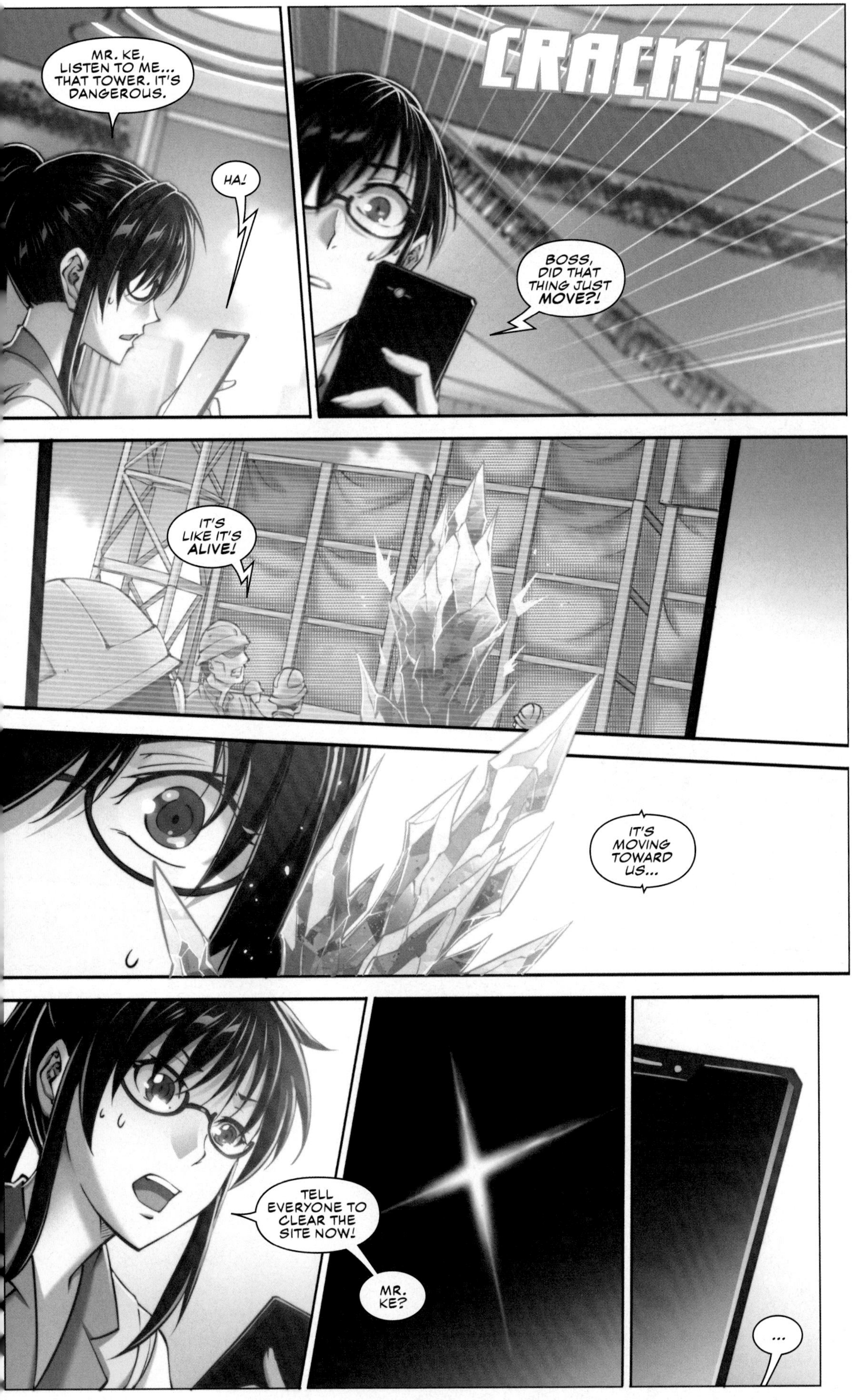
MR. KE, LISTEN TO ME... THAT TOWER. IT'S DANGEROUS.
HA!
CRACK!
BOSS, DID THAT THING JUST MOVE?!
IT'S LIKE IT'S ALIVE!
IT'S MOVING TOWARD US...
TELL EVERYONE TO CLEAR THE SITE NOW!
MR. KE?
...

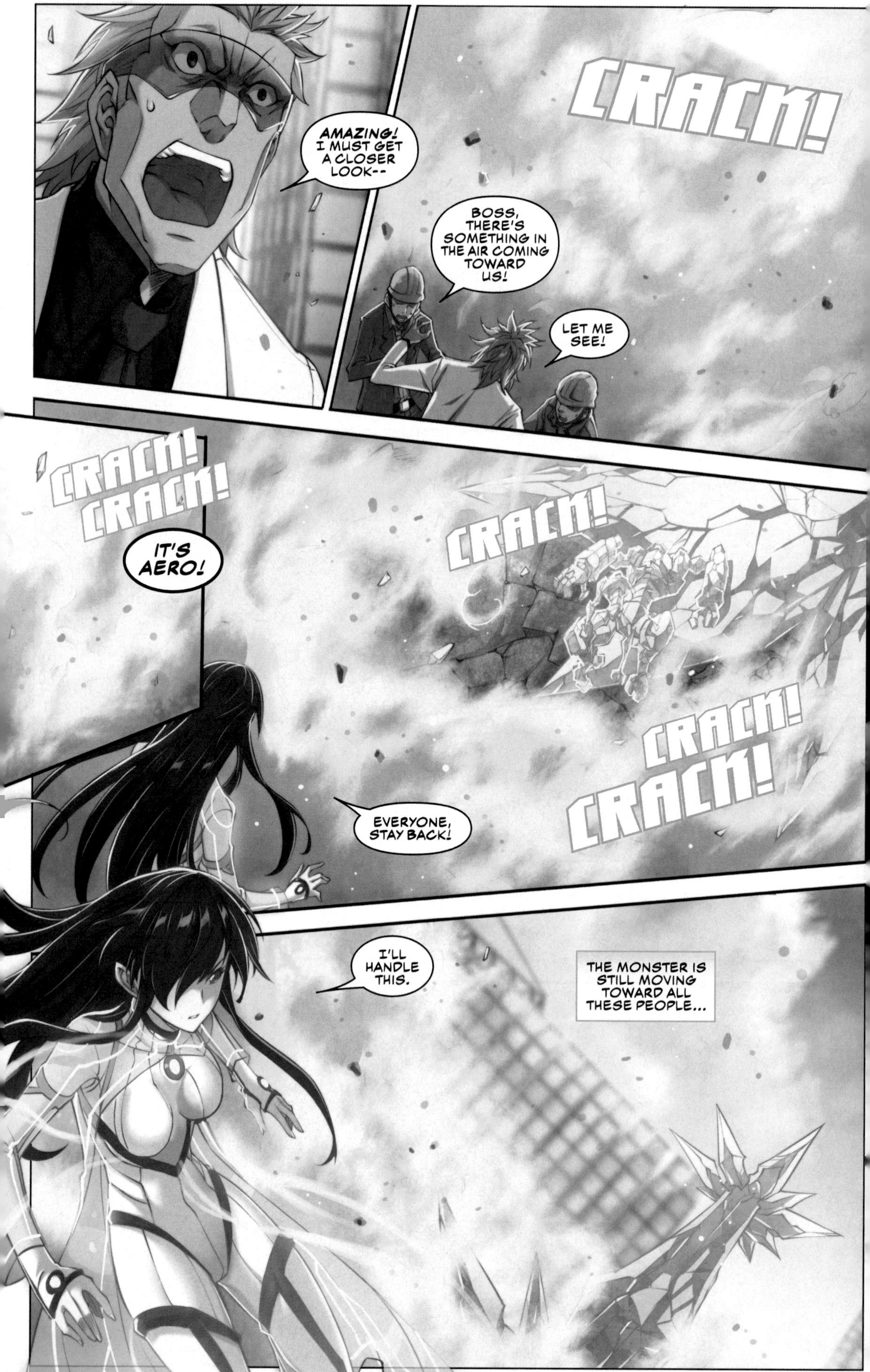
AMAZING! I MUST GET A CLOSER LOOK--
CRACK!
BOSS, THERE'S SOMETHING IN THE AIR COMING TOWARD US!
LET ME SEE!
CRACK! CRACK!
IT'S AERO!
CRACK!
CRACK! CRACK!
EVERYONE, STAY BACK!
I'LL HANDLE THIS.
THE MONSTER IS STILL MOVING TOWARD ALL THESE PEOPLE...

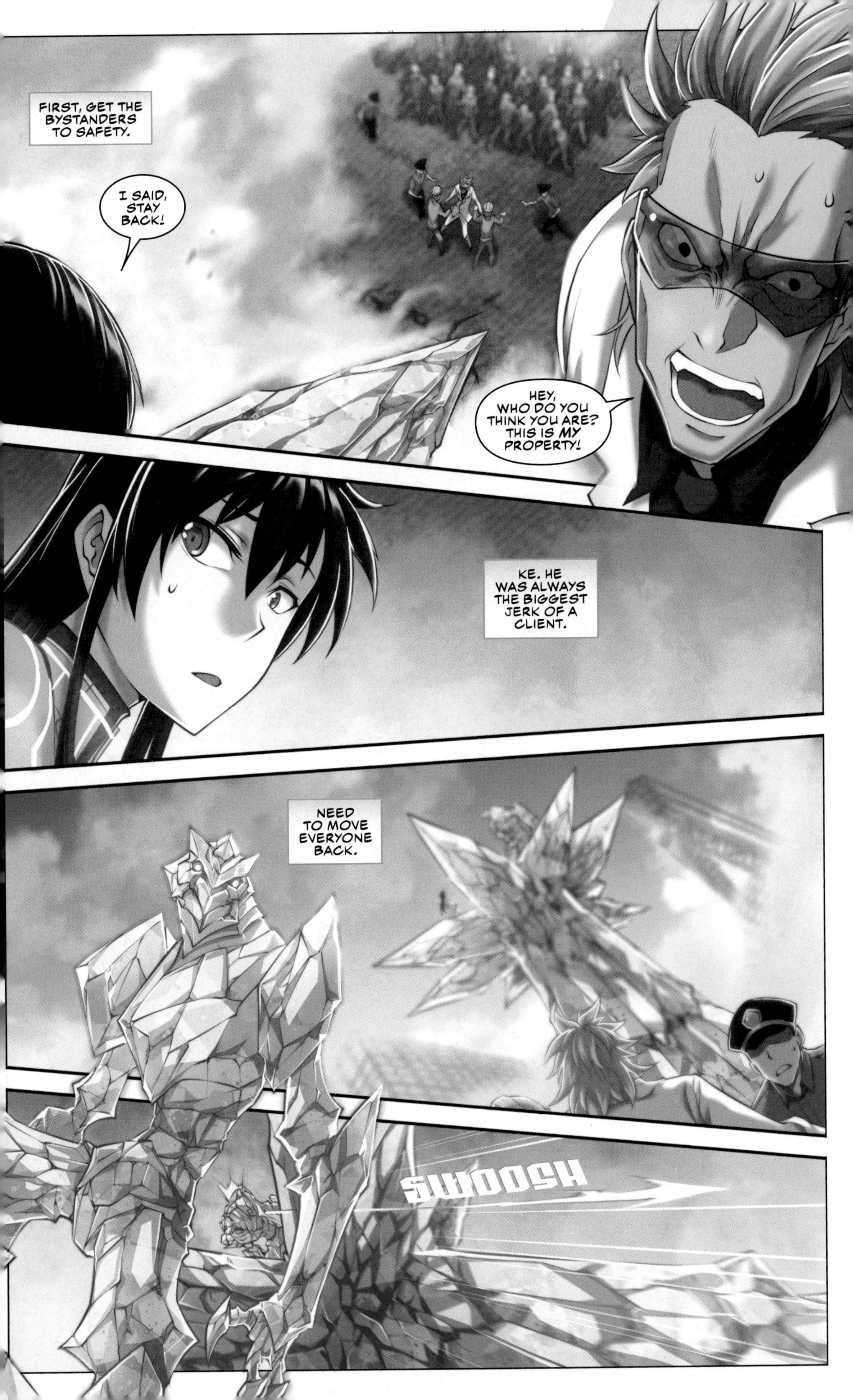
FIRST, GET THE BYSTANDERS TO SAFETY.
I SAID, STAY BACK!
HEY, WHO DO YOU THINK YOU ARE? THIS IS MY PROPERTY!
KE. HE WAS ALWAYS THE BIGGEST JERK OF A CLIENT.
NEED TO MOVE EVERYONE BACK.
SWOOSH

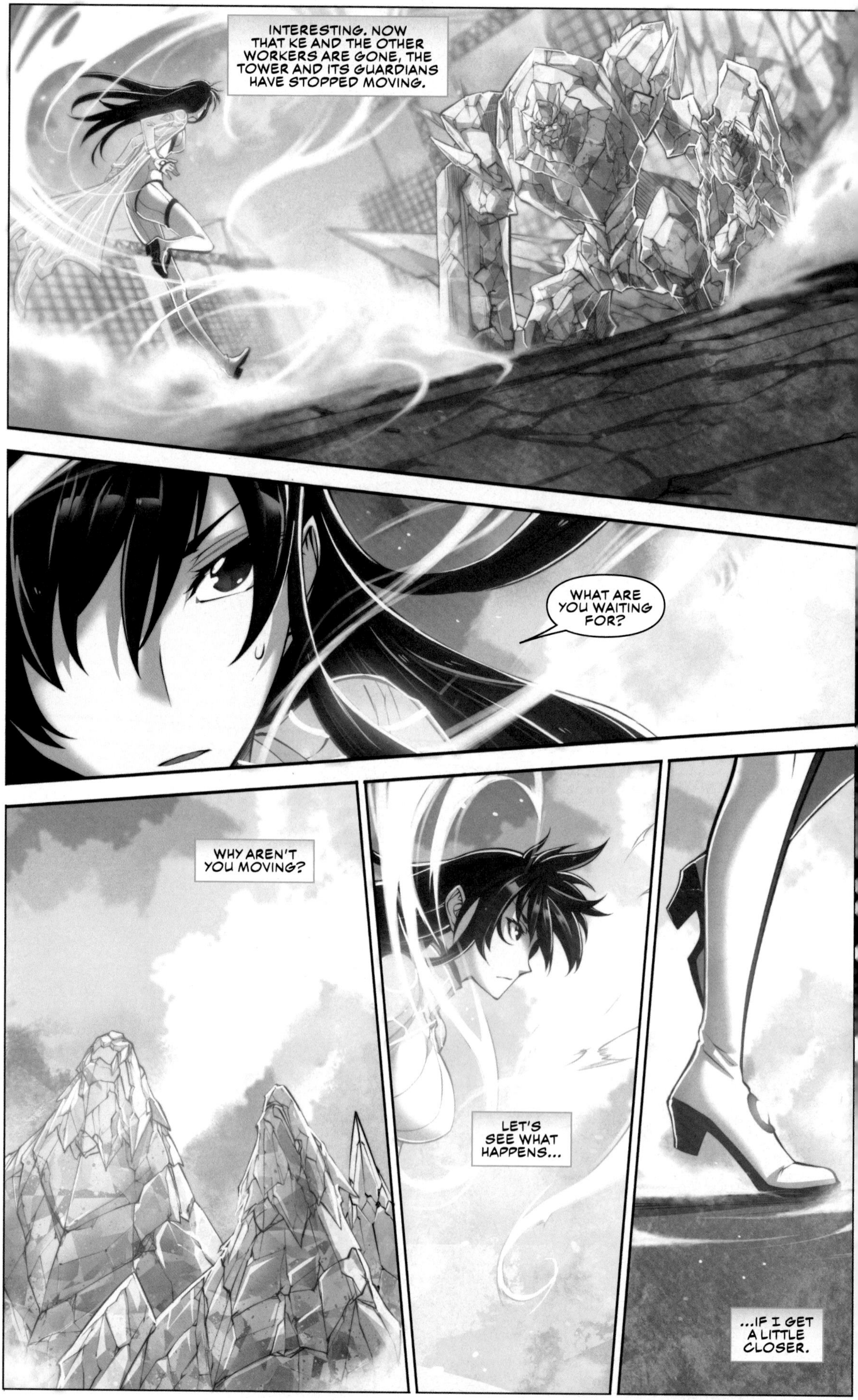
INTERESTING. NOW THAT KE AND THE OTHER WORKERS ARE GONE, THE TOWER AND ITS GUARDIANS HAVE STOPPED MOVING.
WHAT ARE YOU WAITING FOR?
WHY AREN'T YOU MOVING?
LET'S SEE WHAT HAPPENS...
...IF I GET A LITTLE CLOSER.

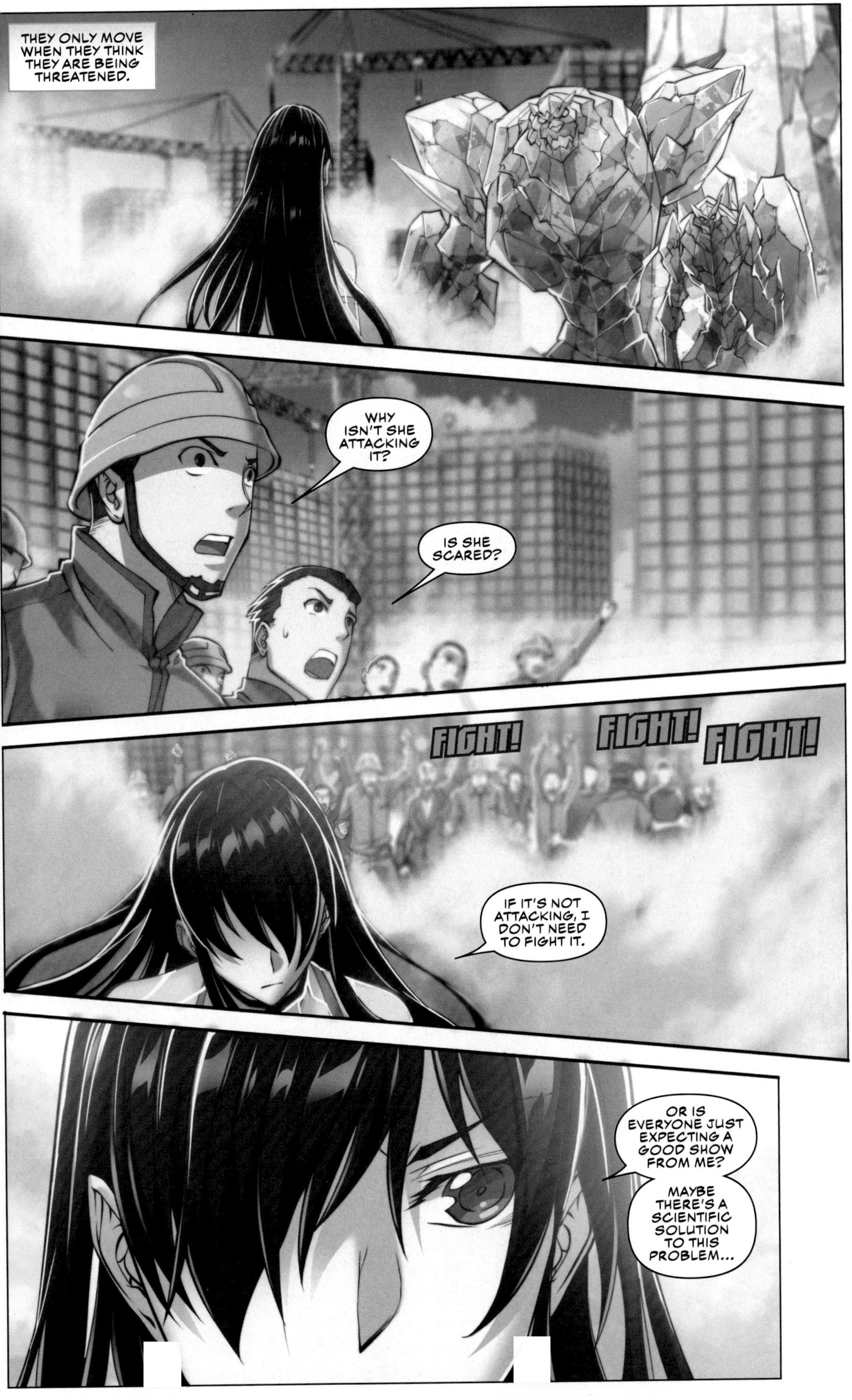
THEY ONLY MOVE WHEN THEY THINK THEY ARE BEING THREATENED.
WHY ISN'T SHE ATTACKING IT?
IS SHE SCARED?
FIGHT! FIGHT! FIGHT!
IF IT'S NOT ATTACKING, I DON'T NEED TO FIGHT IT.
OR IS EVERYONE JUST EXPECTING A GOOD SHOW FROM ME?
MAYBE THERE'S A SCIENTIFIC SOLUTION TO THIS PROBLEM...

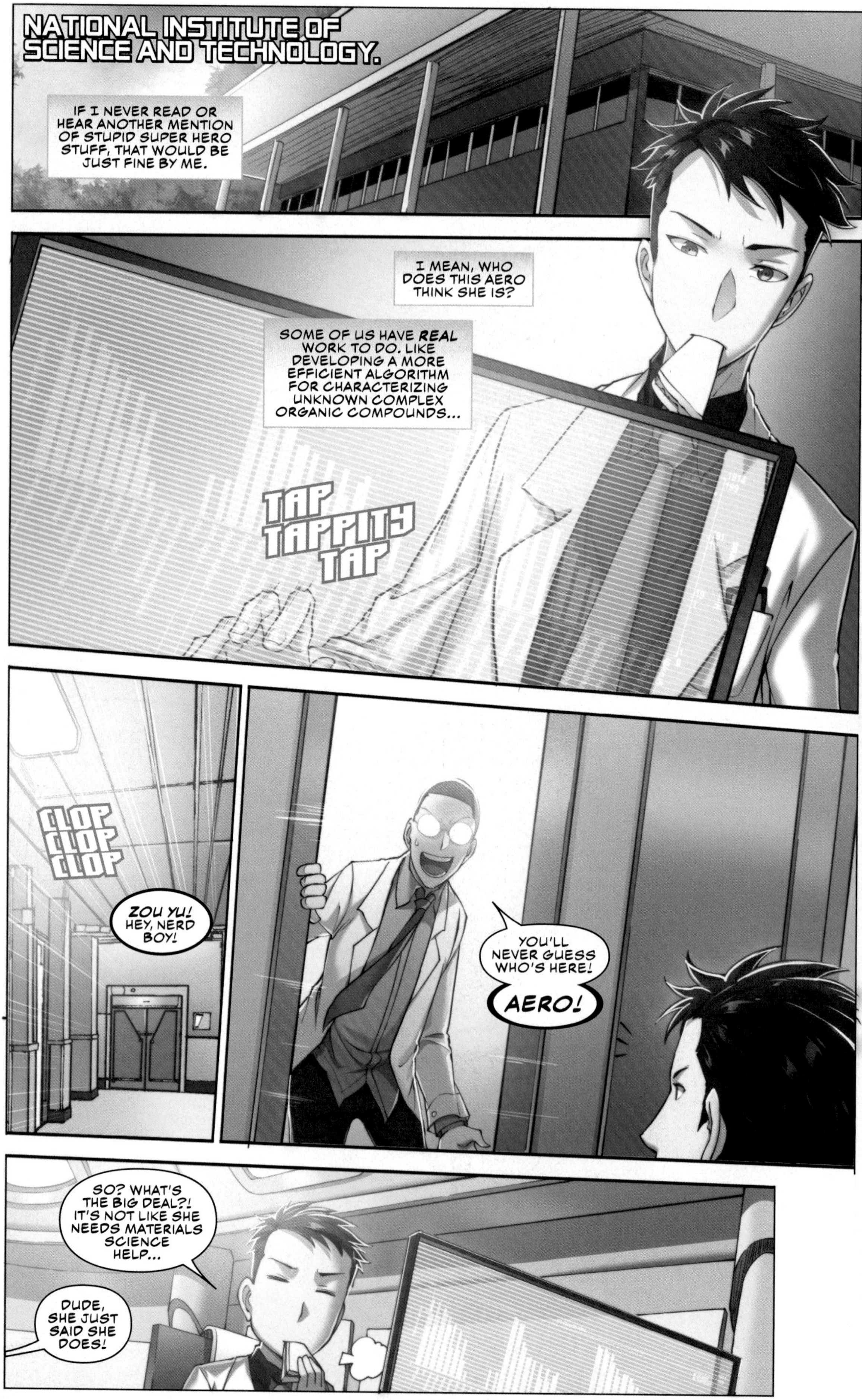
NATIONAL INSTITUTE OF SCIENCE AND TECHNOLOGY.
IF I NEVER READ OR HEAR ANOTHER MENTION OF STUPID SUPER HERO STUFF, THAT WOULD BE JUST FINE BY ME.
I MEAN, WHO DOES THIS AERO THINK SHE IS?
SOME OF US HAVE REAL WORK TO DO. LIKE DEVELOPING A MORE EFFICIENT ALGORITHM FOR CHARACTERIZING UNKNOWN COMPLEX ORGANIC COMPOUNDS...
TAP TAPPITY TAP
CLOP CLOP CLOP
ZOU YU! HEY, NERD BOY!
YOU'LL NEVER GUESS WHO'S HERE!
AERO!
SO? WHAT'S THE BIG DEAL?! IT'S NOT LIKE SHE NEEDS MATERIALS SCIENCE HELP...
DUDE, SHE JUST SAID SHE DOES!

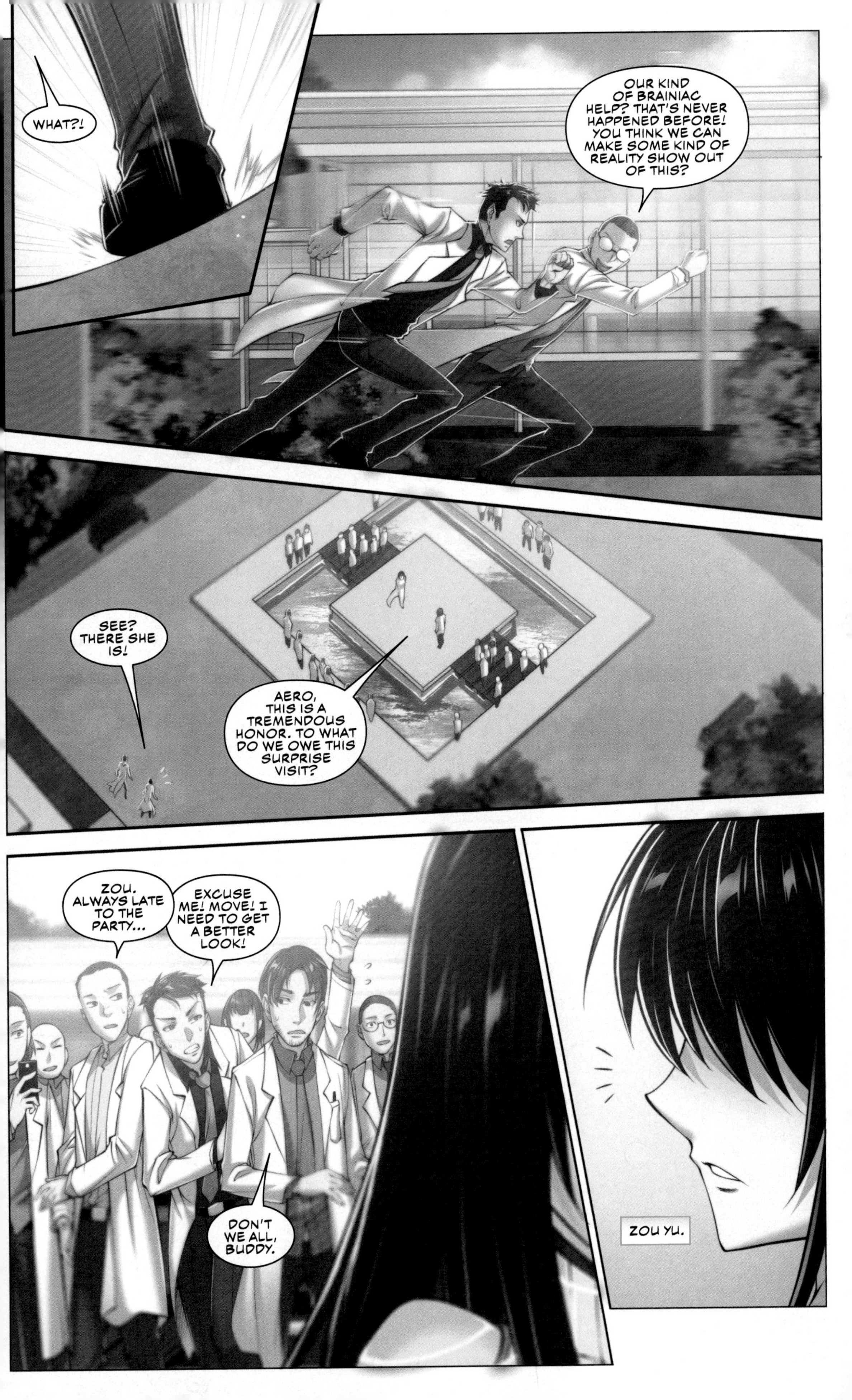
WHAT?!
OUR KIND OF BRAINIAC HELP? THAT'S NEVER HAPPENED BEFORE! YOU THINK WE CAN MAKE SOME KIND OF REALITY SHOW OUT OF THIS?
SEE? THERE SHE IS!
AERO, THIS IS A TREMENDOUS HONOR. TO WHAT DO WE OWE THIS SURPRISE VISIT?
ZOU. ALWAYS LATE TO THE PARTY...
EXCUSE ME! MOVE! I NEED TO GET A BETTER LOOK!
DON'T WE ALL, BUDDY.
ZOU YU.

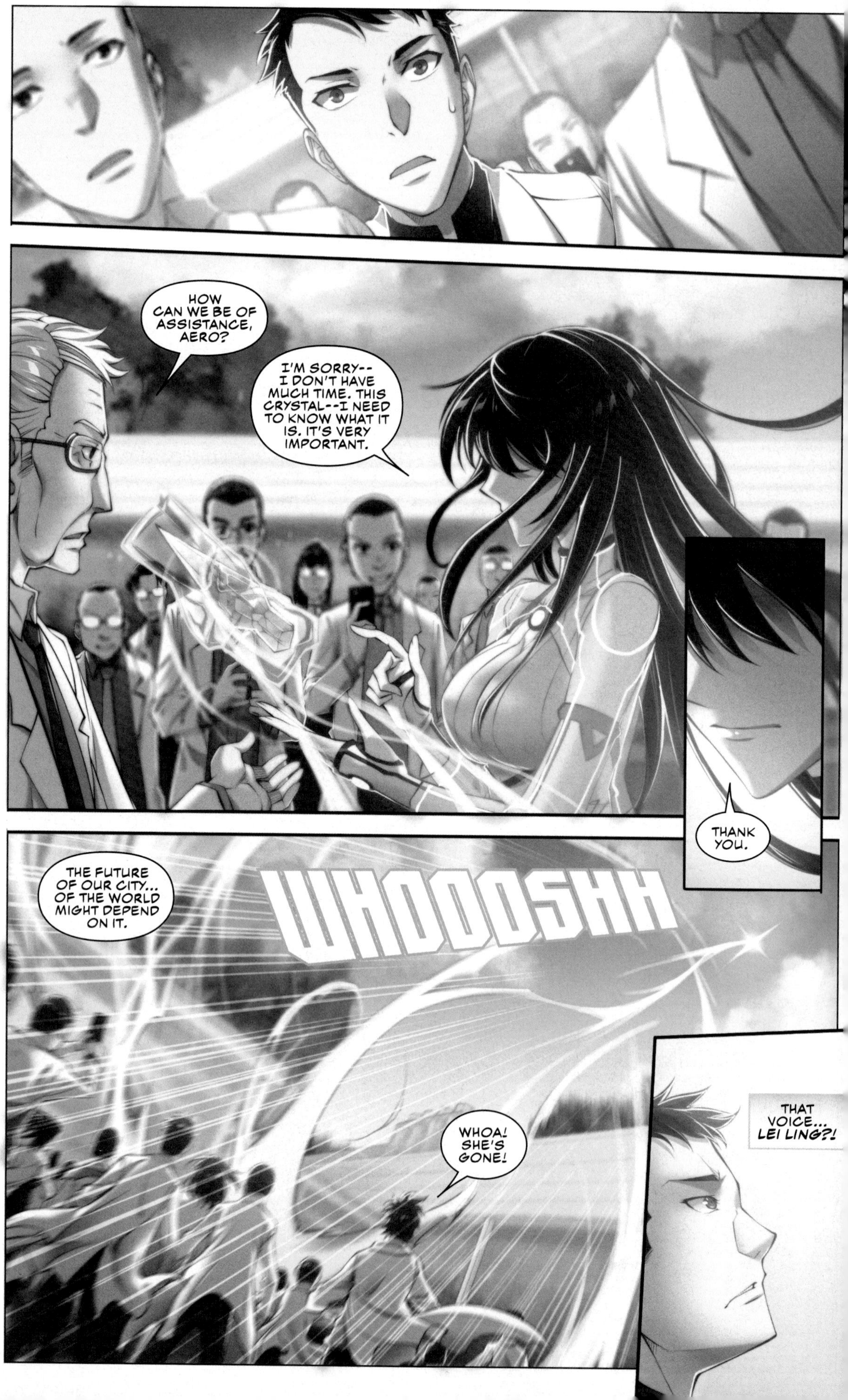
HOW CAN WE BE OF ASSISTANCE, AERO?
I'M SORRY-- I DON'T HAVE MUCH TIME. THIS CRYSTAL--I NEED TO KNOW WHAT IT IS. IT'S VERY IMPORTANT.
THANK YOU.
THE FUTURE OF OUR CITY... OF THE WORLD MIGHT DEPEND ON IT.
WHOOOSHH
WHOA! SHE'S GONE!
THAT VOICE... LEI LING?!

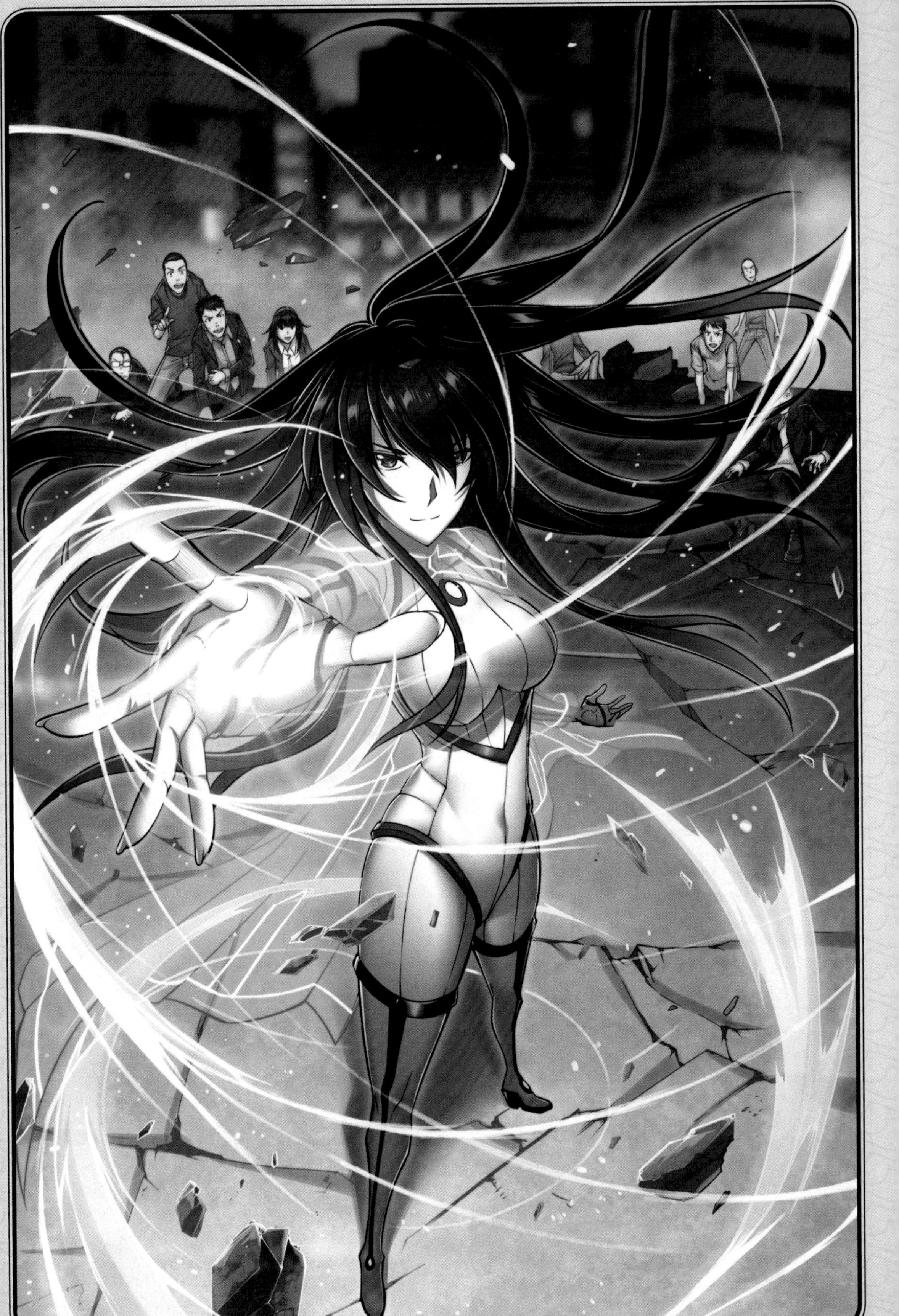

8 Secrets of the Ancients

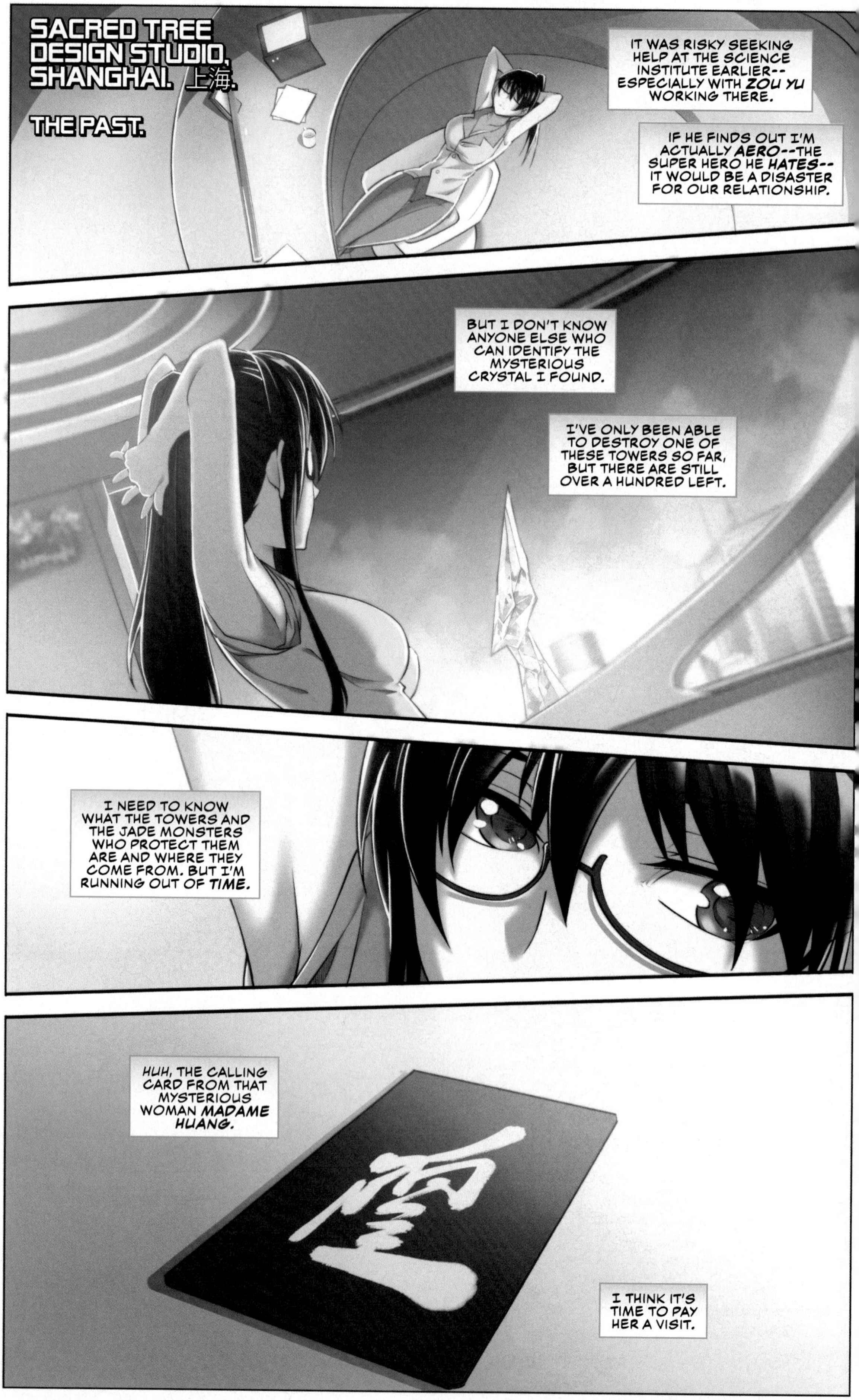
SACRED TREE DESIGN STUDIO, SHANGHAI. 上海.
THE PAST.
IT WAS RISKY SEEKING HELP AT THE SCIENCE INSTITUTE EARLIER--ESPECIALLY WITH ZOU YU WORKING THERE.
IF HE FINDS OUT I'M ACTUALLY AERO--THE SUPER HERO HE HATES--IT WOULD BE A DISASTER FOR OUR RELATIONSHIP.
BUT I DON'T KNOW ANYONE ELSE WHO CAN IDENTIFY THE MYSTERIOUS CRYSTAL I FOUND.
I'VE ONLY BEEN ABLE TO DESTROY ONE OF THESE TOWERS SO FAR, BUT THERE ARE STILL OVER A HUNDRED LEFT.
I NEED TO KNOW WHAT THE TOWERS AND THE JADE MONSTERS WHO PROTECT THEM ARE AND WHERE THEY COME FROM. BUT I'M RUNNING OUT OF TIME.
HUH, THE CALLING CARD FROM THAT MYSTERIOUS WOMAN MADAME HUANG.
I THINK IT'S TIME TO PAY HER A VISIT.

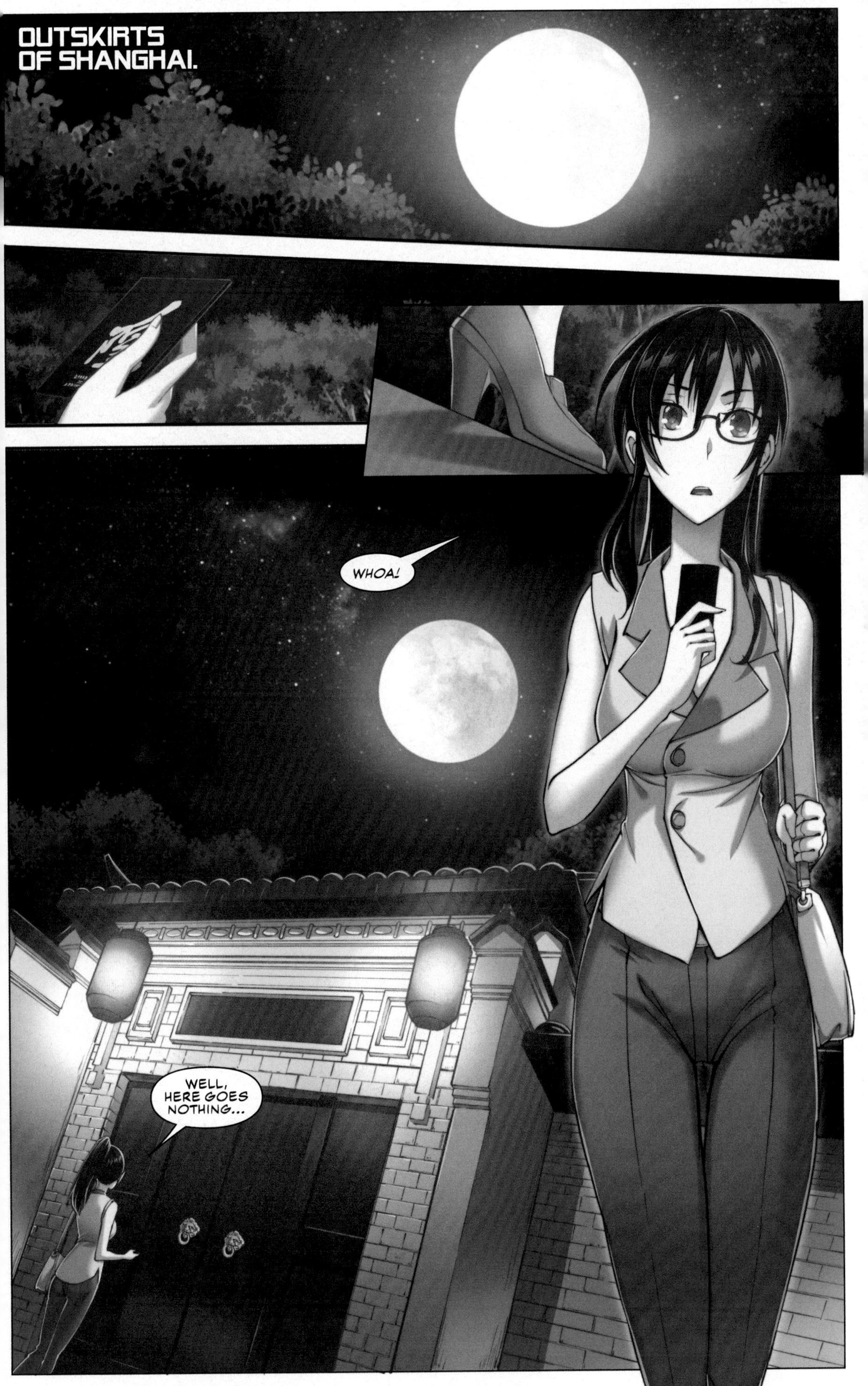
OUTSKIRTS OF SHANGHAI.
WHOA!
WELL, HERE GOES NOTHING...

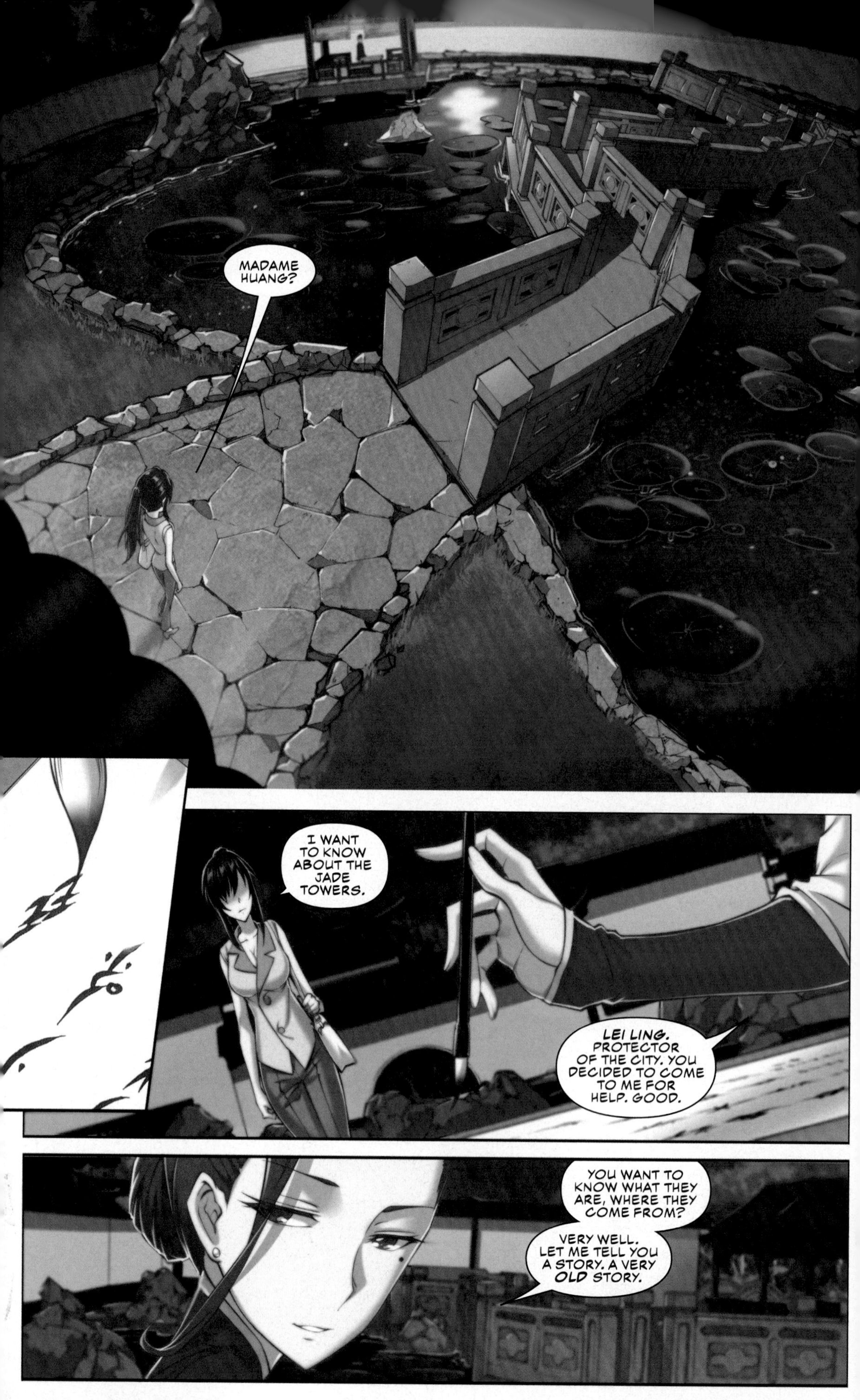
MADAME HUANG?
I WANT TO KNOW ABOUT THE JADE TOWERS.
LEI LING. PROTECTOR OF THE CITY. YOU DECIDED TO COME TO ME FOR HELP. GOOD.
YOU WANT TO KNOW WHAT THEY ARE, WHERE THEY COME FROM?
VERY WELL. LET ME TELL YOU A STORY. A VERY OLD STORY.

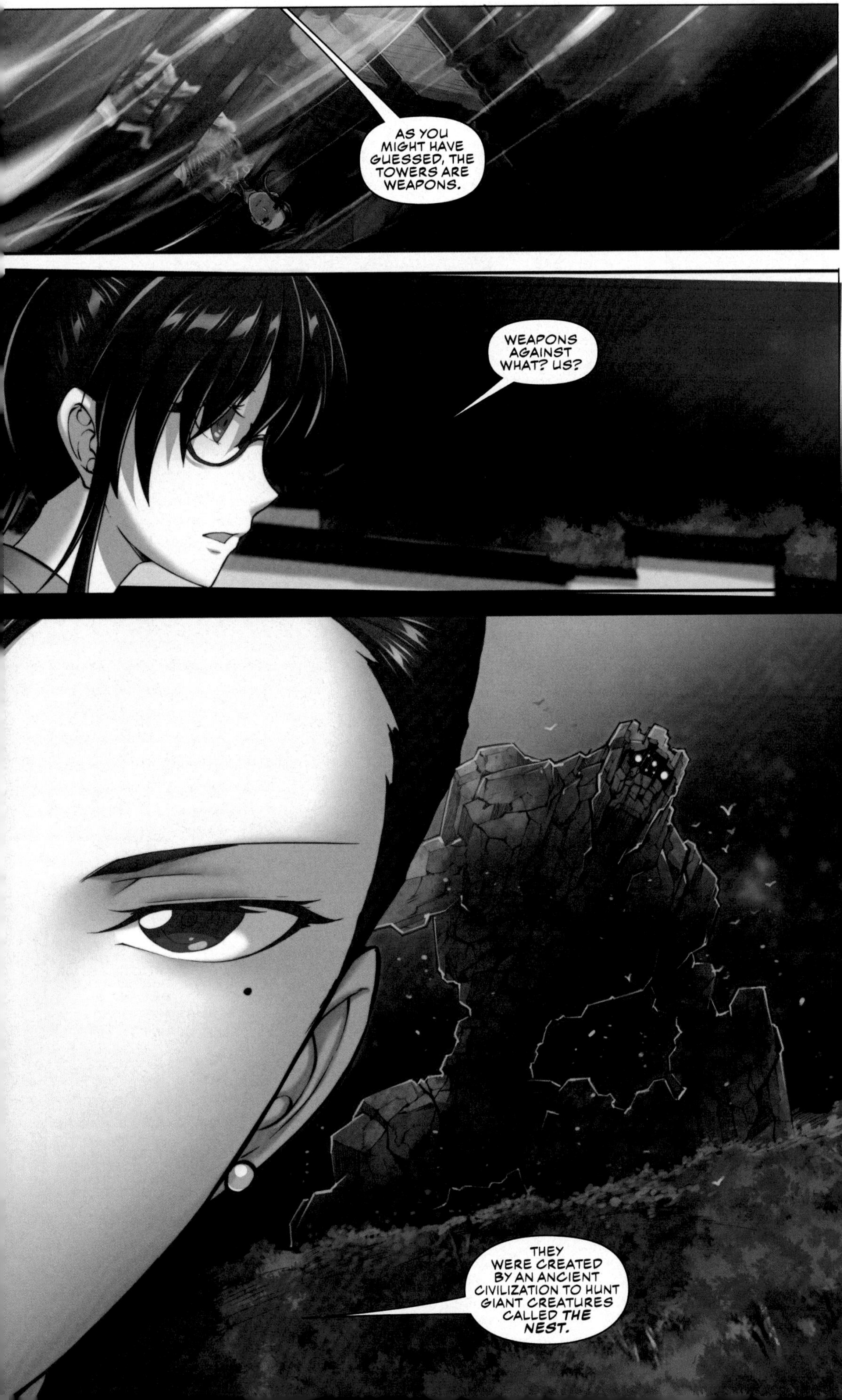
AS YOU MIGHT HAVE GUESSED, THE TOWERS ARE WEAPONS.
WEAPONS AGAINST WHAT? US?
THEY WERE CREATED BY AN ANCIENT CIVILIZATION TO HUNT GIANT CREATURES CALLED THE NEST.

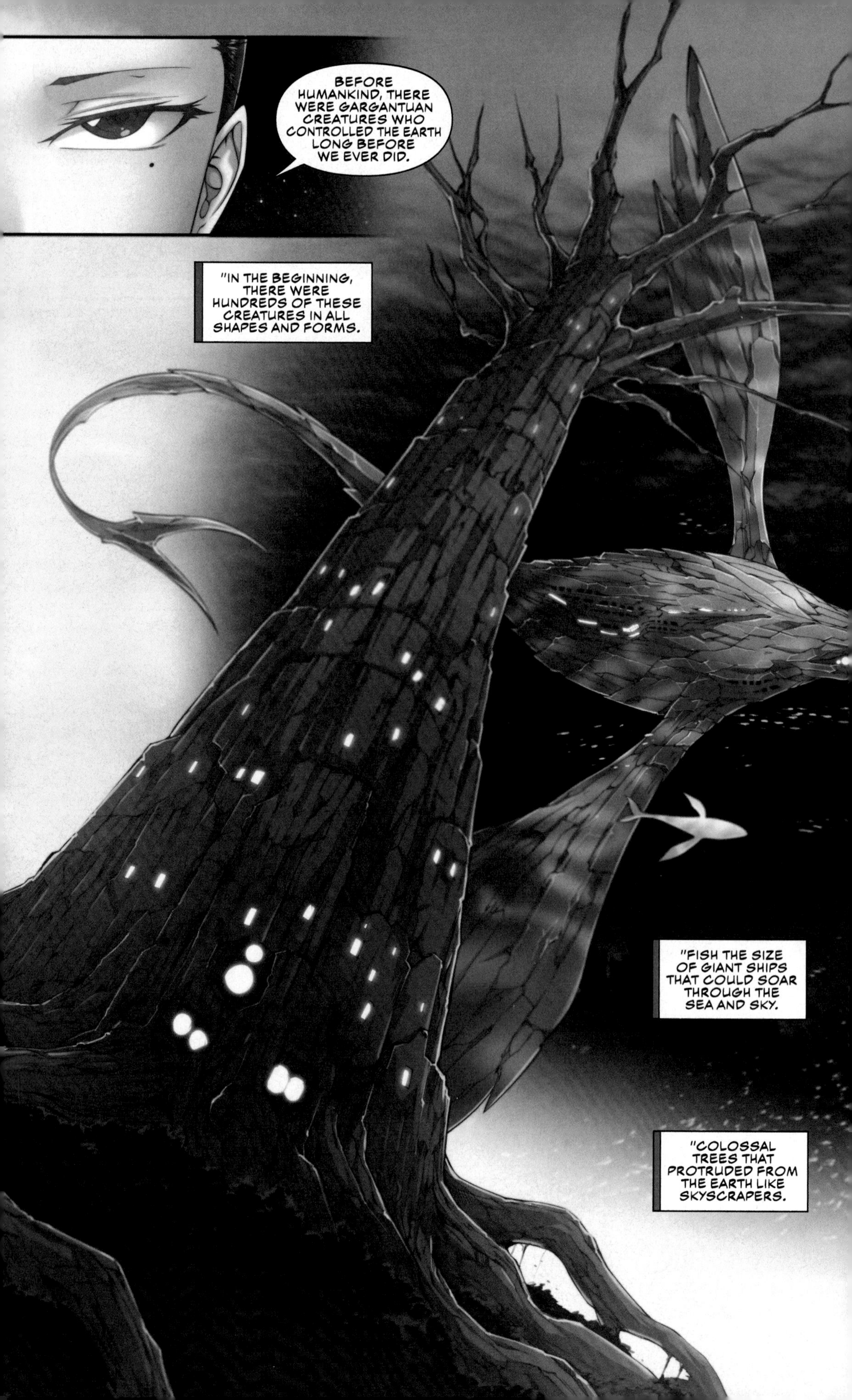
BEFORE HUMANKIND, THERE WERE GARGANTUAN CREATURES WHO CONTROLLED THE EARTH LONG BEFORE WE EVER DID.
"IN THE BEGINNING, THERE WERE HUNDREDS OF THESE CREATURES IN ALL SHAPES AND FORMS.
"FISH THE SIZE OF GIANT SHIPS THAT COULD SOAR THROUGH THE SEA AND SKY.
"COLOSSAL TREES THAT PROTRUDED FROM THE EARTH LIKE SKYSCRAPERS.

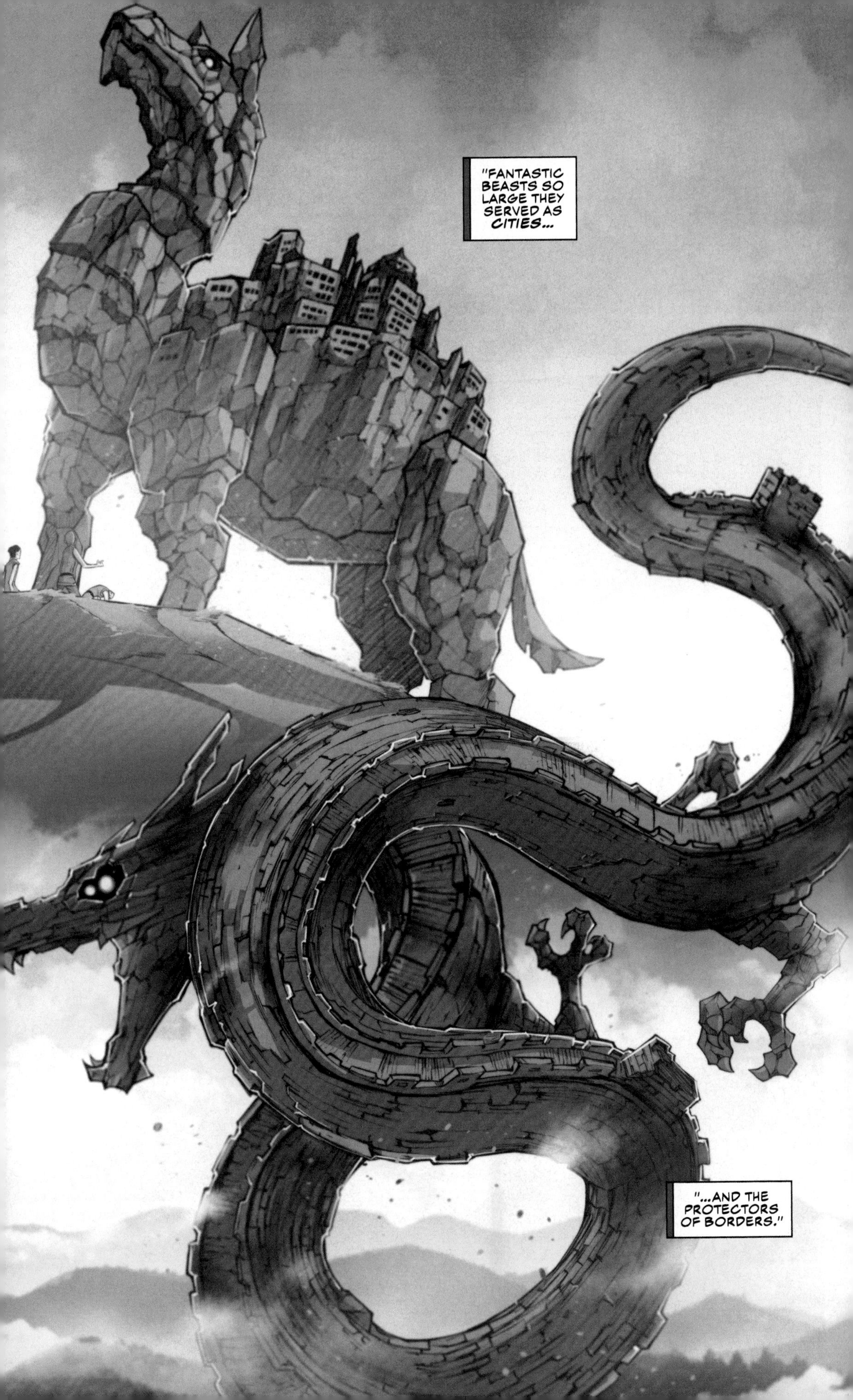
"FANTASTIC BEASTS SO LARGE THEY SERVED AS CITIES...
"...AND THE PROTECTORS OF BORDERS."

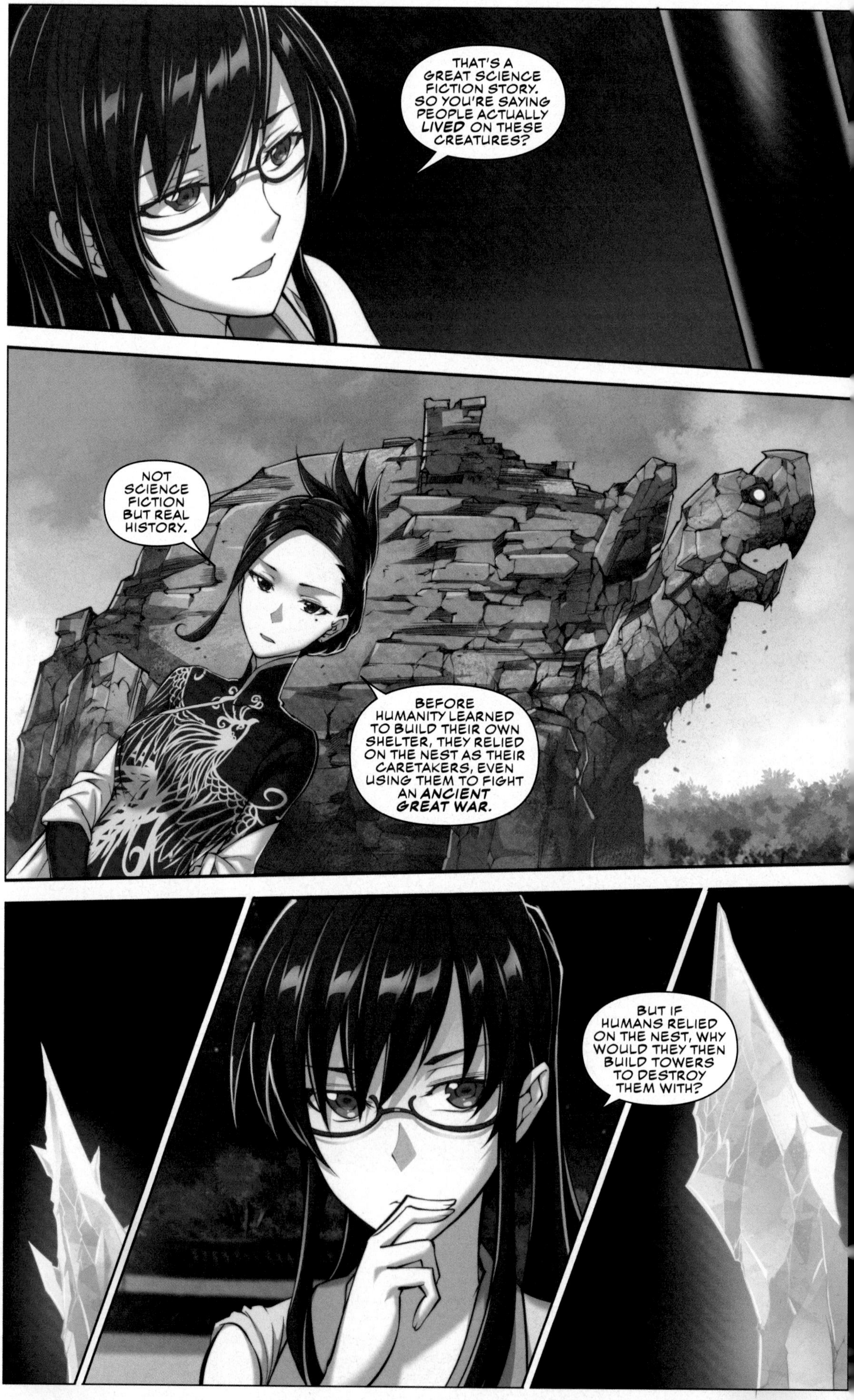
THAT'S A GREAT SCIENCE FICTION STORY. SO YOU'RE SAYING PEOPLE ACTUALLY LIVED ON THESE CREATURES?
NOT SCIENCE FICTION BUT REAL HISTORY.
BEFORE HUMANITY LEARNED TO BUILD THEIR OWN SHELTER, THEY RELIED ON THE NEST AS THEIR CARETAKERS, EVEN USING THEM TO FIGHT AN ANCIENT GREAT WAR.
BUT IF HUMANS RELIED ON THE NEST, WHY WOULD THEY THEN BUILD TOWERS TO DESTROY THEM WITH?

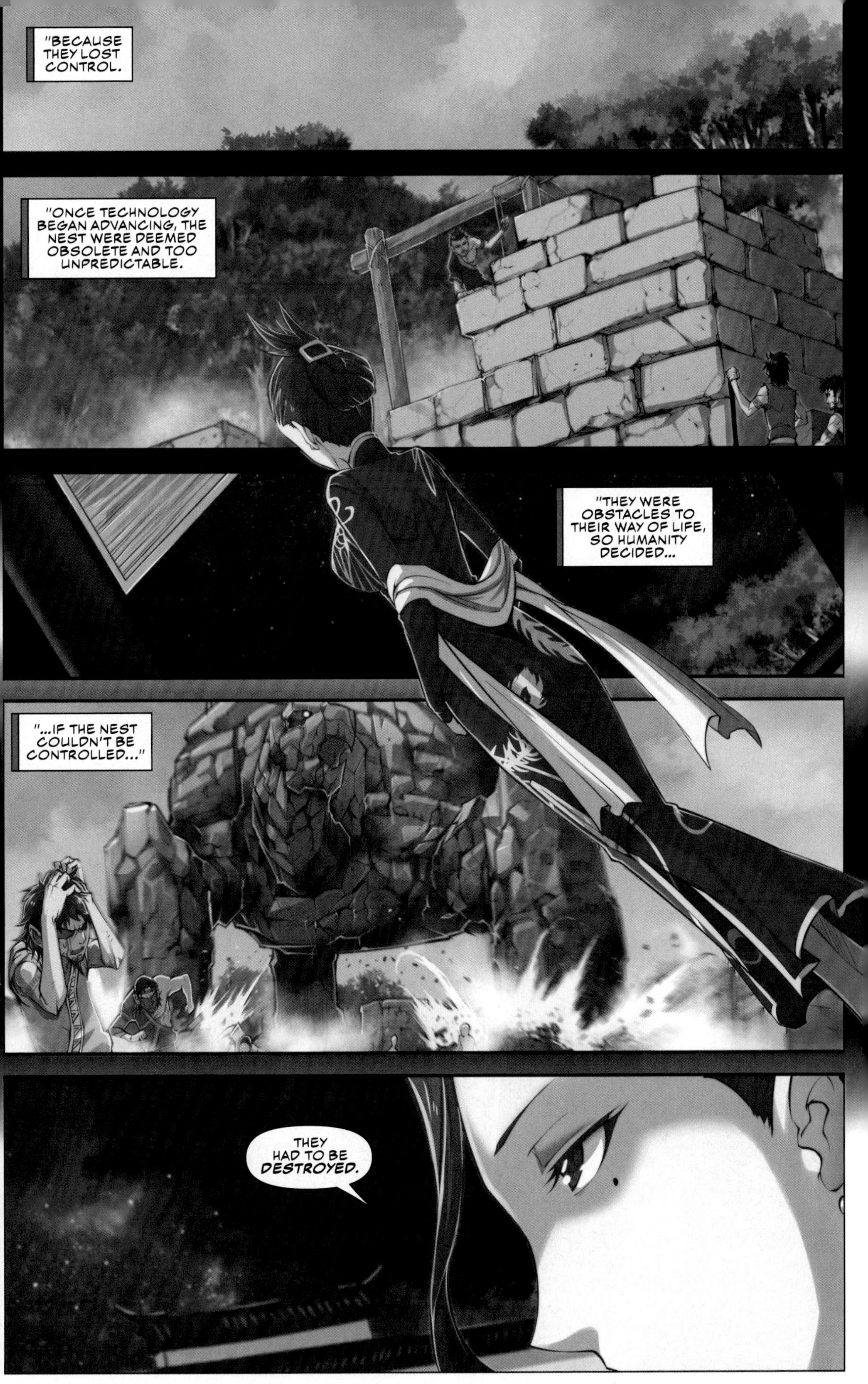
"BECAUSE THEY LOST CONTROL.
"ONCE TECHNOLOGY BEGAN ADVANCING, THE NEST WERE DEEMED OBSOLETE AND TOO UNPREDICTABLE.
"THEY WERE OBSTACLES TO THEIR WAY OF LIFE, SO HUMANITY DECIDED...
"...IF THE NEST COULDN'T BE CONTROLLED..."
THEY HAD TO BE DESTROYED.

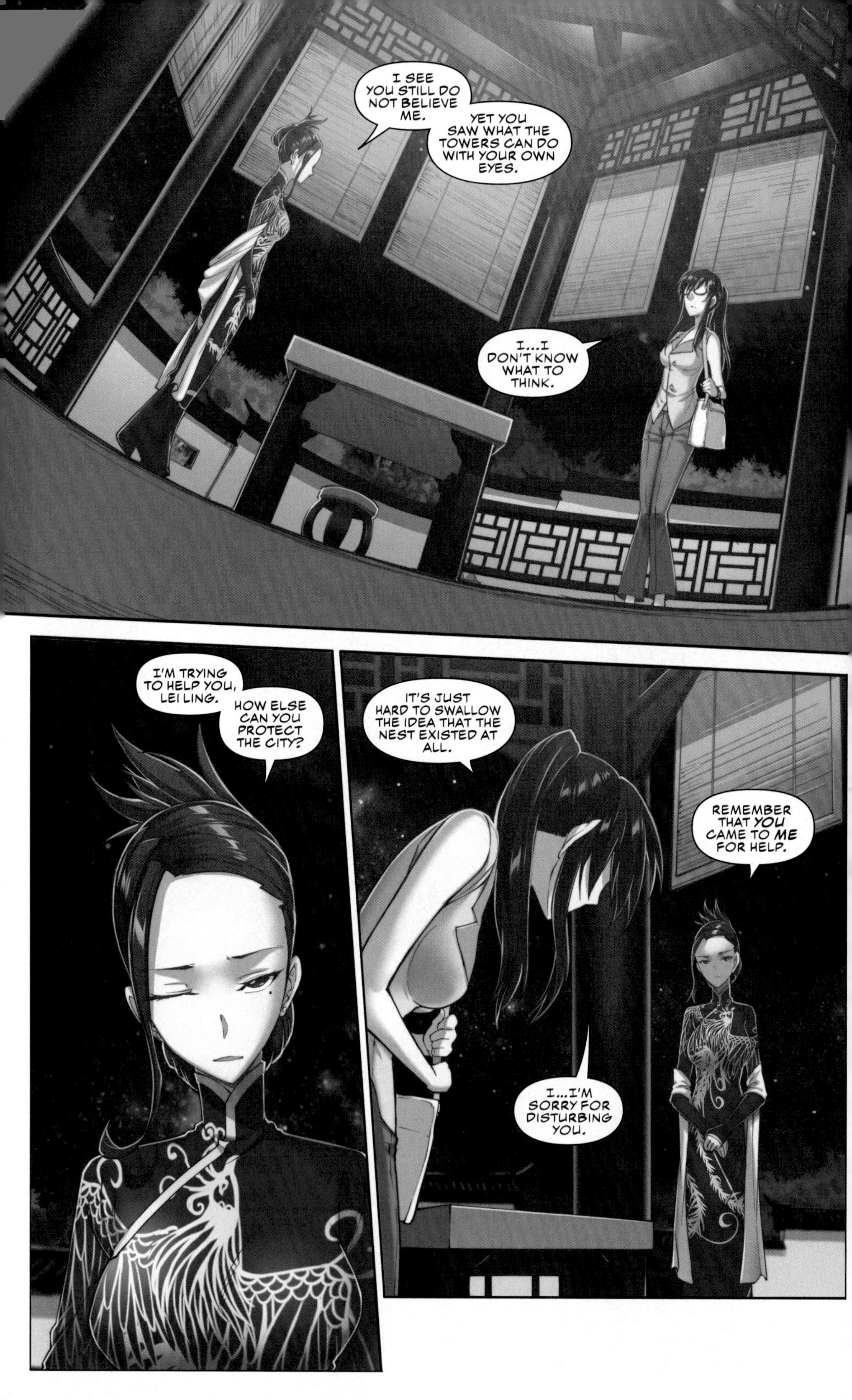
I SEE YOU STILL DO NOT BELIEVE ME.
YET YOU SAW WHAT THE TOWERS CAN DO WITH YOUR OWN EYES.
I...I DON'T KNOW WHAT TO THINK.
I'M TRYING TO HELP YOU, LEI LING.
HOW ELSE CAN YOU PROTECT THE CITY?
IT'S JUST HARD TO SWALLOW THE IDEA THAT THE NEST EXISTED AT ALL.
REMEMBER THAT YOU CAME TO ME FOR HELP.
I...I'M SORRY FOR DISTURBING YOU.

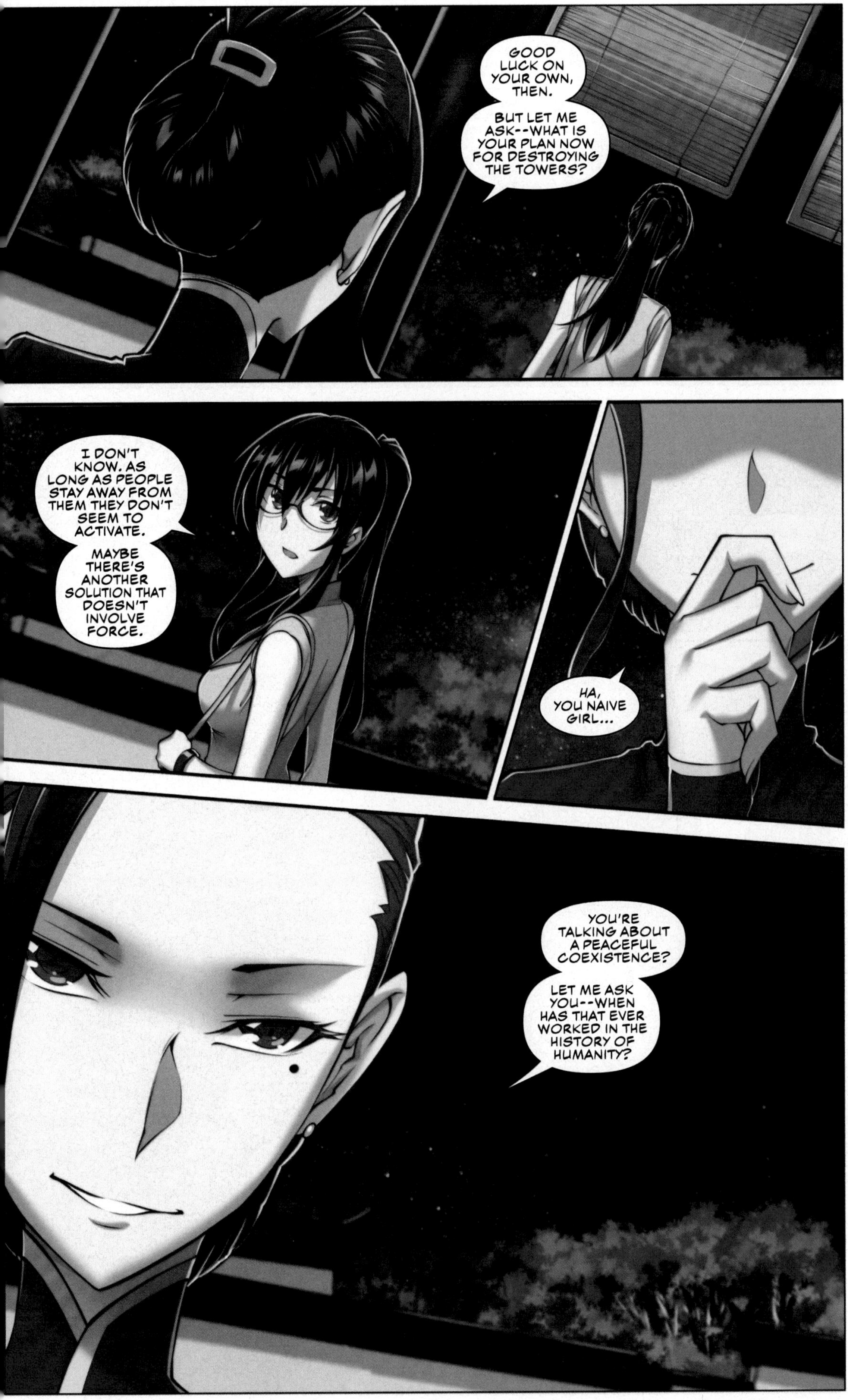
GOOD LUCK ON YOUR OWN, THEN.
BUT LET ME ASK--WHAT IS YOUR PLAN NOW FOR DESTROYING THE TOWERS?
I DON'T KNOW. AS LONG AS PEOPLE STAY AWAY FROM THEM THEY DON'T SEEM TO ACTIVATE.
MAYBE THERE'S ANOTHER SOLUTION THAT DOESN'T INVOLVE FORCE.
HA, YOU NAIVE GIRL...
YOU'RE TALKING ABOUT A PEACEFUL COEXISTENCE?
LET ME ASK YOU--WHEN HAS THAT EVER WORKED IN THE HISTORY OF HUMANITY?

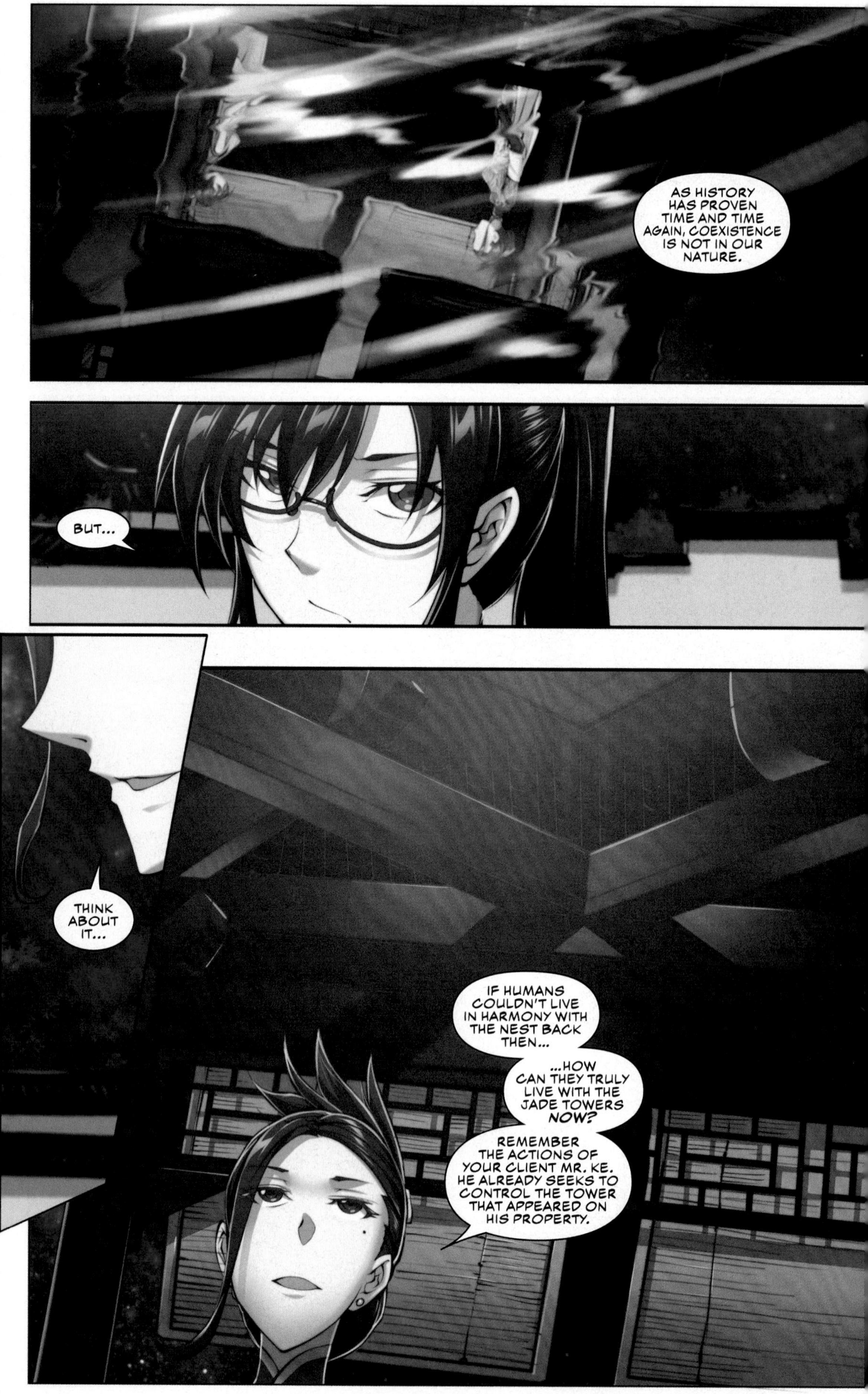
AS HISTORY HAS PROVEN TIME AND TIME AGAIN, COEXISTENCE IS NOT IN OUR NATURE.
BUT...
THINK ABOUT IT...
IF HUMANS COULDN'T LIVE IN HARMONY WITH THE NEST BACK THEN...
...HOW CAN THEY TRULY LIVE WITH THE JADE TOWERS NOW?
REMEMBER THE ACTIONS OF YOUR CLIENT MR. KE. HE ALREADY SEEKS TO CONTROL THE TOWER THAT APPEARED ON HIS PROPERTY.

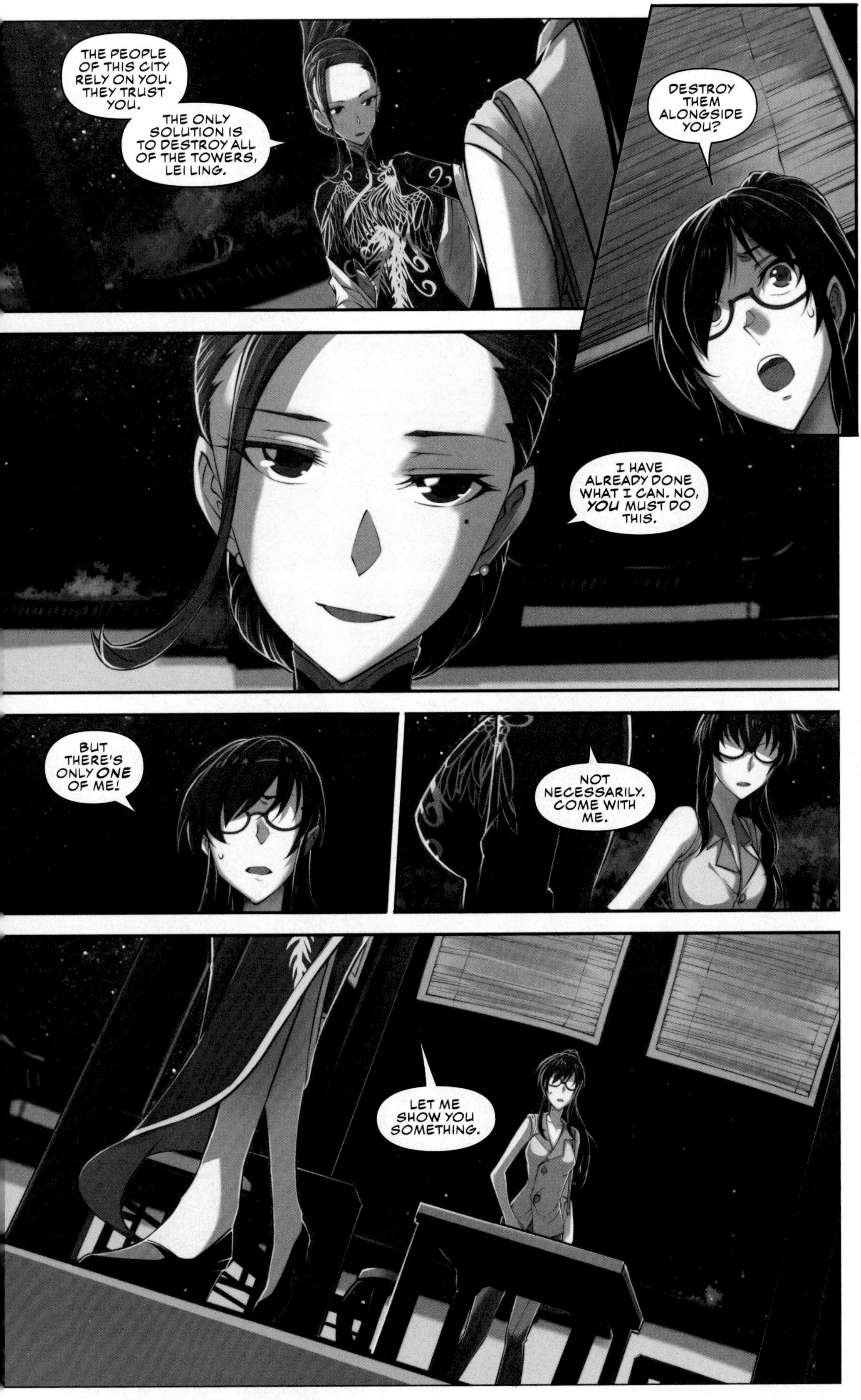
THE PEOPLE OF THIS CITY RELY ON YOU. THEY TRUST YOU.
THE ONLY SOLUTION IS TO DESTROY ALL OF THE TOWERS, LEI LING.
DESTROY THEM ALONGSIDE YOU?
I HAVE ALREADY DONE WHAT I CAN. NO, *YOU* MUST DO THIS.
BUT THERE'S ONLY *ONE* OF ME!
NOT NECESSARILY. COME WITH ME.
LET ME SHOW YOU SOMETHING.

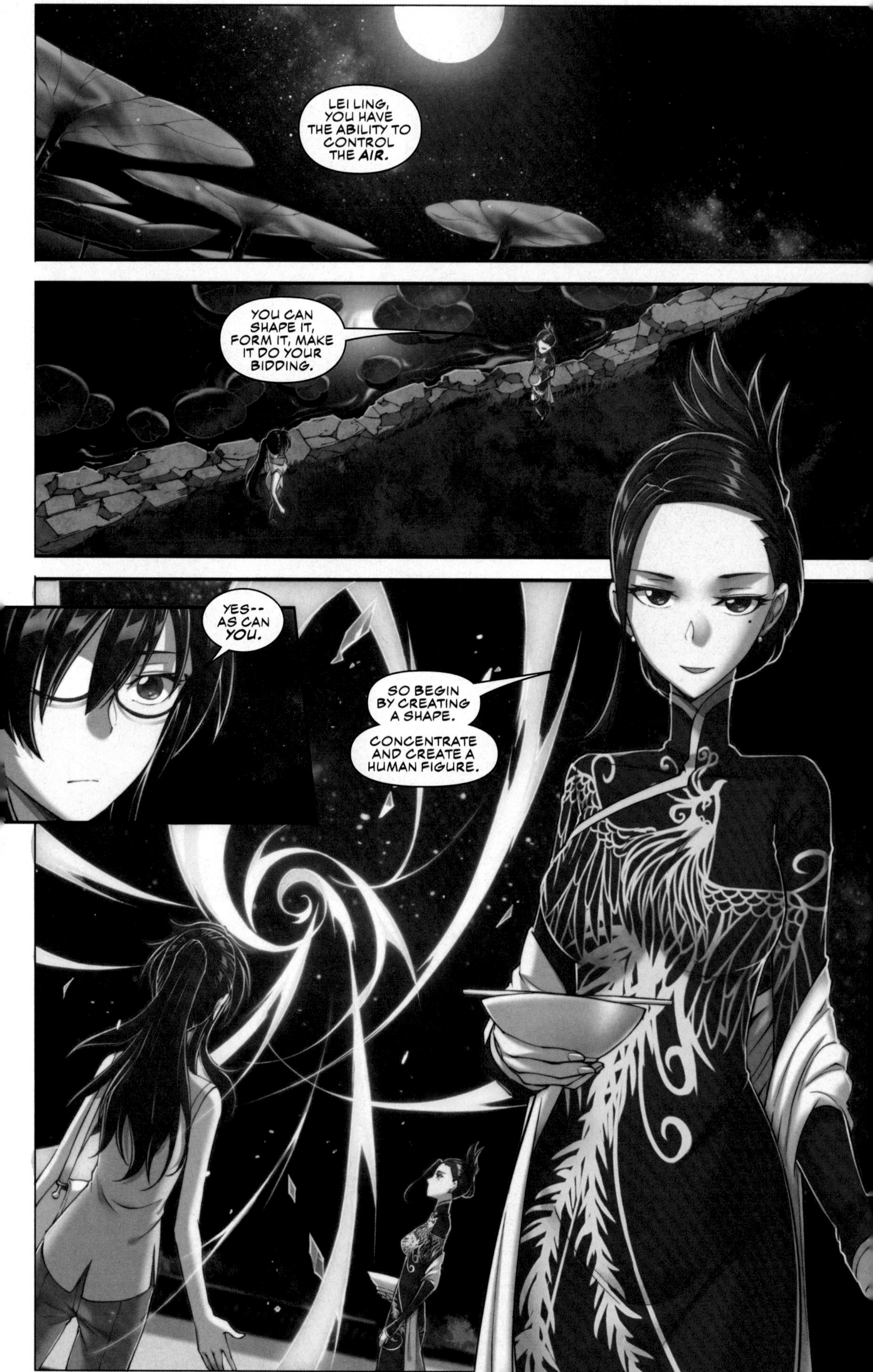
LEI LING, YOU HAVE THE ABILITY TO CONTROL THE AIR.
YOU CAN SHAPE IT, FORM IT, MAKE IT DO YOUR BIDDING.
YES-- AS CAN YOU.
SO BEGIN BY CREATING A SHAPE.
CONCENTRATE AND CREATE A HUMAN FIGURE.

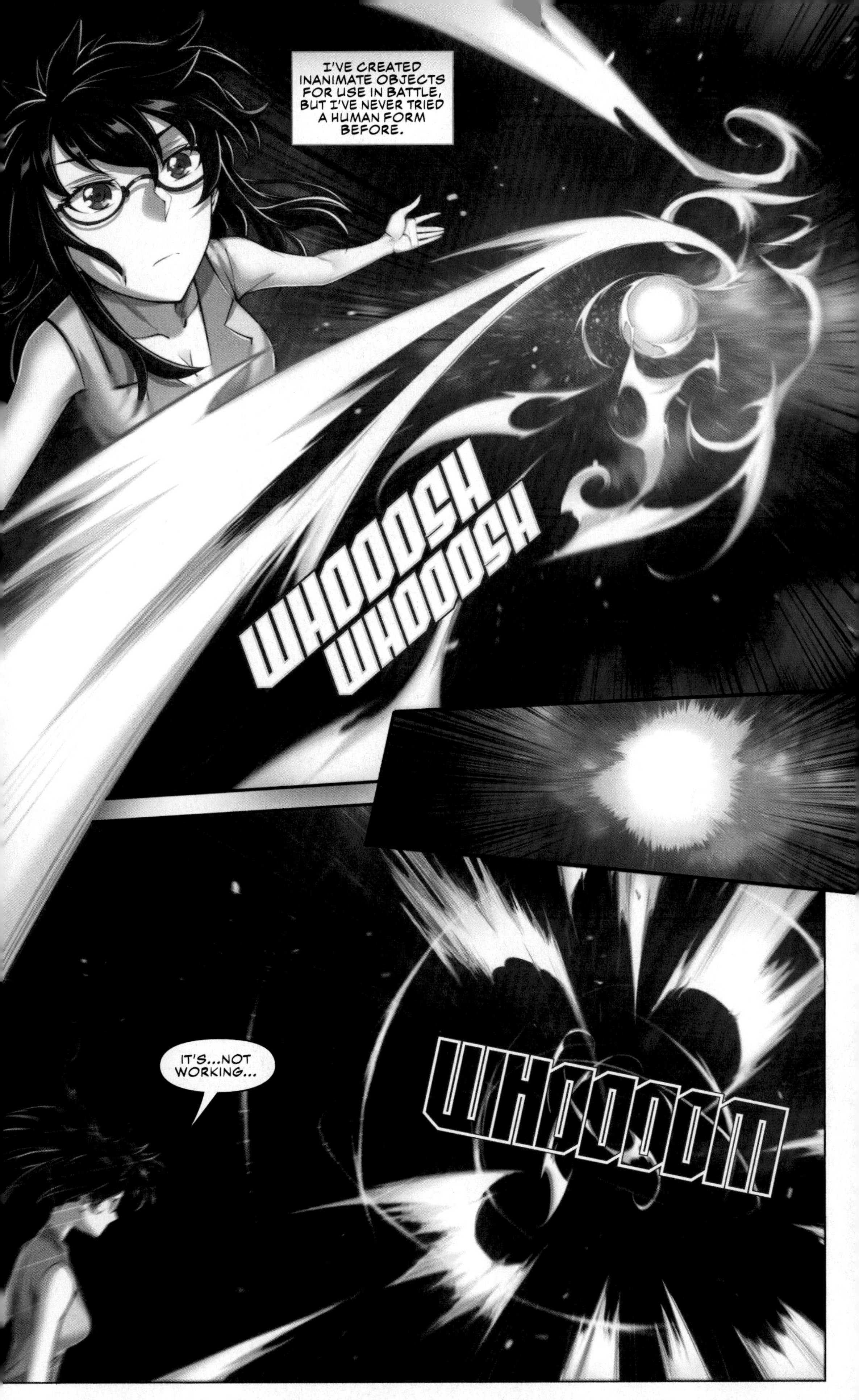
I'VE CREATED INANIMATE OBJECTS FOR USE IN BATTLE, BUT I'VE NEVER TRIED A HUMAN FORM BEFORE.
WHOOOSH
WHOOOSH
IT'S...NOT WORKING...
WHOOOOM

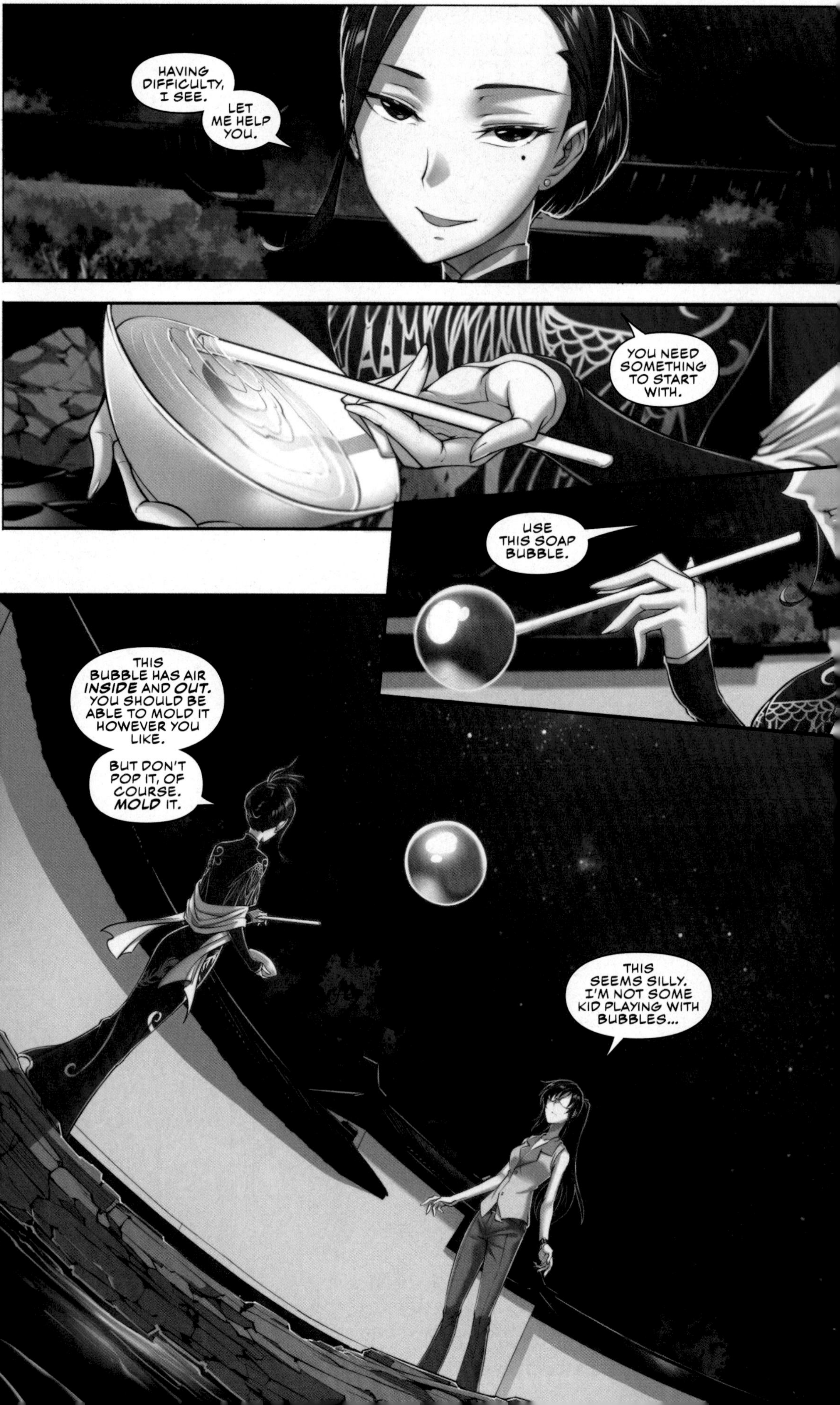
HAVING DIFFICULTY, I SEE.
LET ME HELP YOU.
YOU NEED SOMETHING TO START WITH.
USE THIS SOAP BUBBLE.
THIS BUBBLE HAS AIR *INSIDE* AND *OUT*. YOU SHOULD BE ABLE TO MOLD IT HOWEVER YOU LIKE.
BUT DON'T POP IT, OF COURSE. *MOLD* IT.
THIS SEEMS SILLY. I'M NOT SOME KID PLAYING WITH BUBBLES...

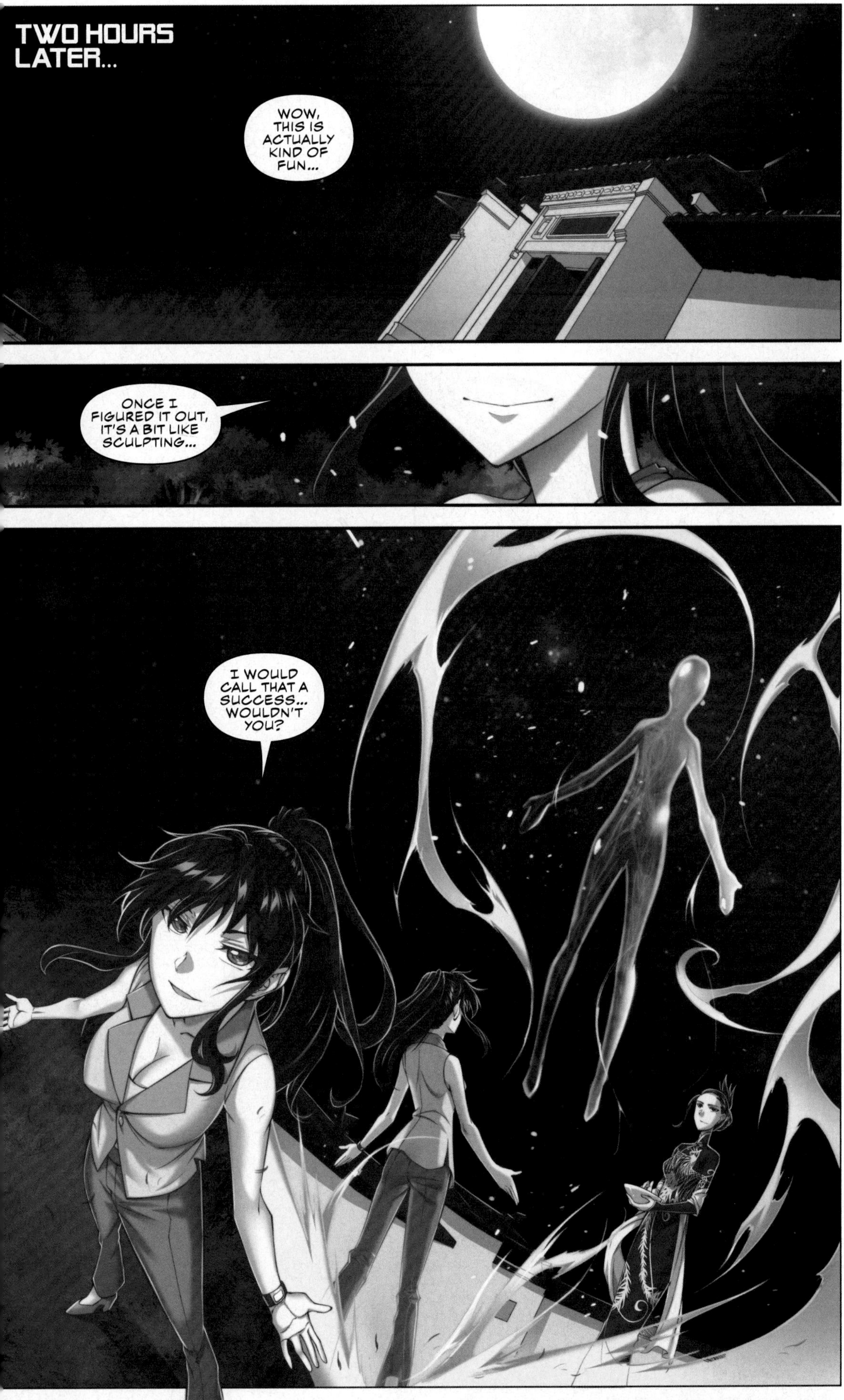
TWO HOURS LATER...
WOW, THIS IS ACTUALLY KIND OF FUN...
ONCE I FIGURED IT OUT, IT'S A BIT LIKE SCULPTING...
I WOULD CALL THAT A SUCCESS... WOULDN'T YOU?

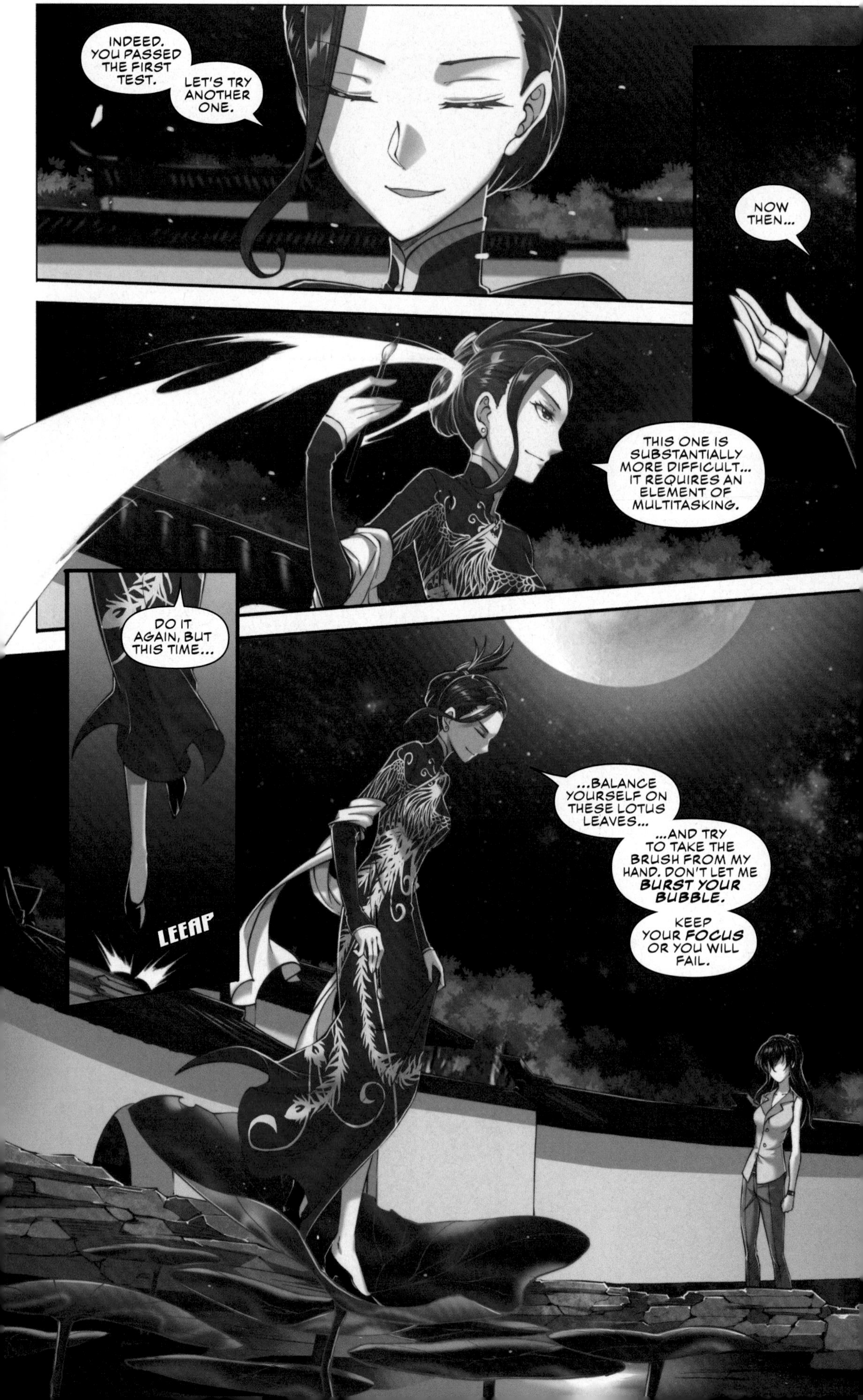
INDEED. YOU PASSED THE FIRST TEST.
LET'S TRY ANOTHER ONE.
NOW THEN...
THIS ONE IS SUBSTANTIALLY MORE DIFFICULT... IT REQUIRES AN ELEMENT OF MULTITASKING.
DO IT AGAIN, BUT THIS TIME...
LEEAP
...BALANCE YOURSELF ON THESE LOTUS LEAVES...
...AND TRY TO TAKE THE BRUSH FROM MY HAND. DON'T LET ME BURST YOUR BUBBLE.
KEEP YOUR FOCUS OR YOU WILL FAIL.

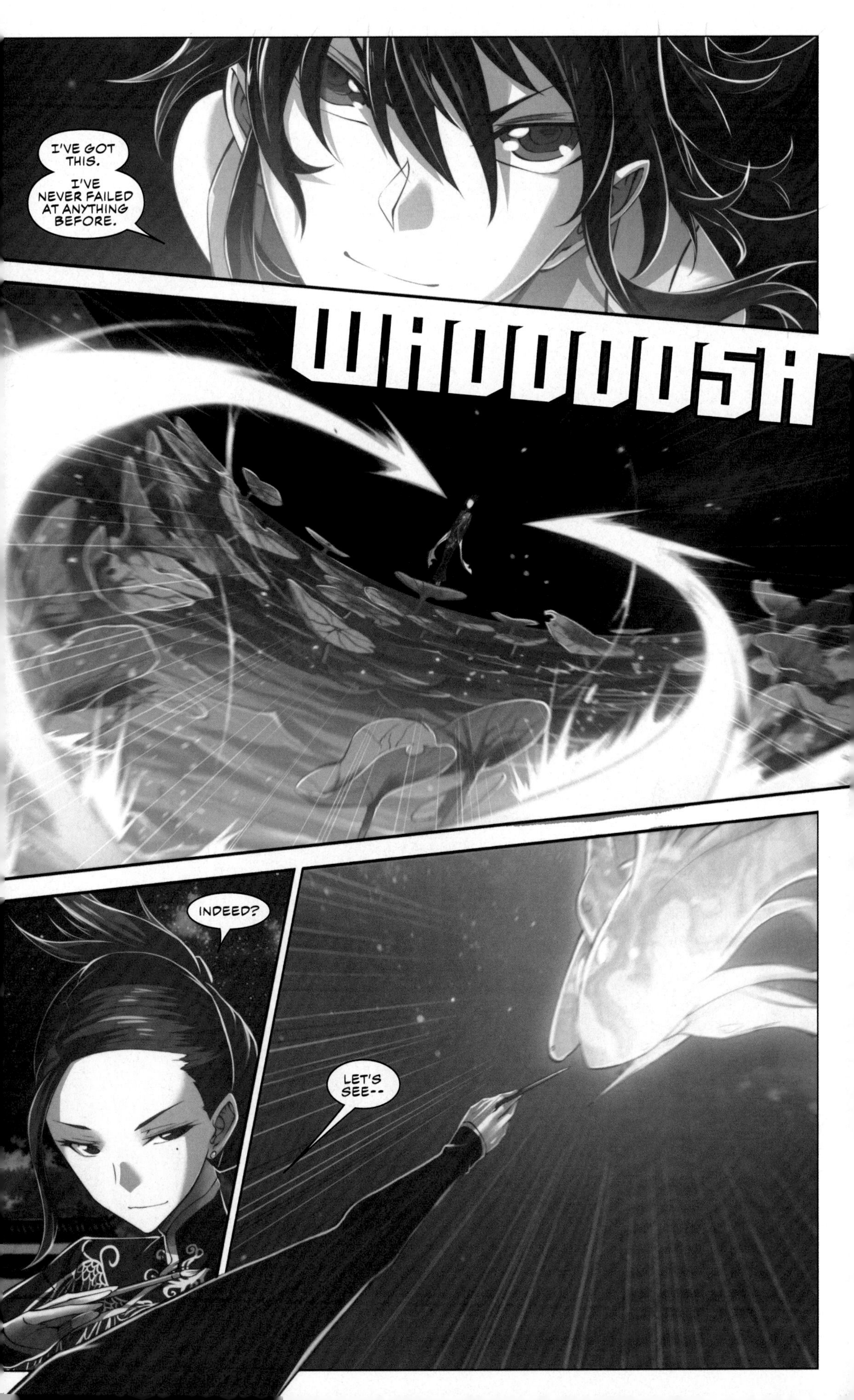

I'VE GOT THIS.
I'VE NEVER FAILED AT ANYTHING BEFORE.
WHOOOOSH
INDEED?
LET'S SEE--

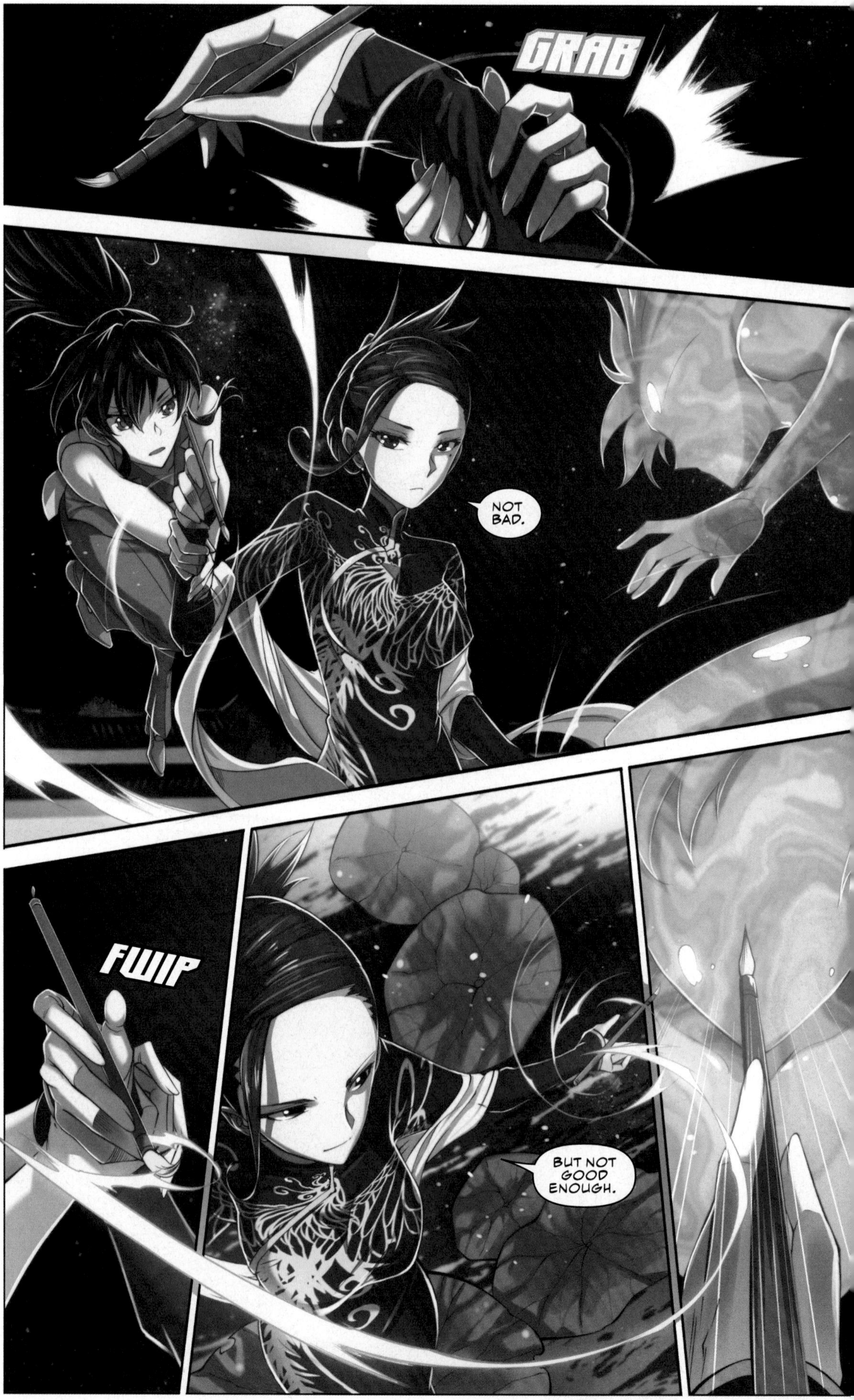
GRAB
NOT BAD.
FWIP
BUT NOT GOOD ENOUGH.

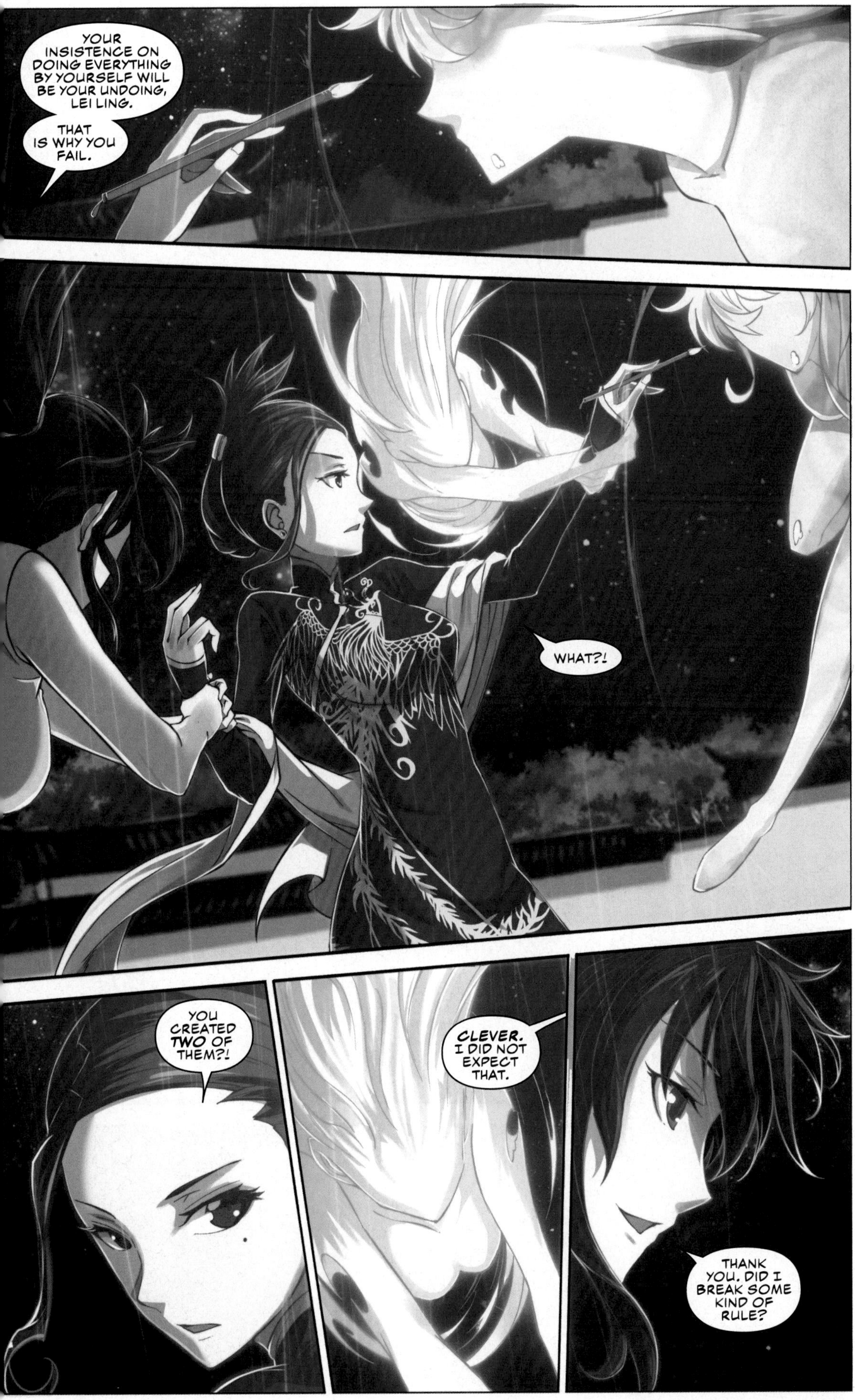
YOUR INSISTENCE ON DOING EVERYTHING BY YOURSELF WILL BE YOUR UNDOING, LEI LING.
THAT IS WHY YOU FAIL.
WHAT?!
YOU CREATED TWO OF THEM?!
CLEVER. I DID NOT EXPECT THAT.
THANK YOU. DID I BREAK SOME KIND OF RULE?

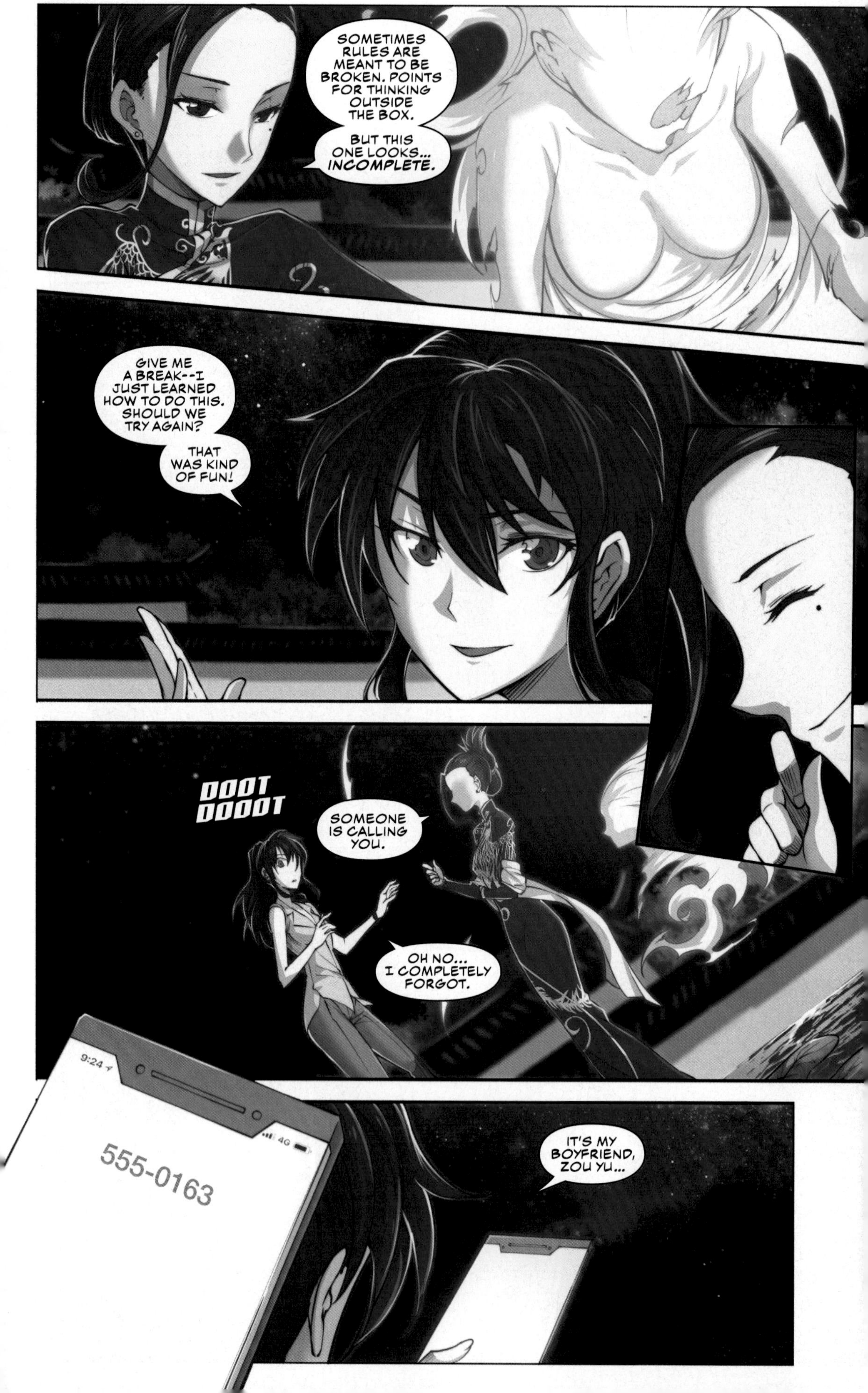
SOMETIMES RULES ARE MEANT TO BE BROKEN. POINTS FOR THINKING OUTSIDE THE BOX.
BUT THIS ONE LOOKS... INCOMPLETE.
GIVE ME A BREAK--I JUST LEARNED HOW TO DO THIS. SHOULD WE TRY AGAIN?
THAT WAS KIND OF FUN!
DOOT DOOOT
SOMEONE IS CALLING YOU.
OH NO... I COMPLETELY FORGOT.
9:24
4G
555-0163
IT'S MY BOYFRIEND, ZOU YU...

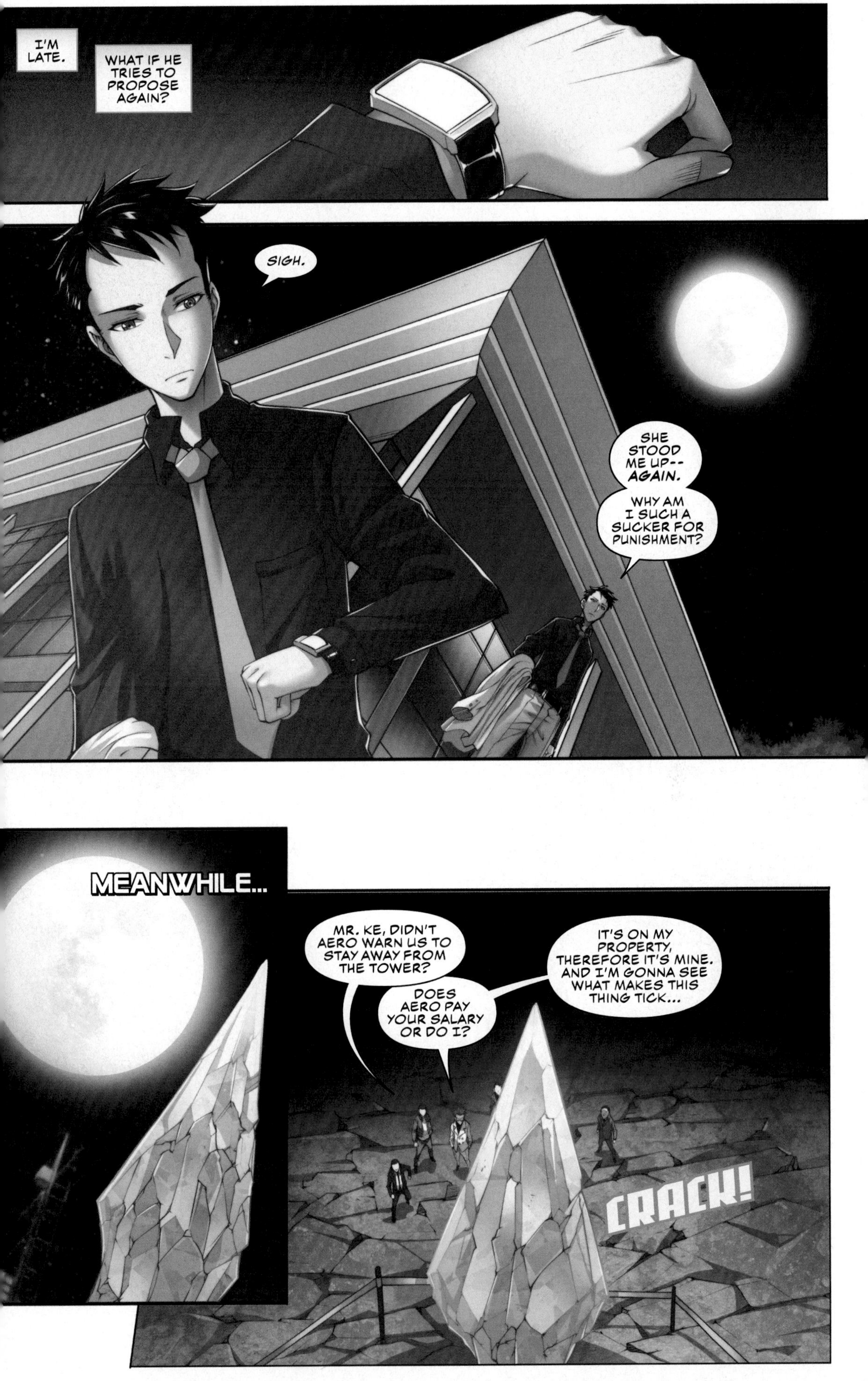
I'M LATE.
WHAT IF HE TRIES TO PROPOSE AGAIN?
SIGH.
SHE STOOD ME UP-- AGAIN.
WHY AM I SUCH A SUCKER FOR PUNISHMENT?
MEANWHILE...
MR. KE, DIDN'T AERO WARN US TO STAY AWAY FROM THE TOWER?
DOES AERO PAY YOUR SALARY OR DO I?
IT'S ON MY PROPERTY, THEREFORE IT'S MINE. AND I'M GONNA SEE WHAT MAKES THIS THING TICK...
CRACK!

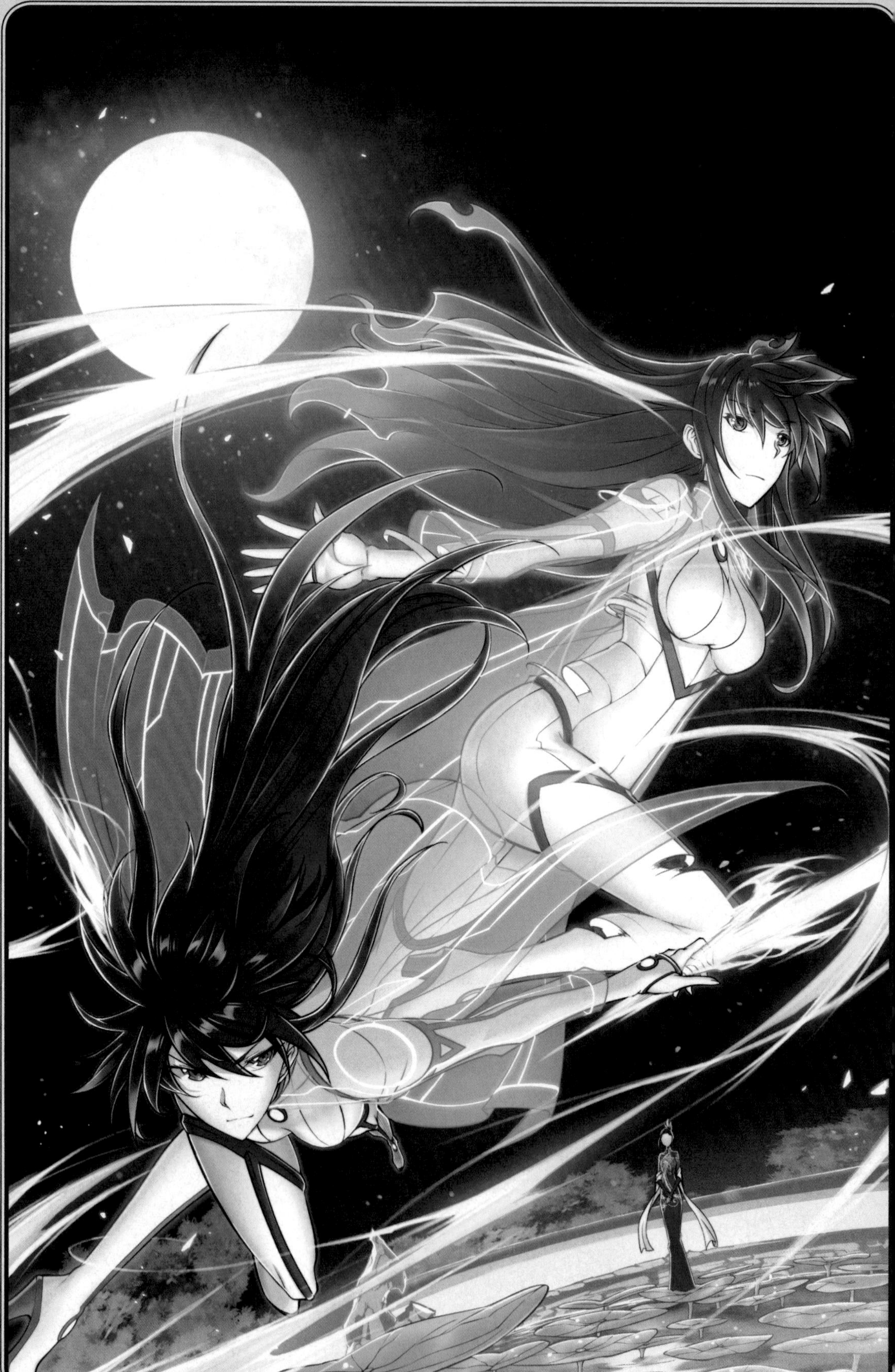

9 Double Trouble

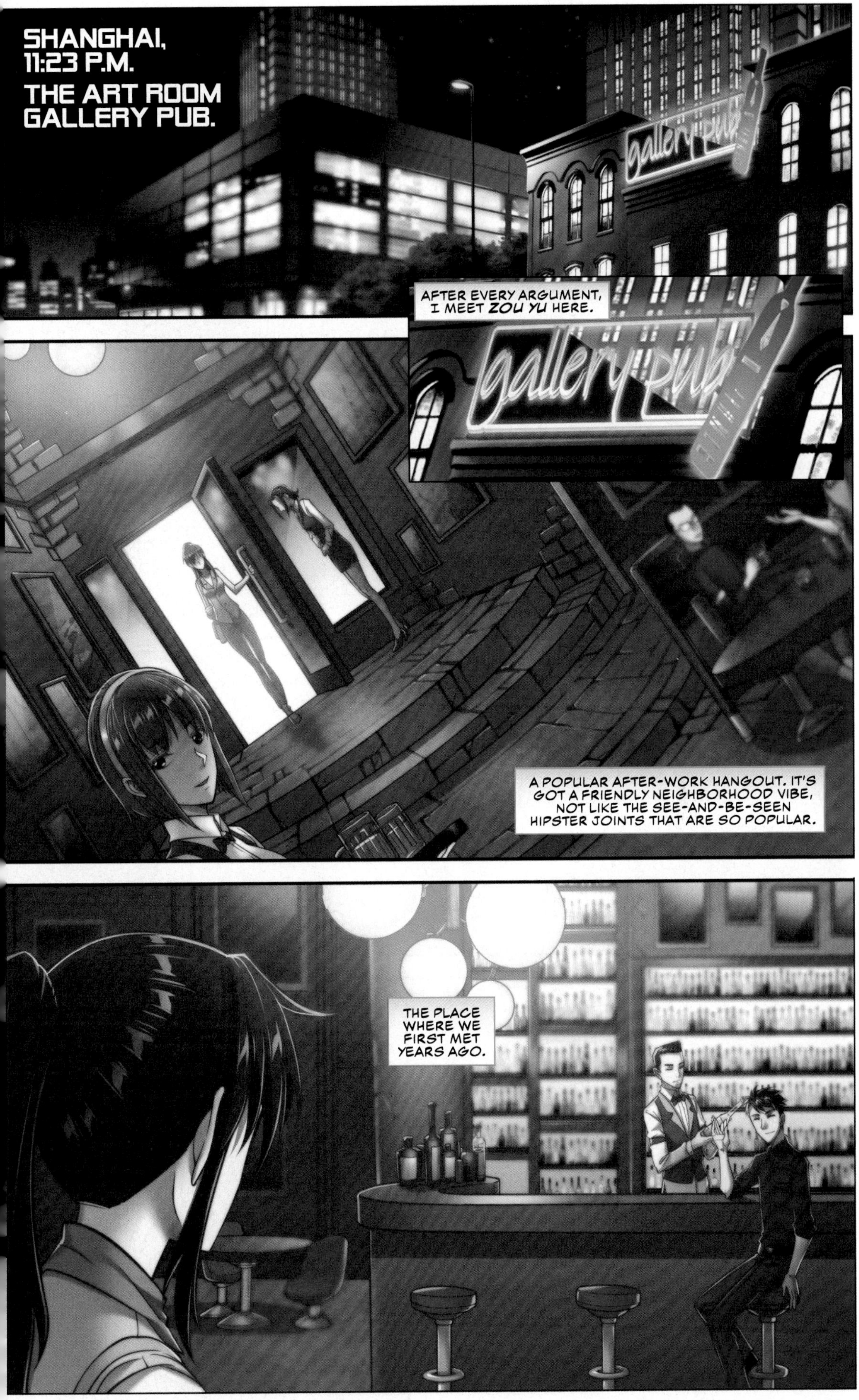
SHANGHAI,
11:23 P.M.
THE ART ROOM
GALLERY PUB.
gallery pub
AFTER EVERY ARGUMENT,
I MEET ZOU YU HERE.
gallery pub
A POPULAR AFTER-WORK HANGOUT. IT'S
GOT A FRIENDLY NEIGHBORHOOD VIBE,
NOT LIKE THE SEE-AND-BE-SEEN
HIPSTER JOINTS THAT ARE SO POPULAR.
THE PLACE
WHERE WE
FIRST MET
YEARS AGO.

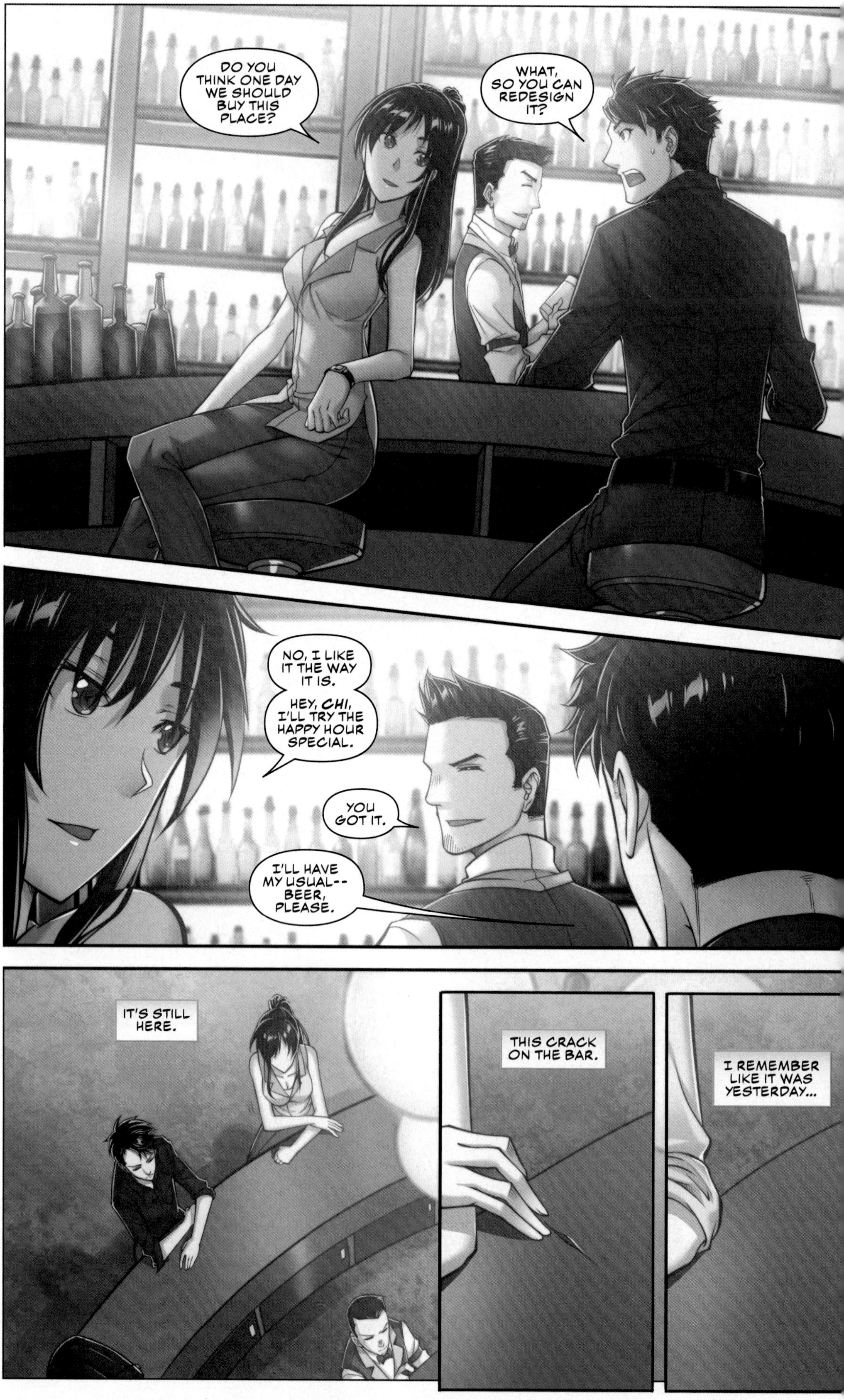
DO YOU THINK ONE DAY WE SHOULD BUY THIS PLACE?
WHAT, SO YOU CAN REDESIGN IT?
NO, I LIKE IT THE WAY IT IS.
HEY, CHI, I'LL TRY THE HAPPY HOUR SPECIAL.
YOU GOT IT.
I'LL HAVE MY USUAL-- BEER, PLEASE.
IT'S STILL HERE.
THIS CRACK ON THE BAR.
I REMEMBER LIKE IT WAS YESTERDAY...

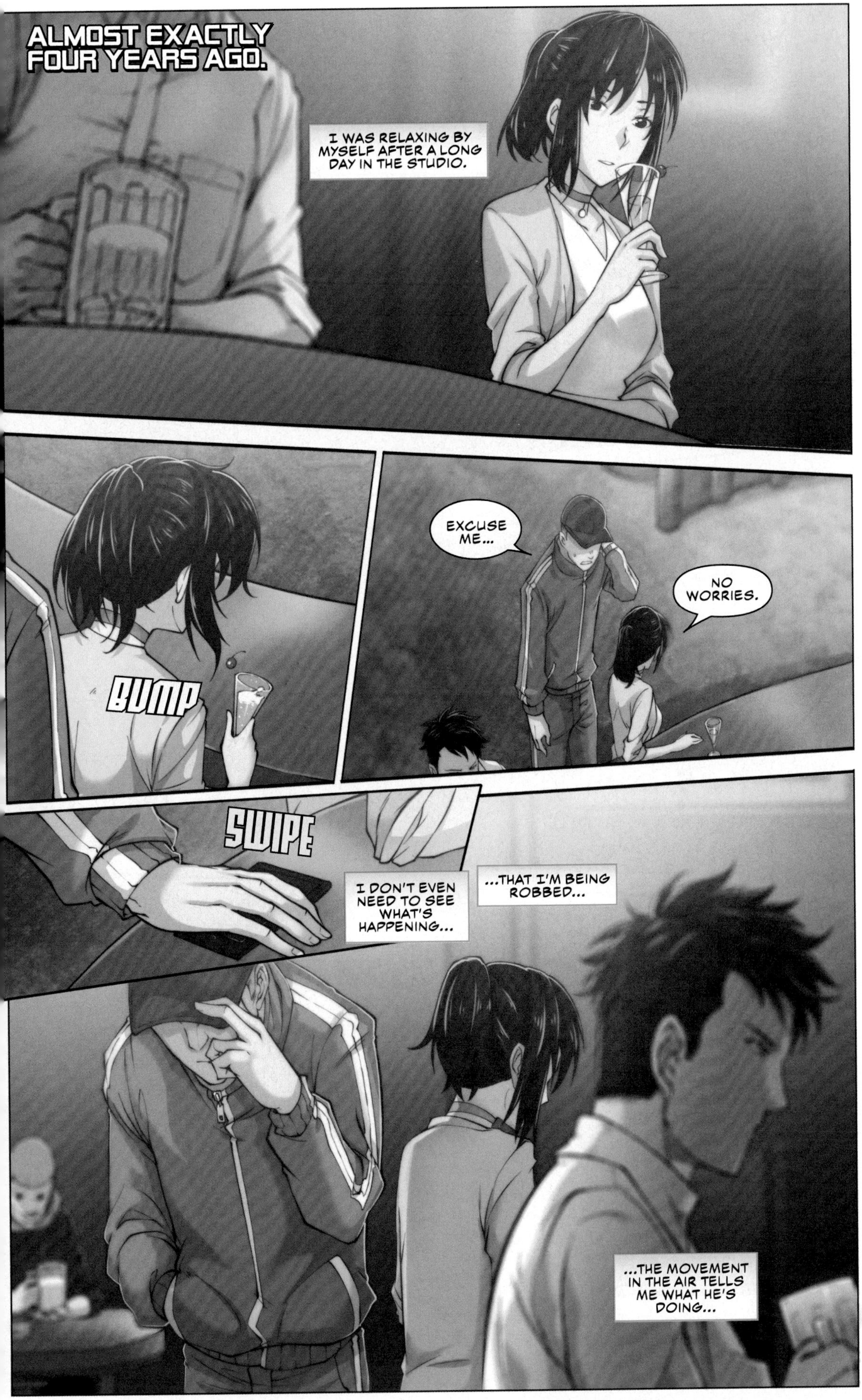
ALMOST EXACTLY FOUR YEARS AGO.
I WAS RELAXING BY MYSELF AFTER A LONG DAY IN THE STUDIO.
BUMP
EXCUSE ME...
NO WORRIES.
SWIPE
I DON'T EVEN NEED TO SEE WHAT'S HAPPENING...
...THAT I'M BEING ROBBED...
...THE MOVEMENT IN THE AIR TELLS ME WHAT HE'S DOING...

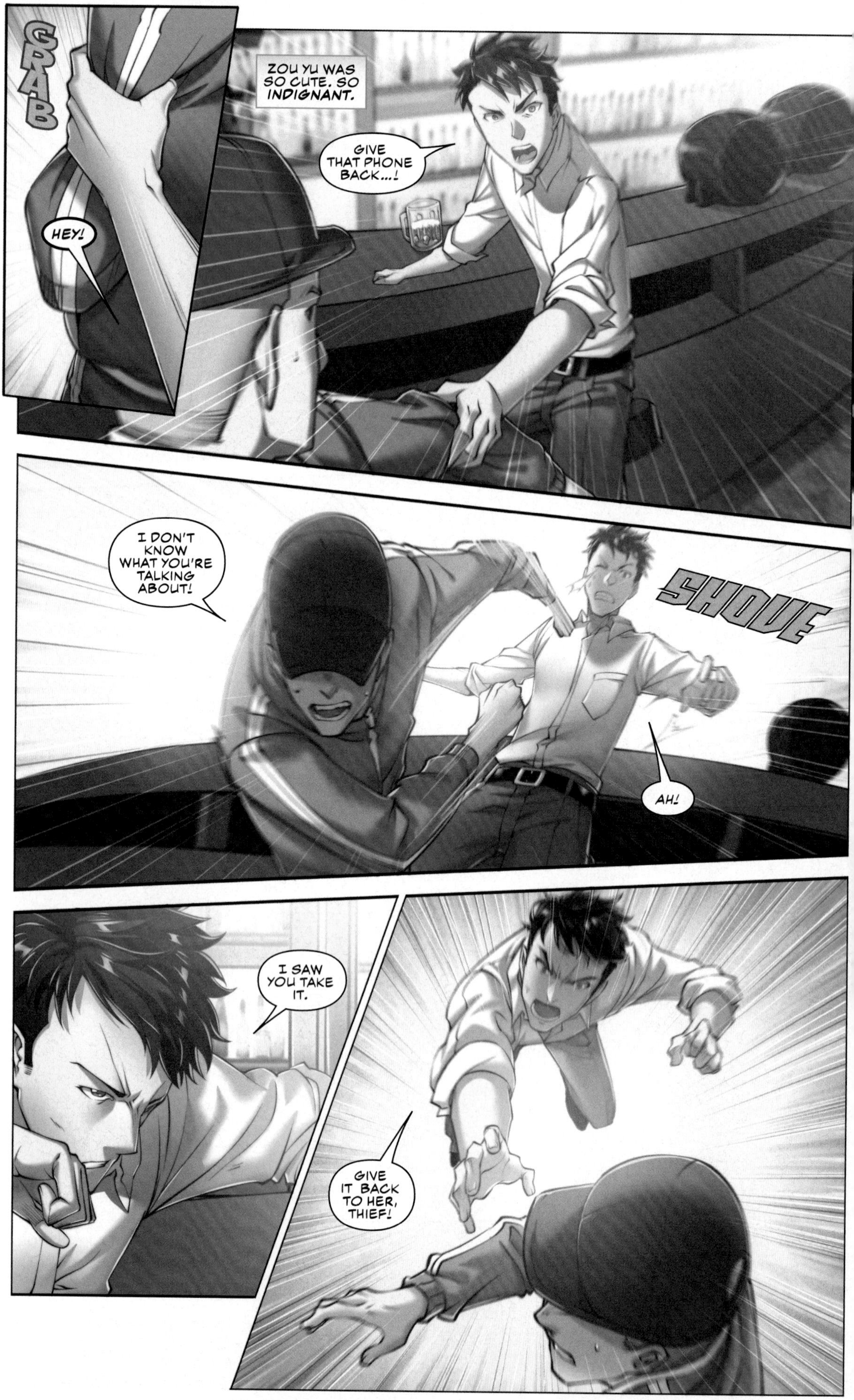
GRAB
ZOU YU WAS SO CUTE. SO INDIGNANT.
GIVE THAT PHONE BACK...!
HEY!
I DON'T KNOW WHAT YOU'RE TALKING ABOUT!
SHOVE
AH!
I SAW YOU TAKE IT.
GIVE IT BACK TO HER, THIEF!

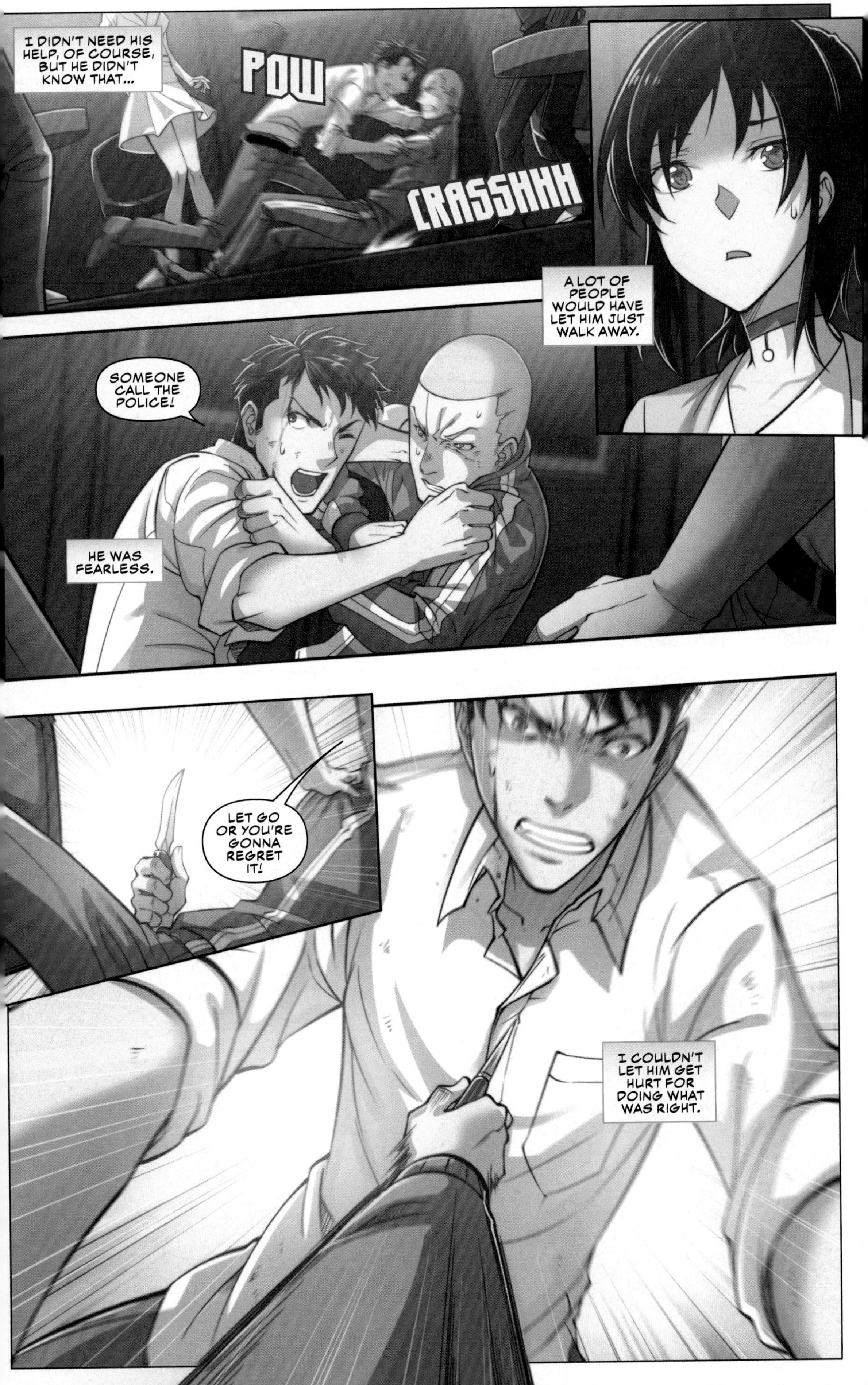
I DIDN'T NEED HIS HELP, OF COURSE, BUT HE DIDN'T KNOW THAT...
POW
CRASSHHH
A LOT OF PEOPLE WOULD HAVE LET HIM JUST WALK AWAY.
SOMEONE CALL THE POLICE!
HE WAS FEARLESS.
LET GO OR YOU'RE GONNA REGRET IT!
I COULDN'T LET HIM GET HURT FOR DOING WHAT WAS RIGHT.

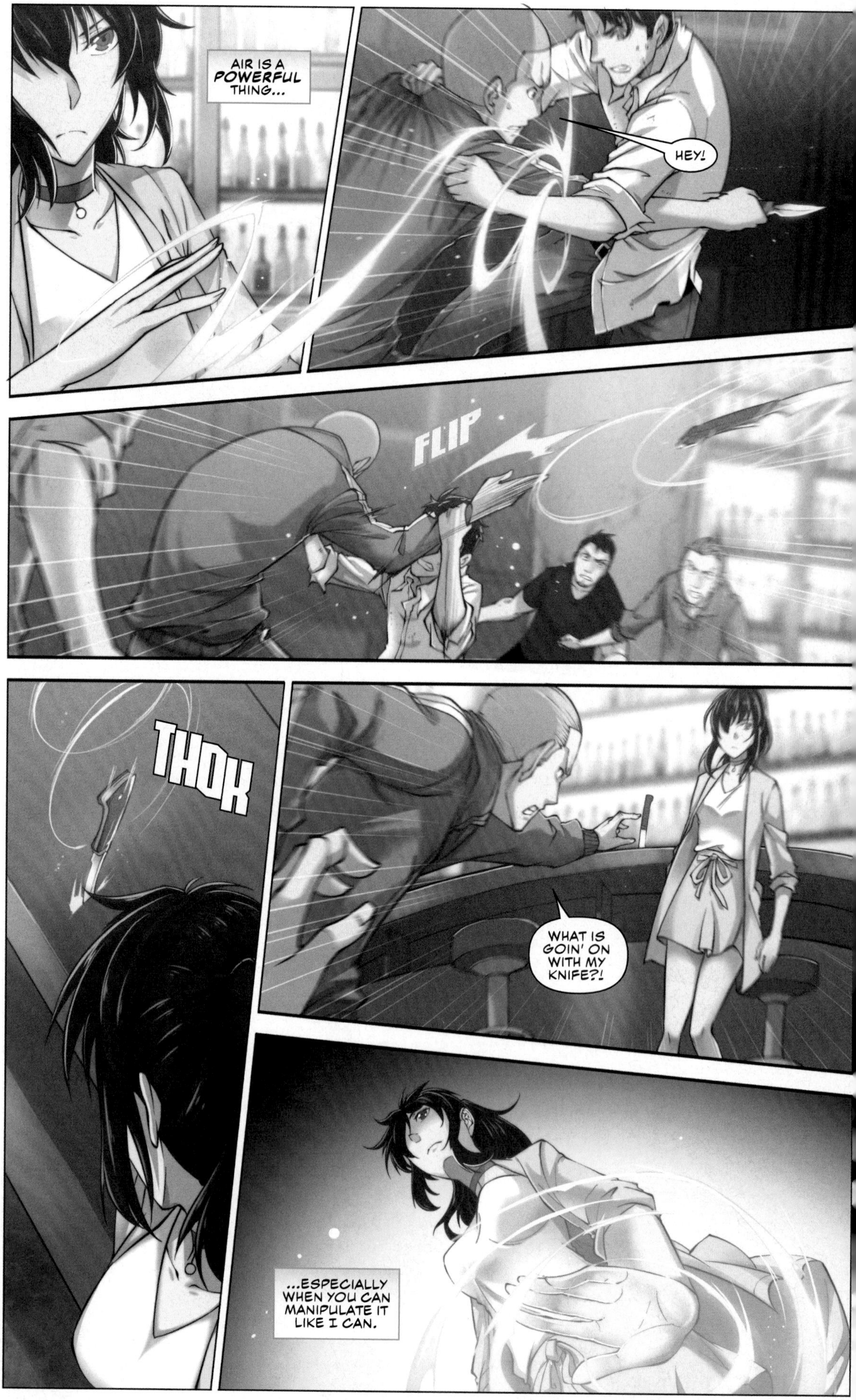
AIR IS A POWERFUL THING...
HEY!
FLIP
THOK
WHAT IS GOIN' ON WITH MY KNIFE?!
...ESPECIALLY WHEN YOU CAN MANIPULATE IT LIKE I CAN.

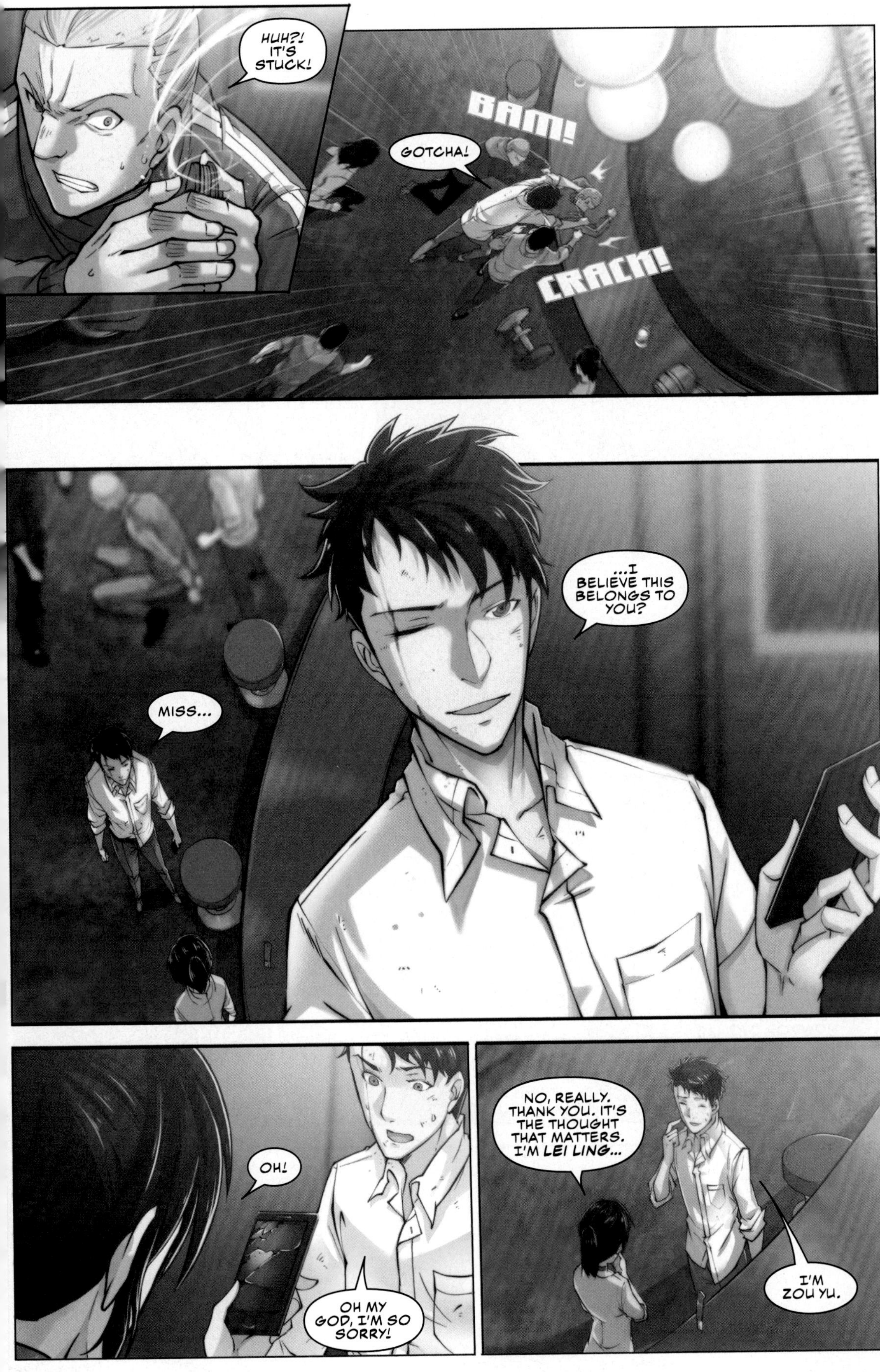
HUH?! IT'S STUCK!
BAM!
GOTCHA!
CRACK!
...I BELIEVE THIS BELONGS TO YOU?
MISS...
OH!
OH MY GOD, I'M SO SORRY!
NO, REALLY. THANK YOU. IT'S THE THOUGHT THAT MATTERS. I'M LEI LING...
I'M ZOU YU.

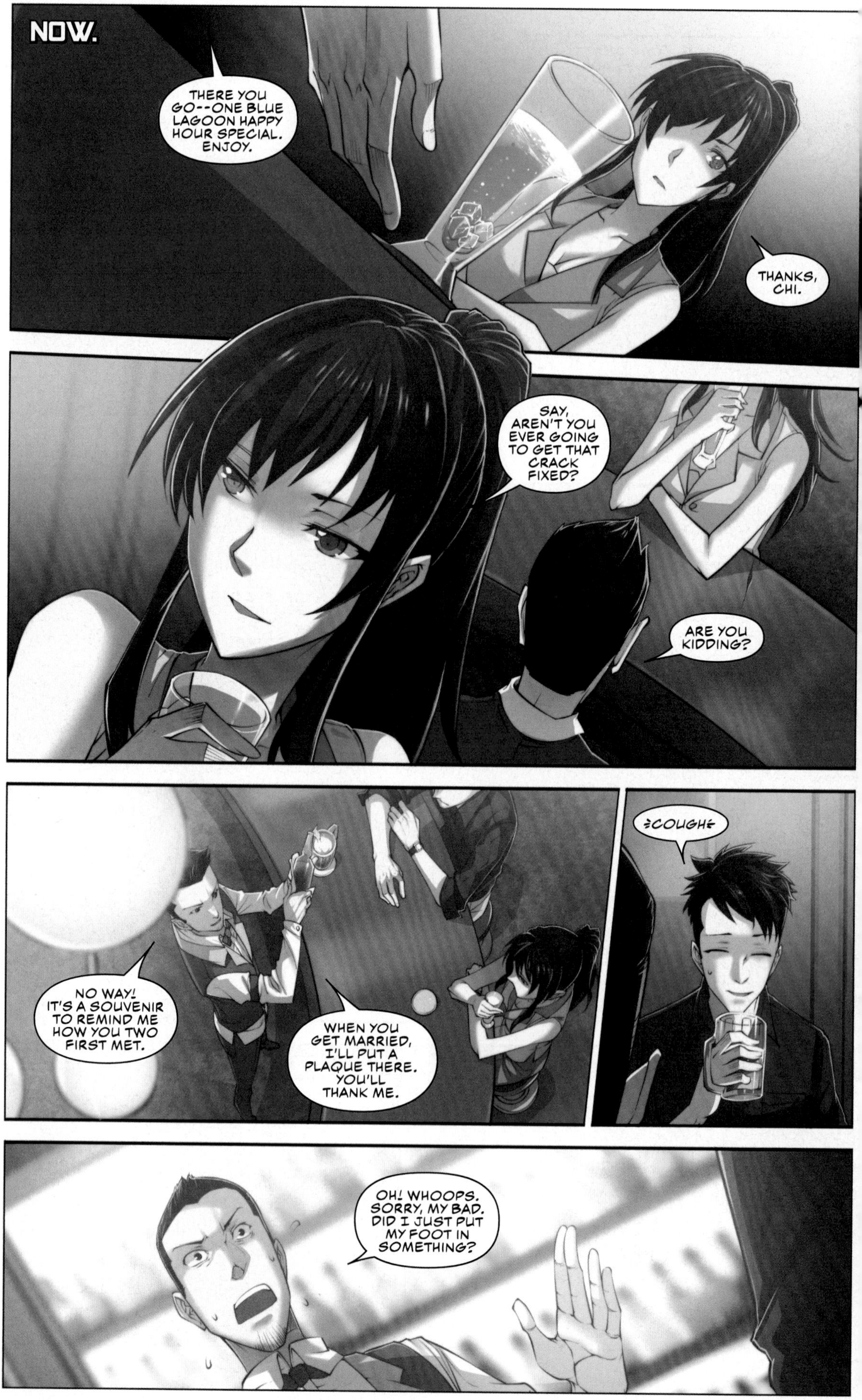
NOW.
THERE YOU GO--ONE BLUE LAGOON HAPPY HOUR SPECIAL. ENJOY.
THANKS, CHI.
SAY, AREN'T YOU EVER GOING TO GET THAT CRACK FIXED?
ARE YOU KIDDING?
NO WAY! IT'S A SOUVENIR TO REMIND ME HOW YOU TWO FIRST MET.
WHEN YOU GET MARRIED, I'LL PUT A PLAQUE THERE. YOU'LL THANK ME.
COUGH
OH! WHOOPS. SORRY, MY BAD. DID I JUST PUT MY FOOT IN SOMETHING?

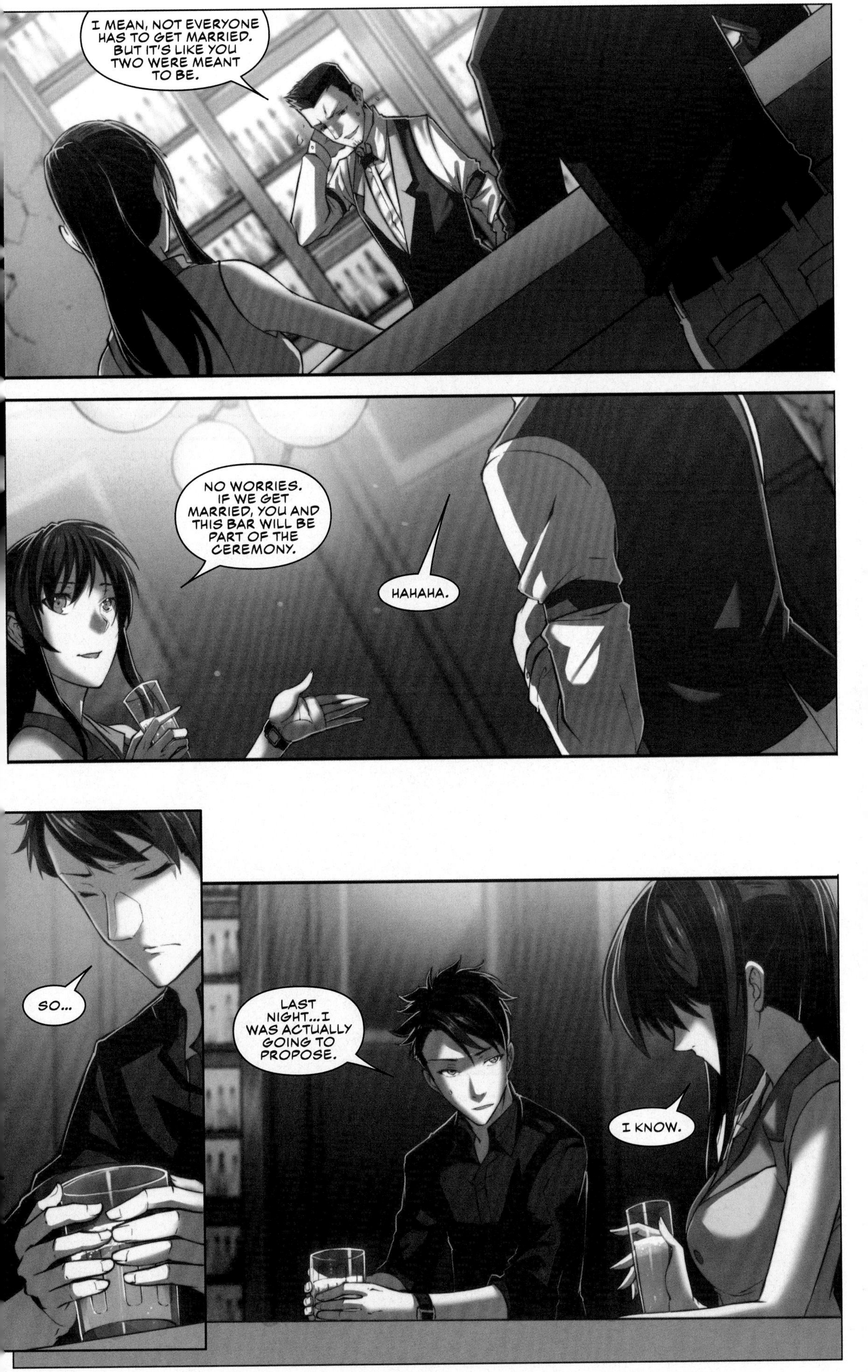
I MEAN, NOT EVERYONE HAS TO GET MARRIED. BUT IT'S LIKE YOU TWO WERE MEANT TO BE.
NO WORRIES. IF WE GET MARRIED, YOU AND THIS BAR WILL BE PART OF THE CEREMONY.
HAHAHA.
SO...
LAST NIGHT...I WAS ACTUALLY GOING TO PROPOSE.
I KNOW.

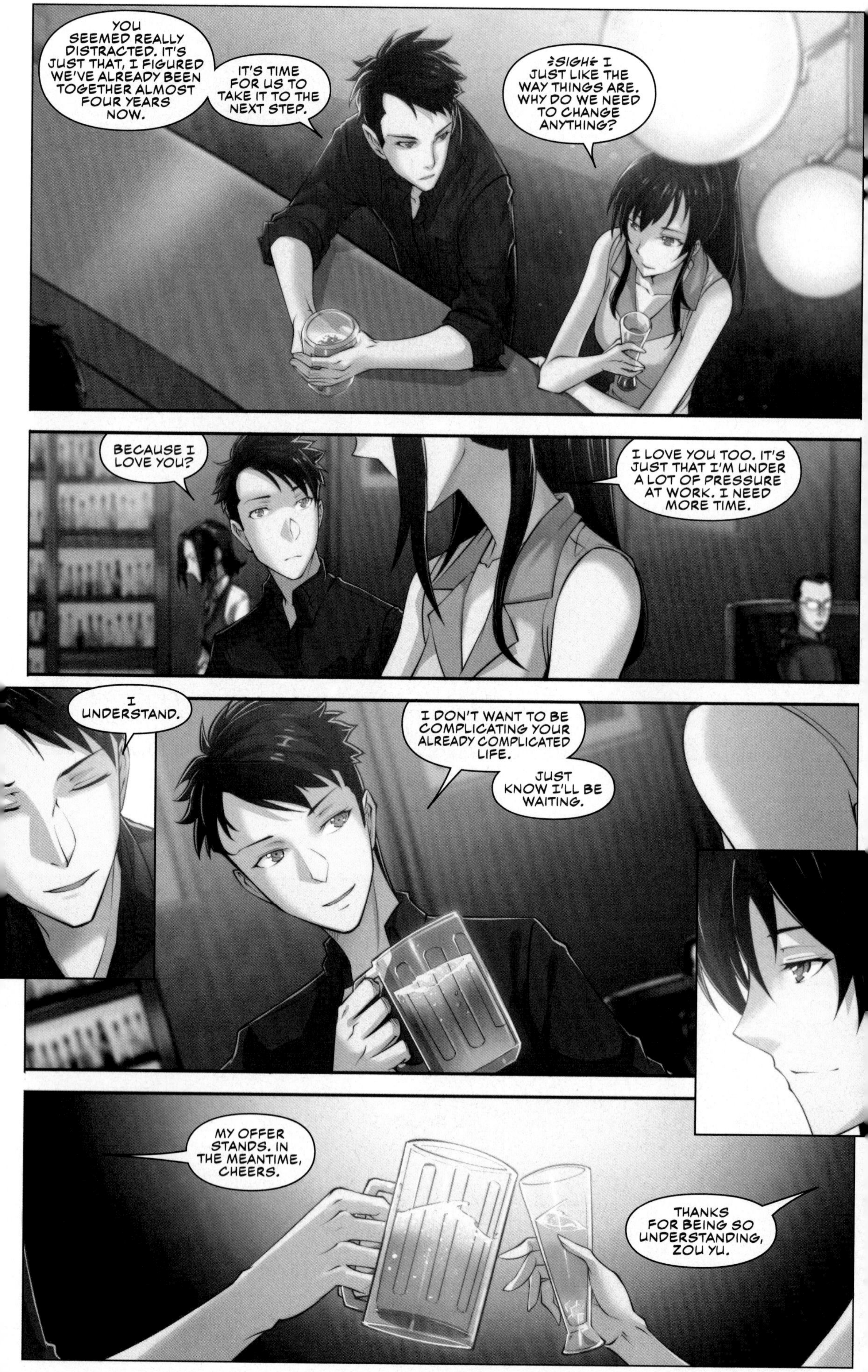
YOU SEEMED REALLY DISTRACTED. IT'S JUST THAT, I FIGURED WE'VE ALREADY BEEN TOGETHER ALMOST FOUR YEARS NOW.
IT'S TIME FOR US TO TAKE IT TO THE NEXT STEP.
SIGH I JUST LIKE THE WAY THINGS ARE. WHY DO WE NEED TO CHANGE ANYTHING?
BECAUSE I LOVE YOU?
I LOVE YOU TOO. IT'S JUST THAT I'M UNDER A LOT OF PRESSURE AT WORK. I NEED MORE TIME.
I UNDERSTAND.
I DON'T WANT TO BE COMPLICATING YOUR ALREADY COMPLICATED LIFE.
JUST KNOW I'LL BE WAITING.
MY OFFER STANDS. IN THE MEANTIME, CHEERS.
THANKS FOR BEING SO UNDERSTANDING, ZOU YU.

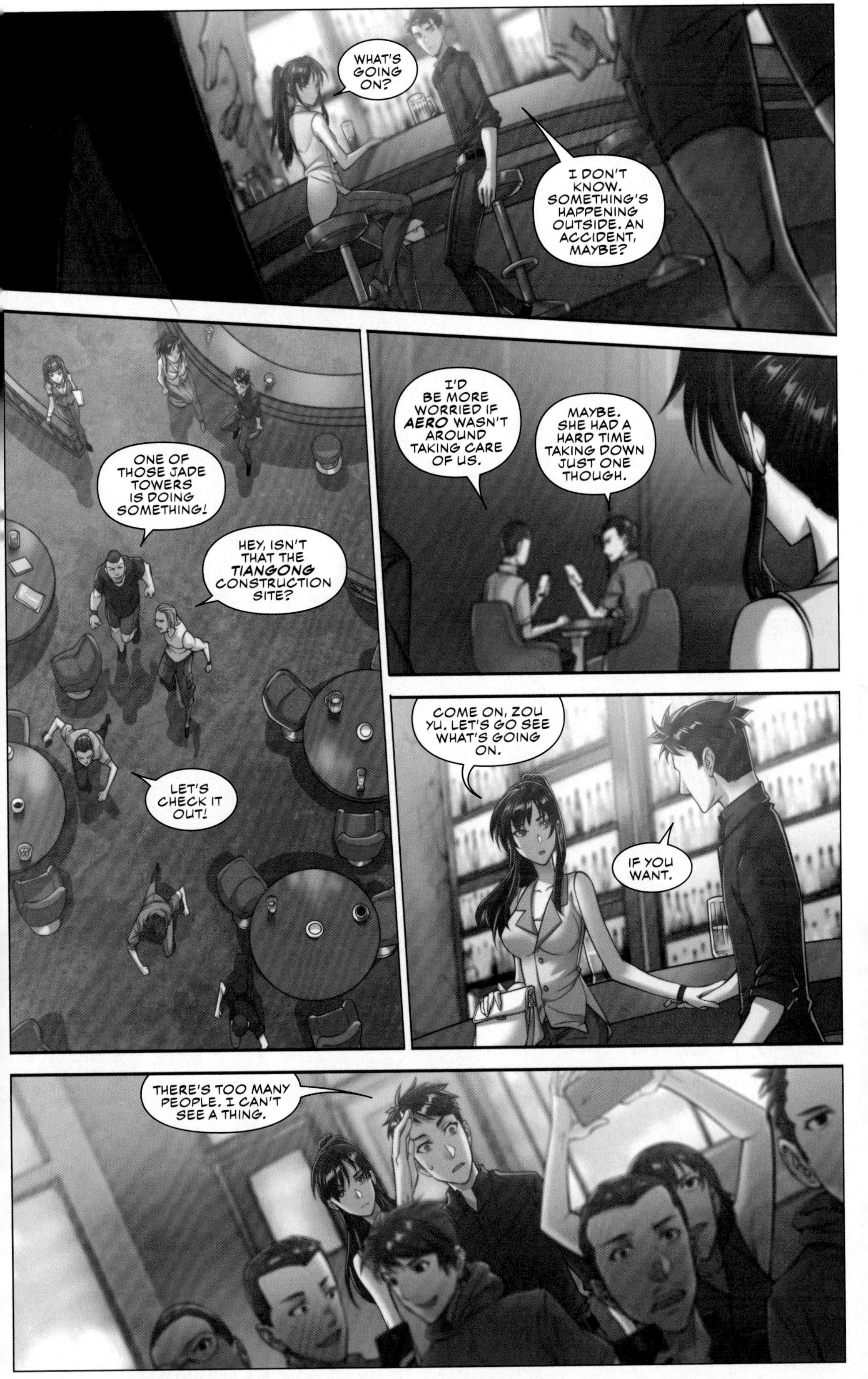
WHAT'S GOING ON?
I DON'T KNOW. SOMETHING'S HAPPENING OUTSIDE. AN ACCIDENT, MAYBE?
ONE OF THOSE JADE TOWERS IS DOING SOMETHING!
HEY, ISN'T THAT THE TIANGONG CONSTRUCTION SITE?
LET'S CHECK IT OUT!
I'D BE MORE WORRIED IF AERO WASN'T AROUND TAKING CARE OF US.
MAYBE. SHE HAD A HARD TIME TAKING DOWN JUST ONE THOUGH.
COME ON, ZOU YU. LET'S GO SEE WHAT'S GOING ON.
IF YOU WANT.
THERE'S TOO MANY PEOPLE. I CAN'T SEE A THING.

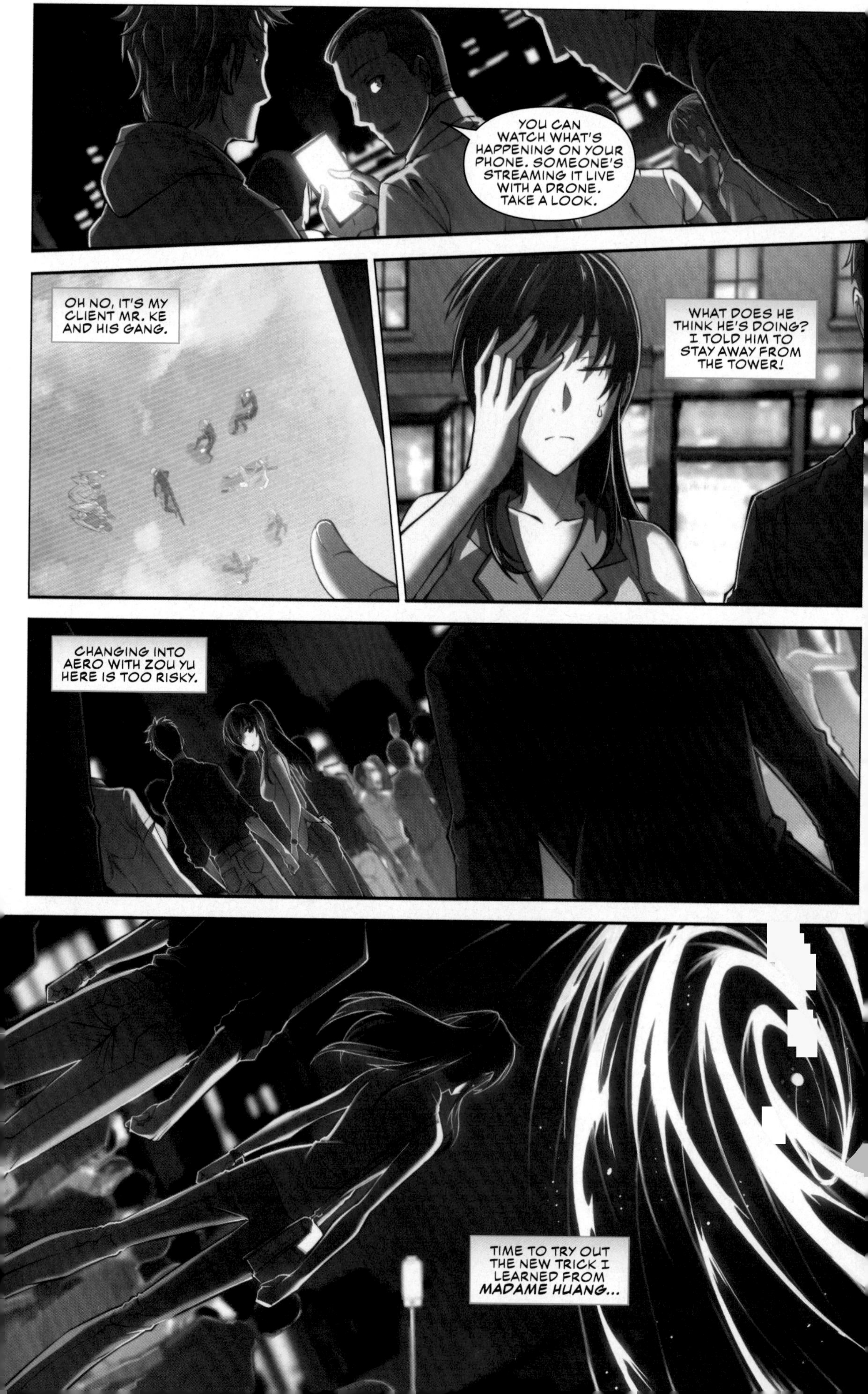
YOU CAN WATCH WHAT'S HAPPENING ON YOUR PHONE. SOMEONE'S STREAMING IT LIVE WITH A DRONE. TAKE A LOOK.
OH NO, IT'S MY CLIENT MR. KE AND HIS GANG.
WHAT DOES HE THINK HE'S DOING? I TOLD HIM TO STAY AWAY FROM THE TOWER!
CHANGING INTO AERO WITH ZOU YU HERE IS TOO RISKY.
TIME TO TRY OUT THE NEW TRICK I LEARNED FROM MADAME HUANG...

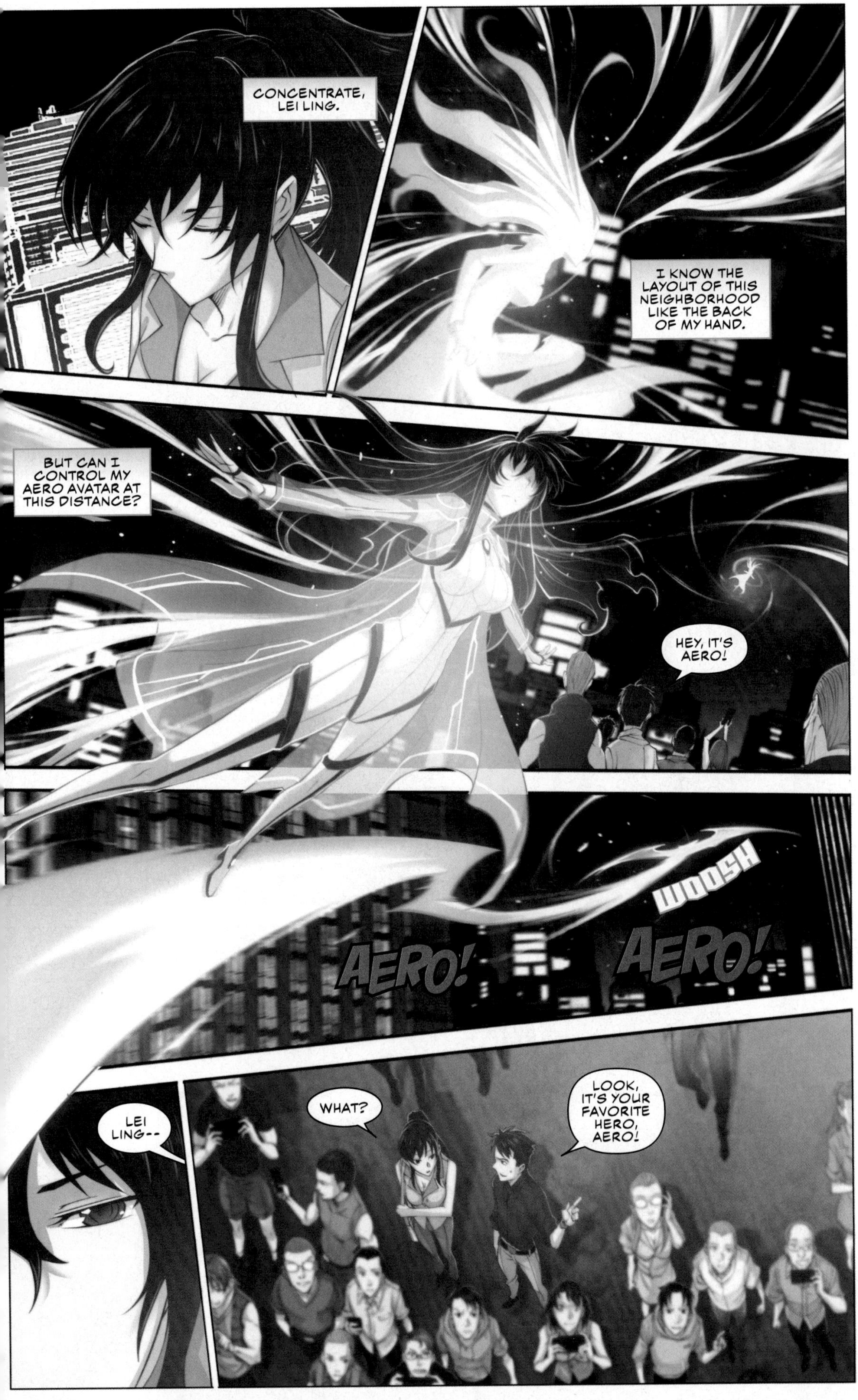
CONCENTRATE, LEI LING.
I KNOW THE LAYOUT OF THIS NEIGHBORHOOD LIKE THE BACK OF MY HAND.
BUT CAN I CONTROL MY AERO AVATAR AT THIS DISTANCE?
HEY, IT'S AERO!
WOOSH
AERO!
AERO!
LEI LING--
WHAT?
LOOK, IT'S YOUR FAVORITE HERO, AERO!

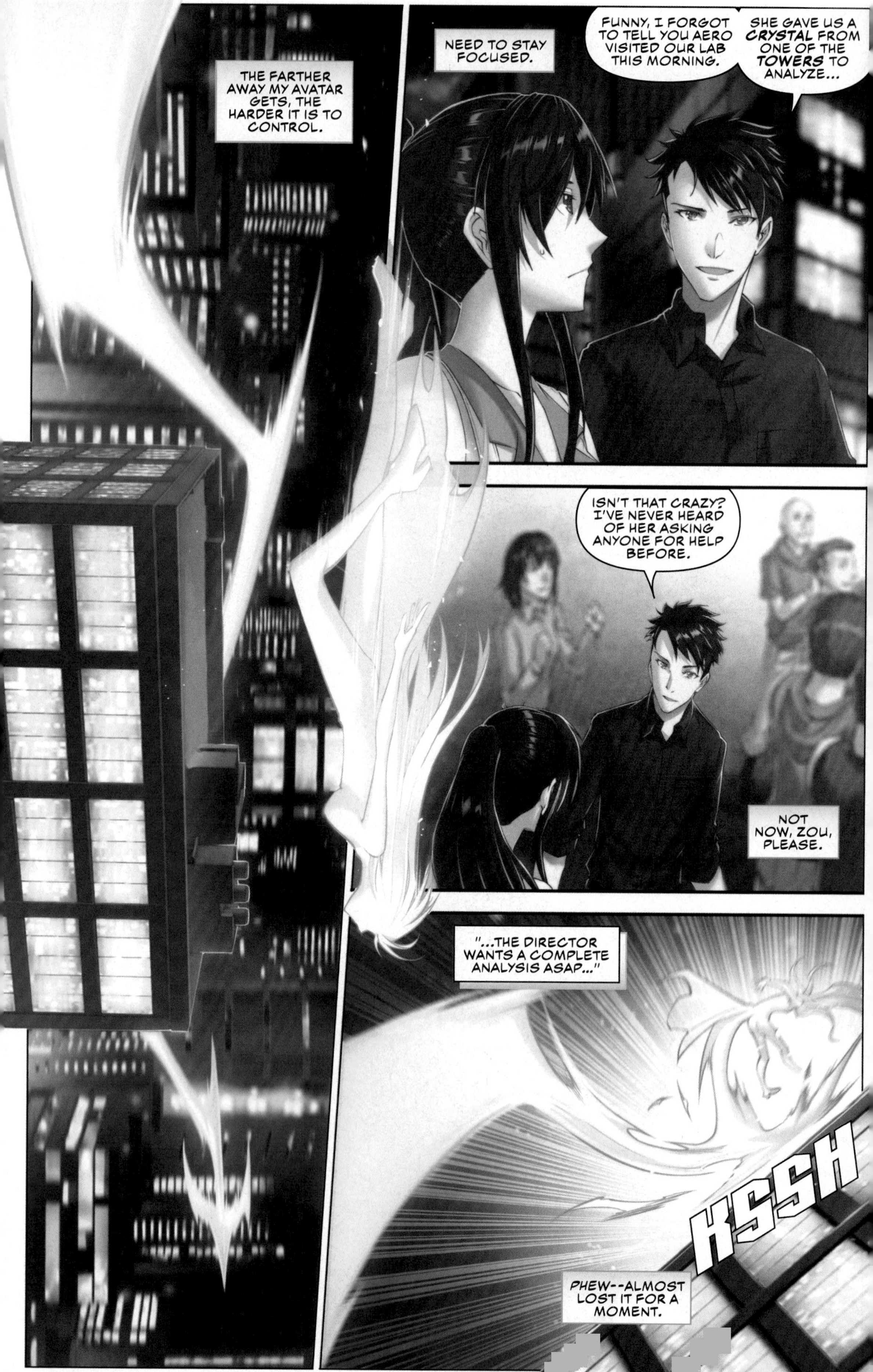
THE FARTHER AWAY MY AVATAR GETS, THE HARDER IT IS TO CONTROL.
NEED TO STAY FOCUSED.
FUNNY, I FORGOT TO TELL YOU AERO VISITED OUR LAB THIS MORNING.
SHE GAVE US A **CRYSTAL** FROM ONE OF THE **TOWERS** TO ANALYZE...
ISN'T THAT CRAZY? I'VE NEVER HEARD OF HER ASKING ANYONE FOR HELP BEFORE.
NOT NOW, ZOU, PLEASE.
"...THE DIRECTOR WANTS A COMPLETE ANALYSIS ASAP..."
KSSH
PHEW--ALMOST LOST IT FOR A MOMENT.

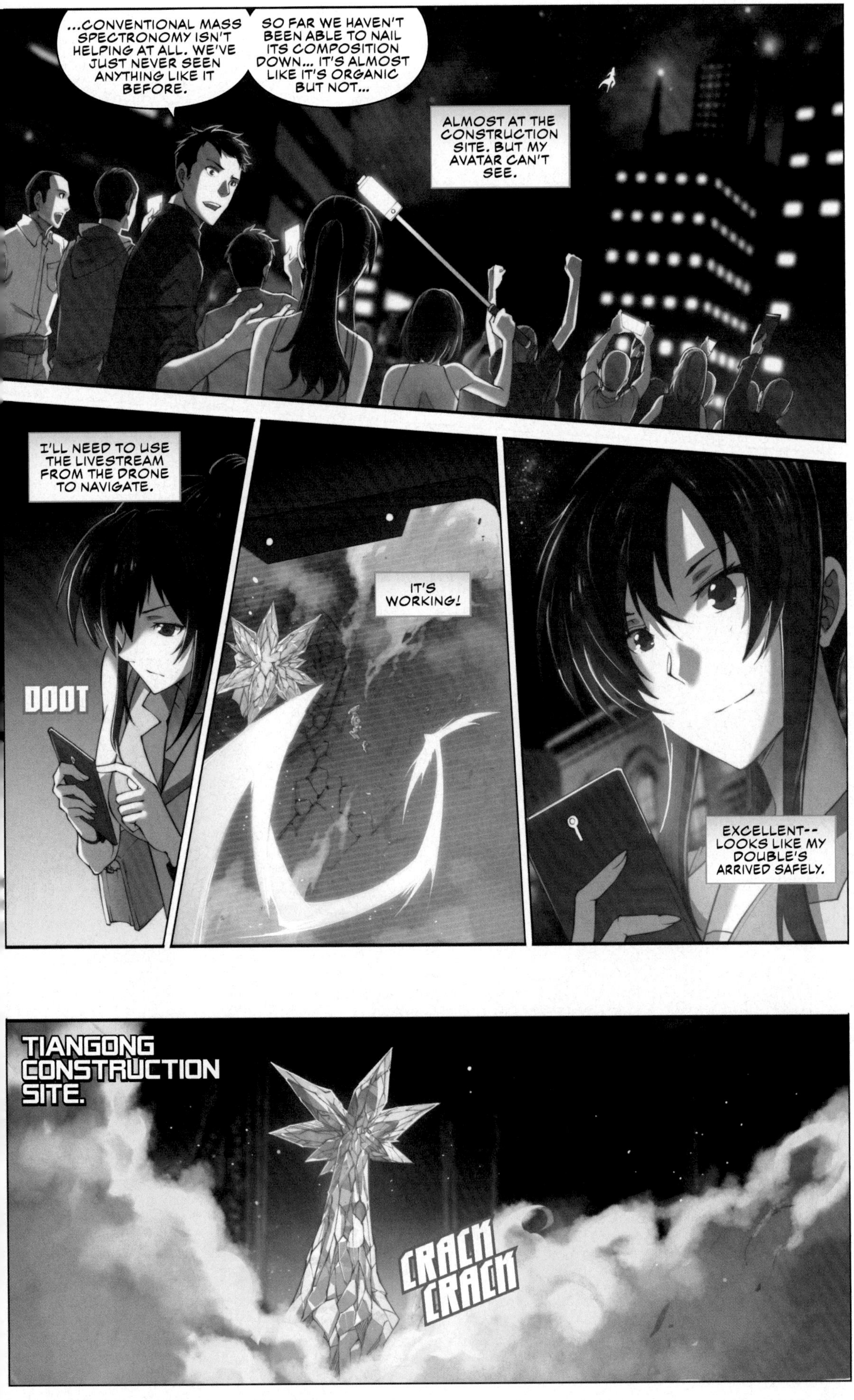
...CONVENTIONAL MASS SPECTRONOMY ISN'T HELPING AT ALL. WE'VE JUST NEVER SEEN ANYTHING LIKE IT BEFORE.
SO FAR WE HAVEN'T BEEN ABLE TO NAIL ITS COMPOSITION DOWN... IT'S ALMOST LIKE IT'S ORGANIC BUT NOT...
ALMOST AT THE CONSTRUCTION SITE. BUT MY AVATAR CAN'T SEE.
I'LL NEED TO USE THE LIVESTREAM FROM THE DRONE TO NAVIGATE.
DOOT
IT'S WORKING!
EXCELLENT-- LOOKS LIKE MY DOUBLE'S ARRIVED SAFELY.
TIANGONG CONSTRUCTION SITE.
CRACK CRACK

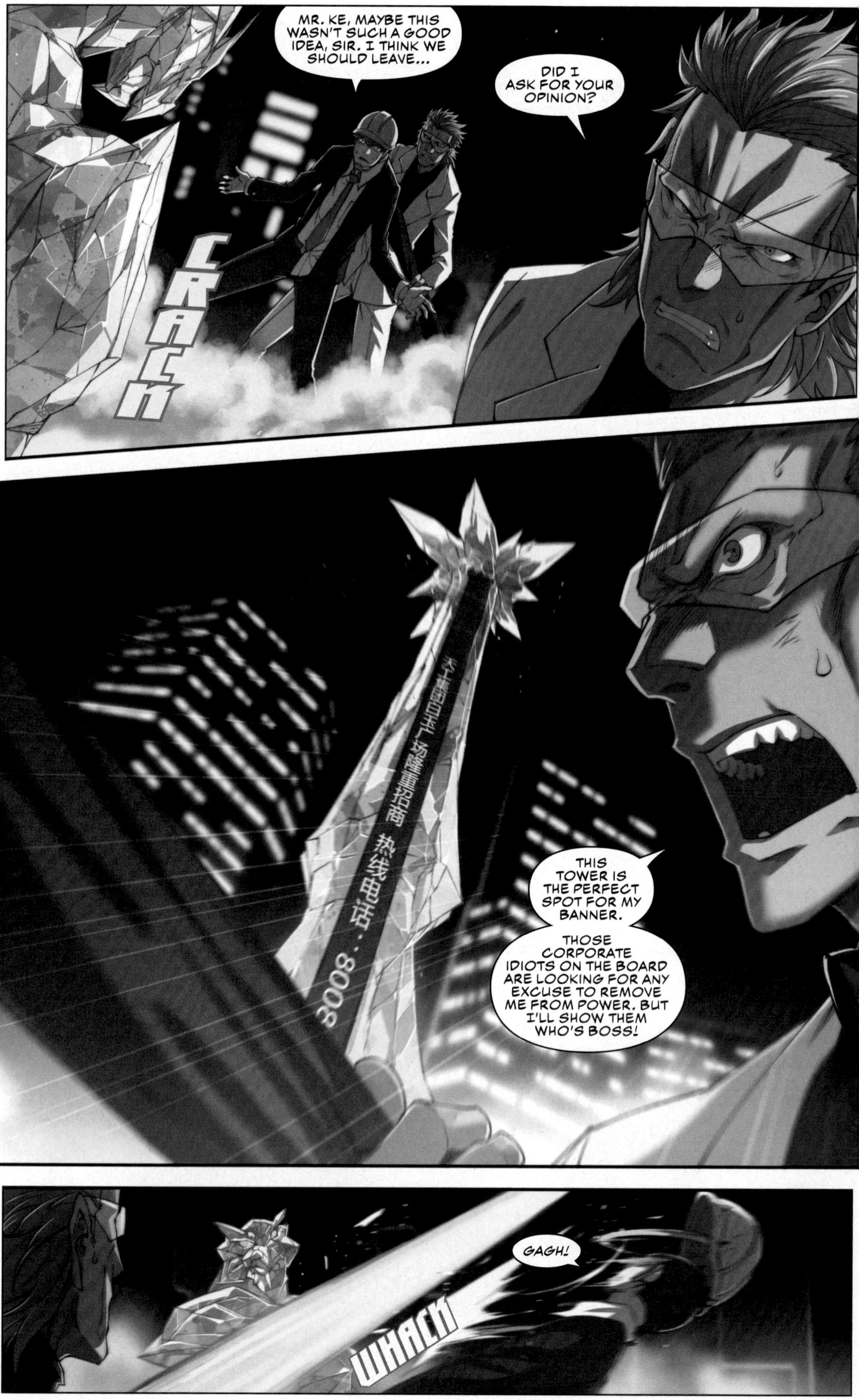
MR. KE, MAYBE THIS WASN'T SUCH A GOOD IDEA, SIR. I THINK WE SHOULD LEAVE...
DID I ASK FOR YOUR OPINION?
CRACK
THIS TOWER IS THE PERFECT SPOT FOR MY BANNER.
THOSE CORPORATE IDIOTS ON THE BOARD ARE LOOKING FOR ANY EXCUSE TO REMOVE ME FROM POWER. BUT I'LL SHOW THEM WHO'S BOSS!
GAGH!
WHACK

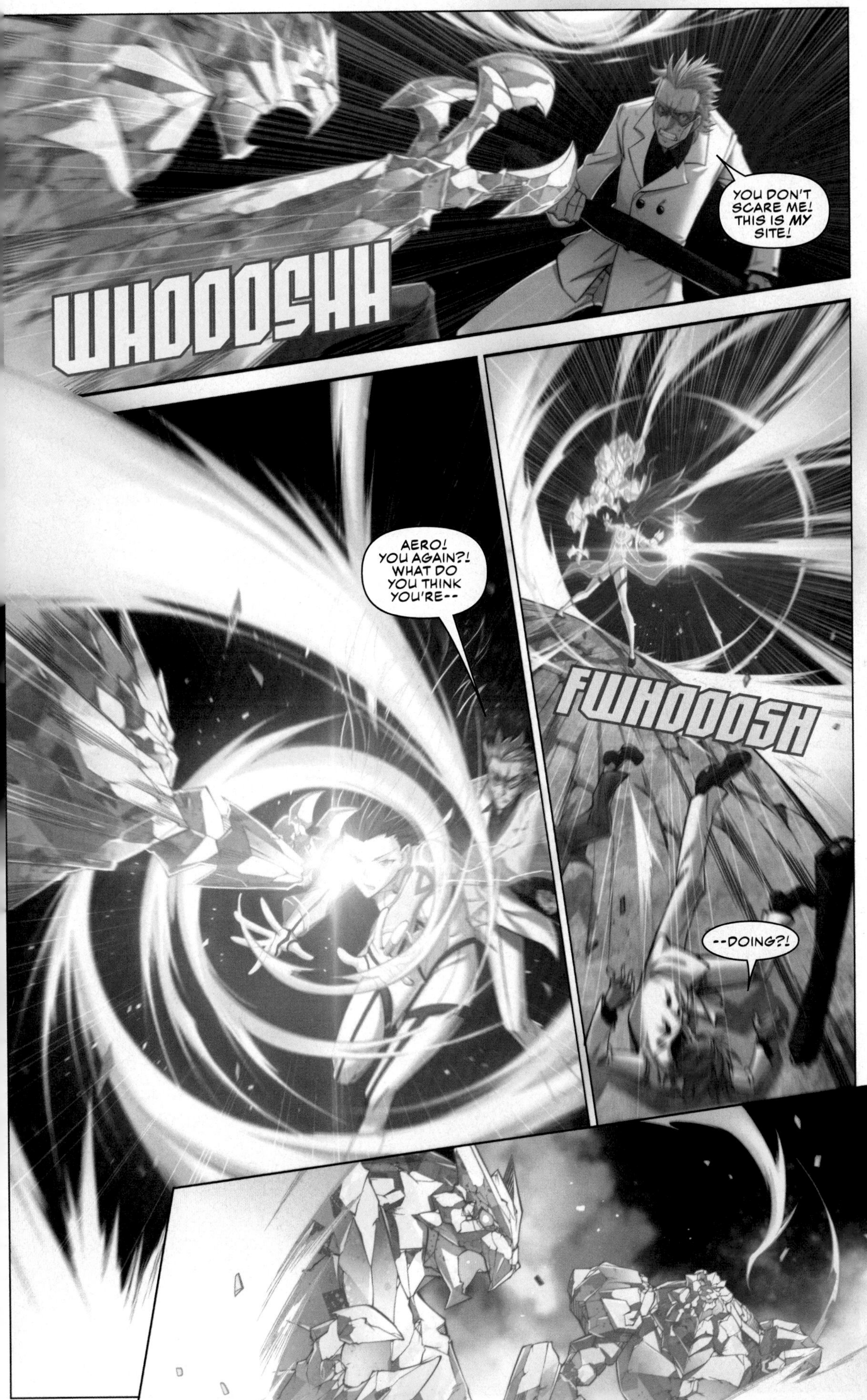
YOU DON'T SCARE ME! THIS IS MY SITE!
WHOOOSH
AERO! YOU AGAIN?! WHAT DO YOU THINK YOU'RE--
FWHOOOSH
--DOING?!

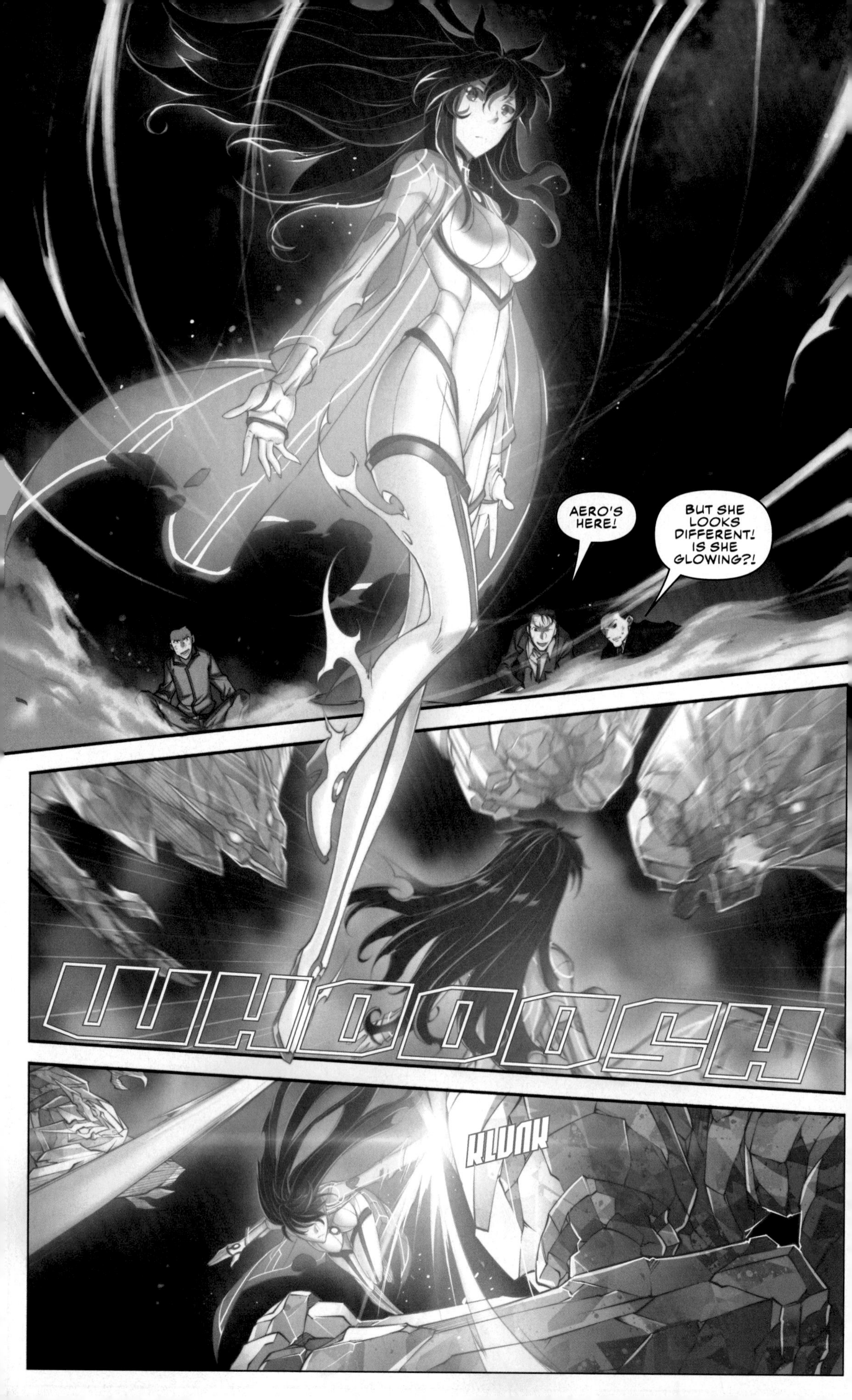
AERO'S HERE!
BUT SHE LOOKS DIFFERENT! IS SHE GLOWING?!
WHOOOSH
KLUNK

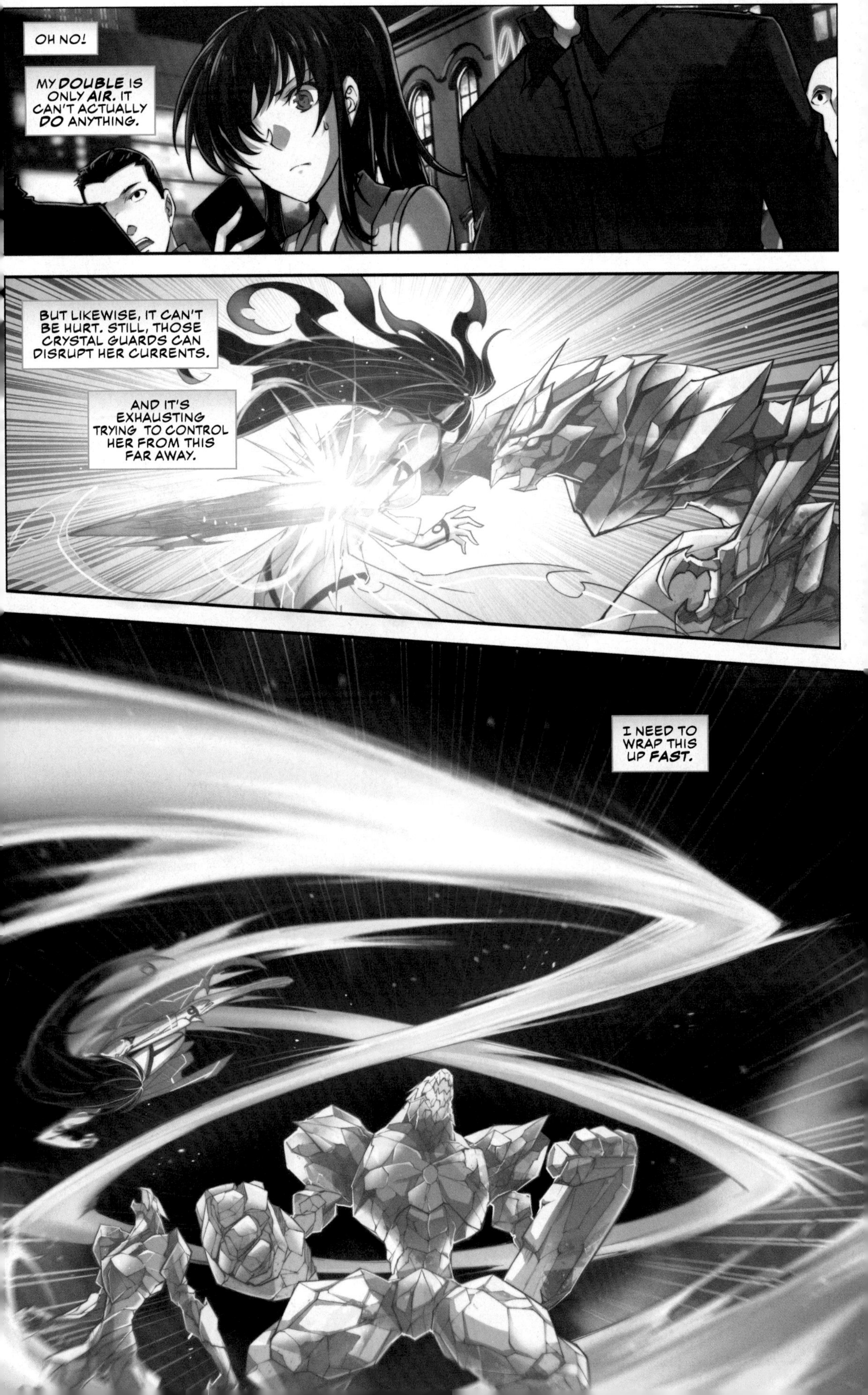
OH NO!
MY DOUBLE IS ONLY AIR. IT CAN'T ACTUALLY DO ANYTHING.
BUT LIKEWISE, IT CAN'T BE HURT. STILL, THOSE CRYSTAL GUARDS CAN DISRUPT HER CURRENTS.
AND IT'S EXHAUSTING TRYING TO CONTROL HER FROM THIS FAR AWAY.
I NEED TO WRAP THIS UP FAST.

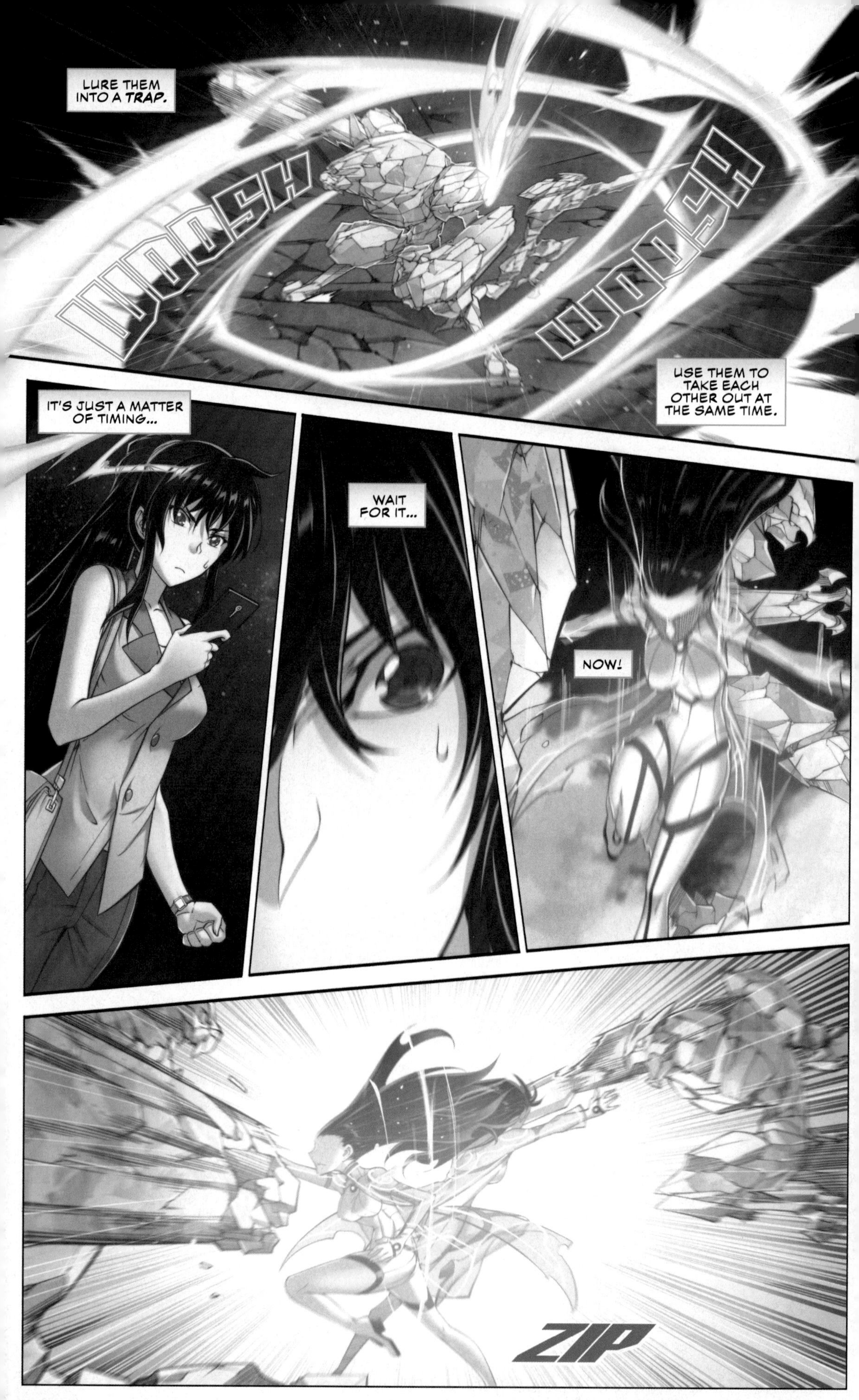
LURE THEM INTO A TRAP.
WHOOSH
WHOOSH
USE THEM TO TAKE EACH OTHER OUT AT THE SAME TIME.
IT'S JUST A MATTER OF TIMING...
WAIT FOR IT...
NOW!
ZIP

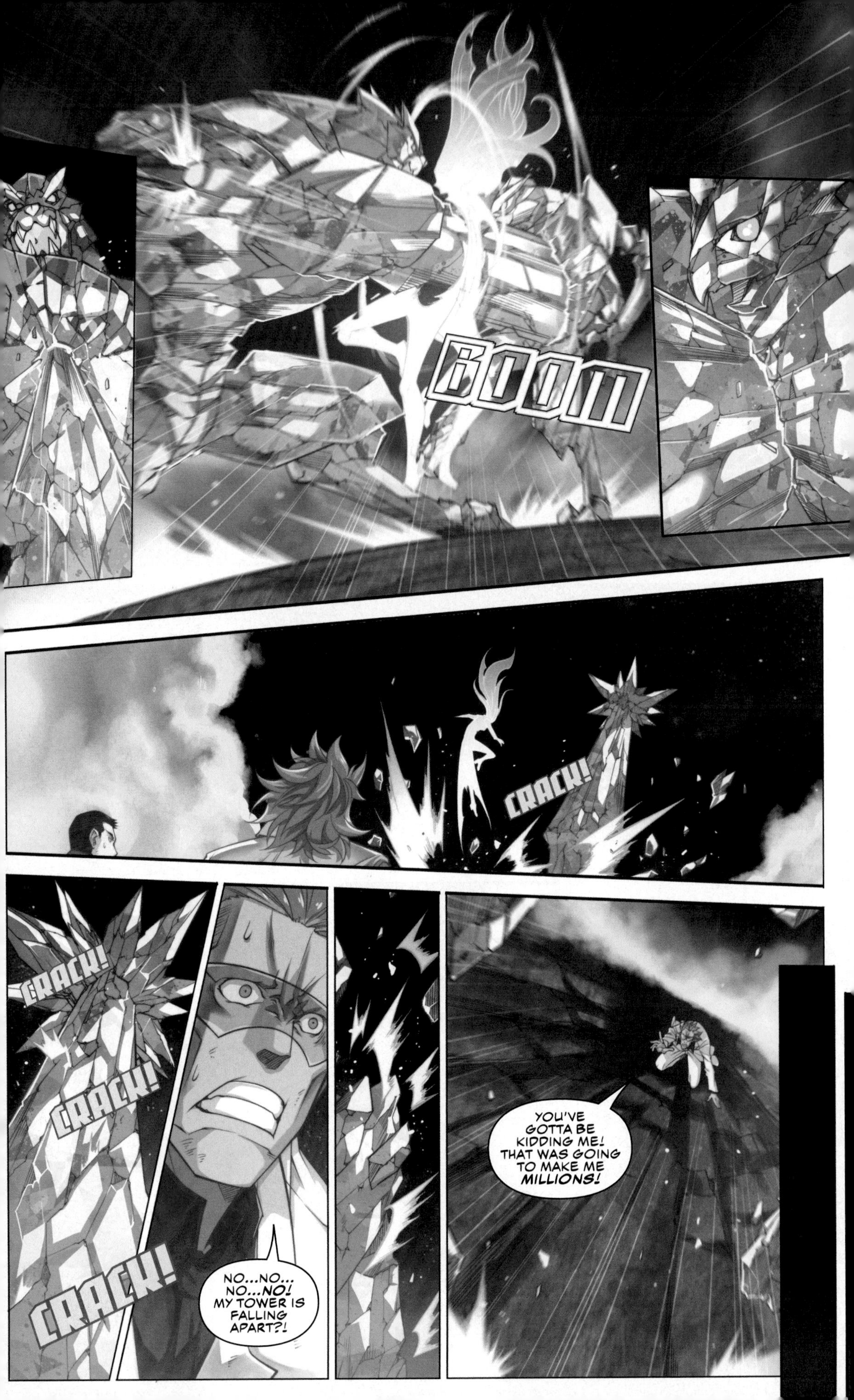
BOOM
CRACK!
CRACK!
CRACK!
CRACK!
NO...NO... NO...NO! MY TOWER IS FALLING APART?!
YOU'VE GOTTA BE KIDDING ME! THAT WAS GOING TO MAKE ME MILLIONS!

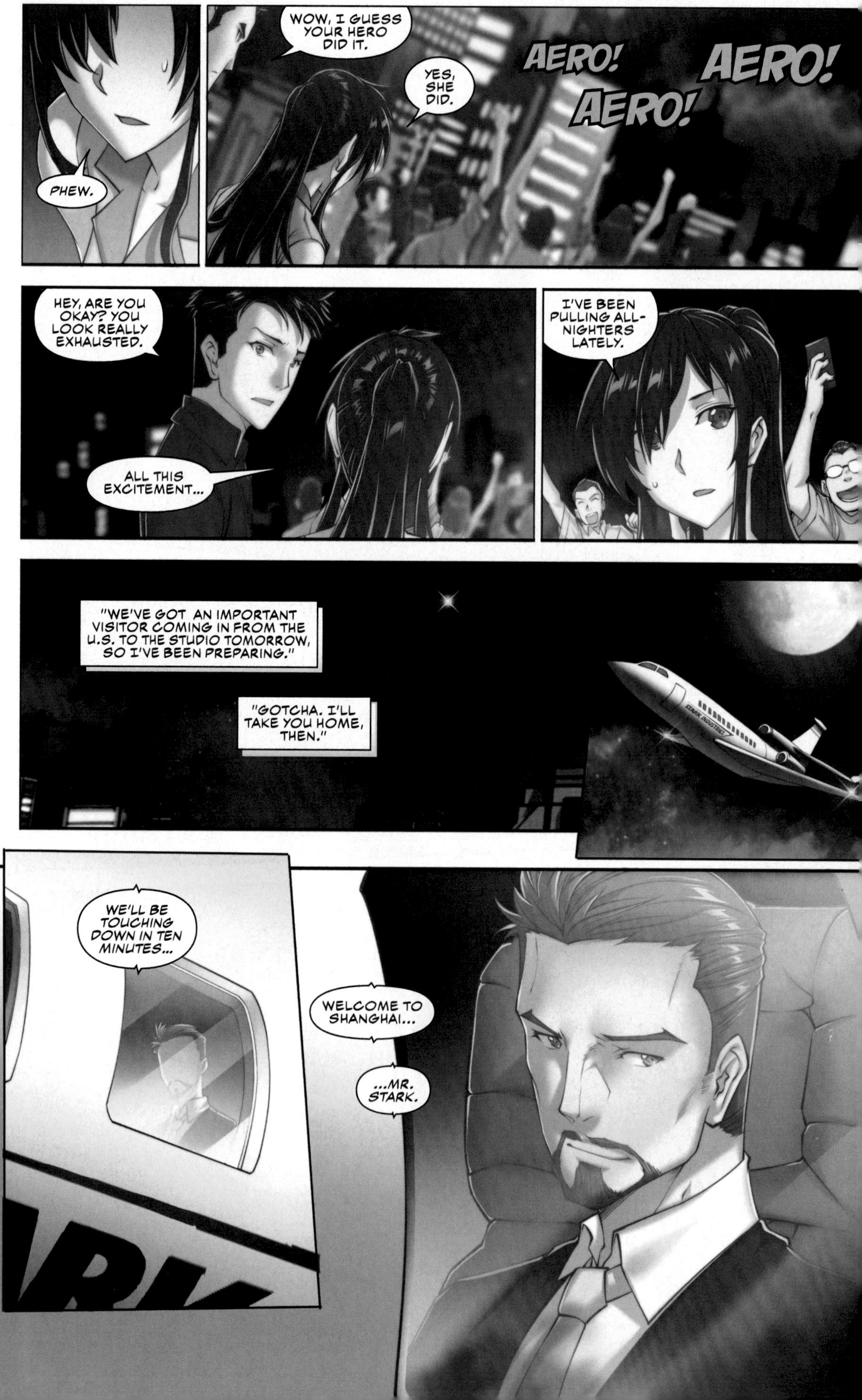
PHEW.
WOW, I GUESS YOUR HERO DID IT.
YES, SHE DID.
AERO!
AERO!
AERO!
HEY, ARE YOU OKAY? YOU LOOK REALLY EXHAUSTED.
ALL THIS EXCITEMENT...
I'VE BEEN PULLING ALL-NIGHTERS LATELY.
"WE'VE GOT AN IMPORTANT VISITOR COMING IN FROM THE U.S. TO THE STUDIO TOMORROW, SO I'VE BEEN PREPARING."
"GOTCHA. I'LL TAKE YOU HOME, THEN."
STARK INDUSTRIES
WE'LL BE TOUCHING DOWN IN TEN MINUTES...
WELCOME TO SHANGHAI...
...MR. STARK.

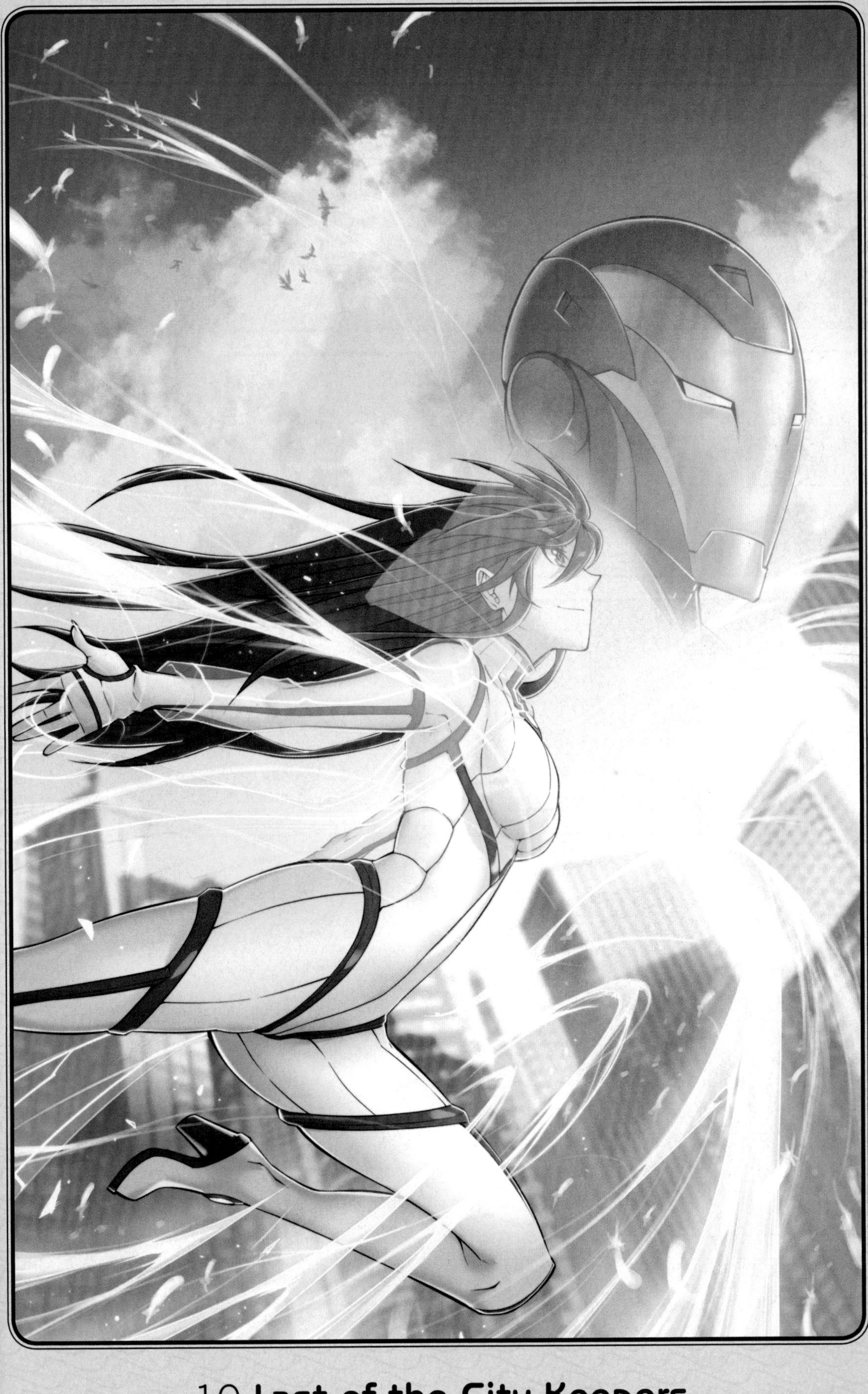

10 Last of the City Keepers

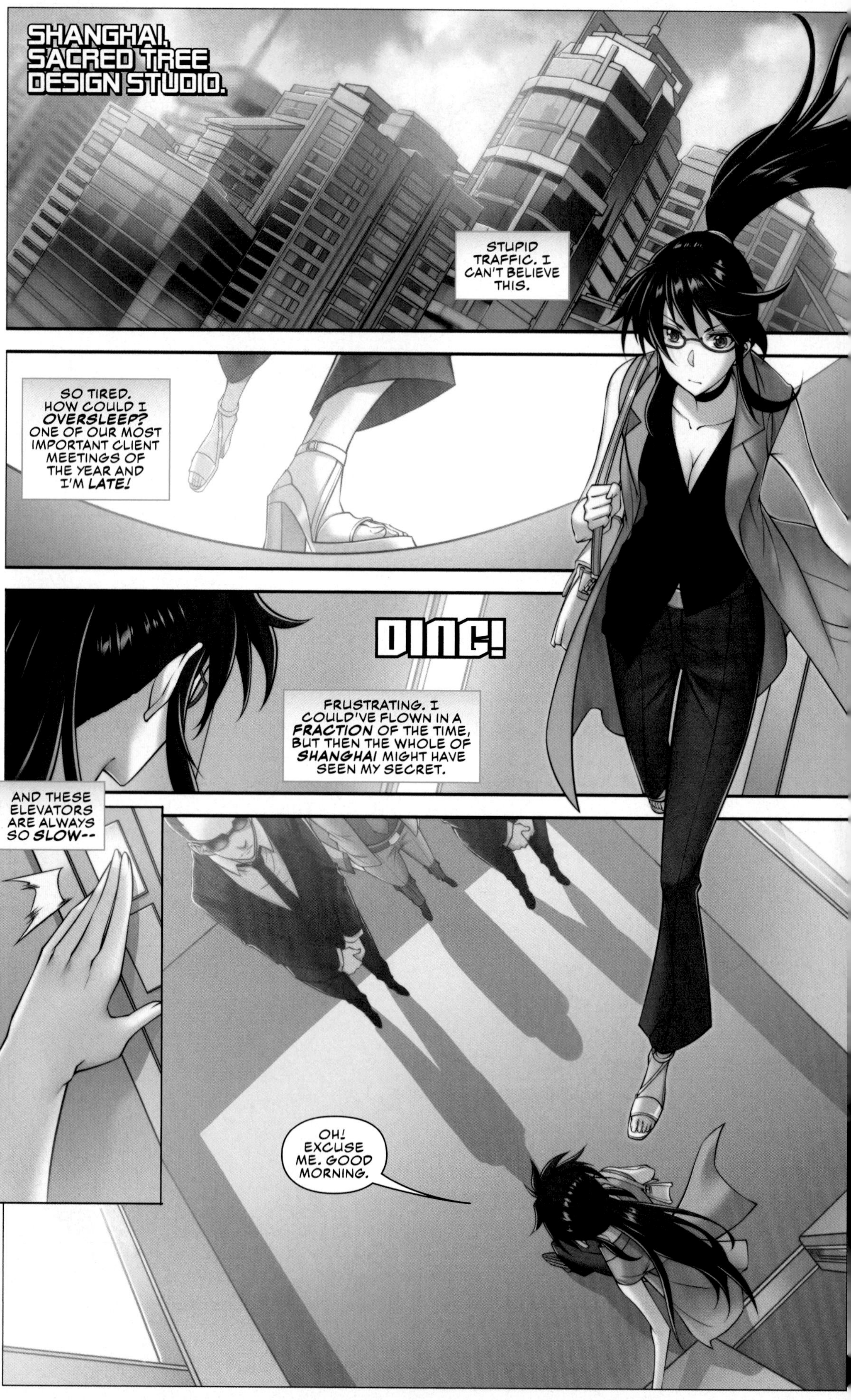
SHANGHAI, SACRED TREE DESIGN STUDIO.
STUPID TRAFFIC. I CAN'T BELIEVE THIS.
SO TIRED. HOW COULD I OVERSLEEP? ONE OF OUR MOST IMPORTANT CLIENT MEETINGS OF THE YEAR AND I'M LATE!
DING!
FRUSTRATING. I COULD'VE FLOWN IN A FRACTION OF THE TIME, BUT THEN THE WHOLE OF SHANGHAI MIGHT HAVE SEEN MY SECRET.
AND THESE ELEVATORS ARE ALWAYS SO SLOW--
OH! EXCUSE ME. GOOD MORNING.

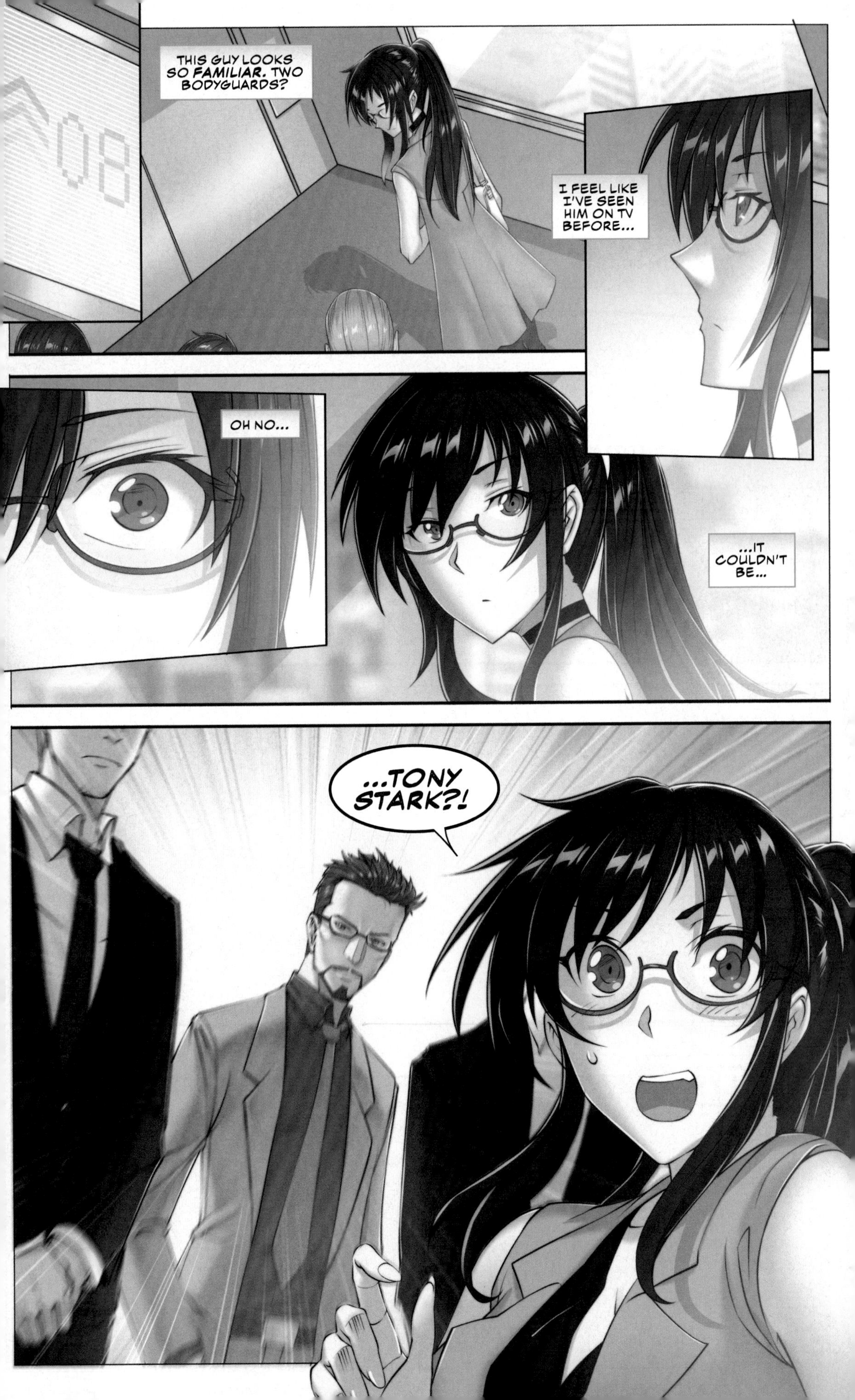
THIS GUY LOOKS SO FAMILIAR. TWO BODYGUARDS?
I FEEL LIKE I'VE SEEN HIM ON TV BEFORE...
OH NO...
...IT COULDN'T BE...
...TONY STARK?!

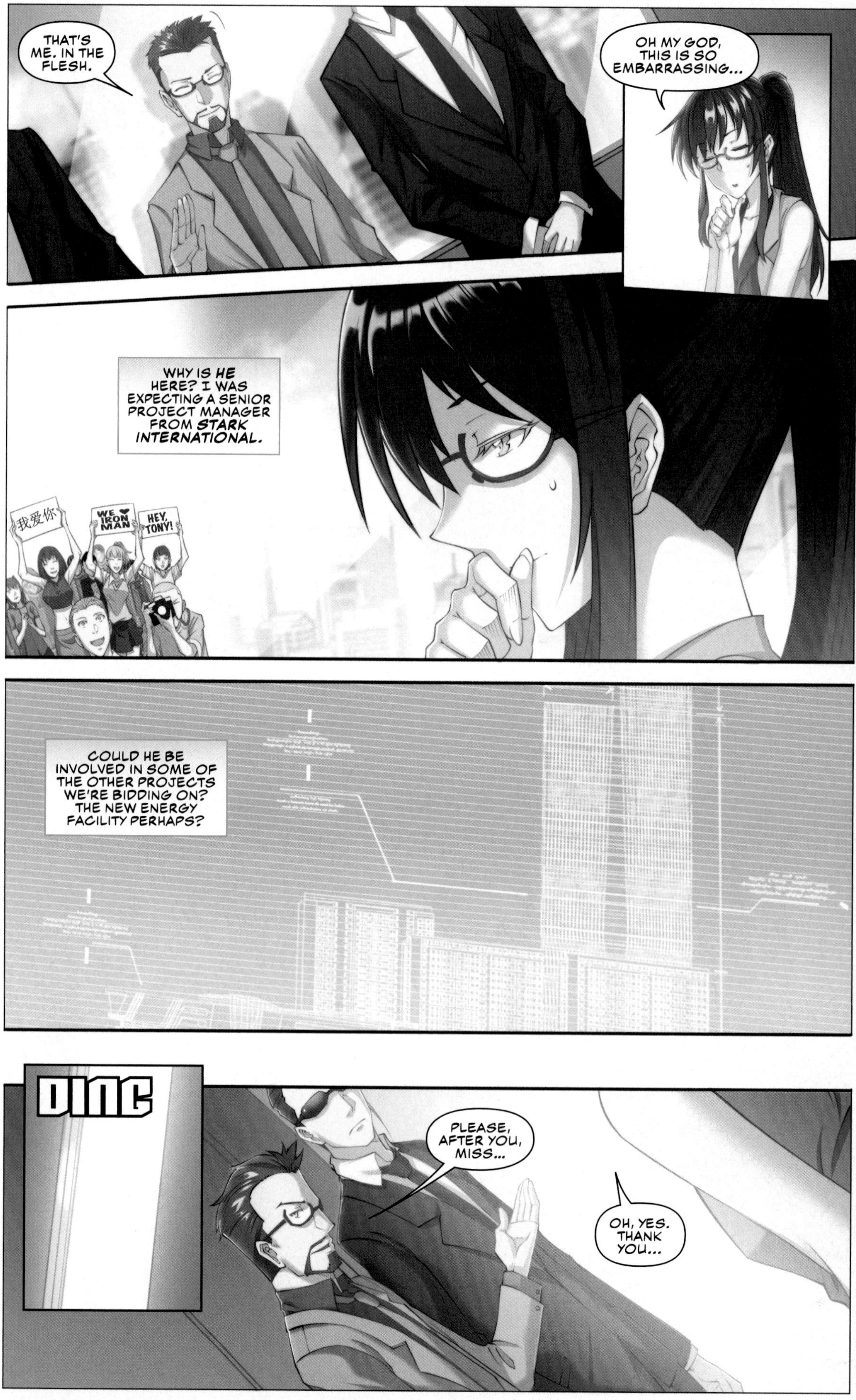
THAT'S ME. IN THE FLESH.
OH MY GOD, THIS IS SO EMBARRASSING...
WHY IS HE HERE? I WAS EXPECTING A SENIOR PROJECT MANAGER FROM STARK INTERNATIONAL.
我爱你
WE ♥ IRON MAN
HEY, TONY!
COULD HE BE INVOLVED IN SOME OF THE OTHER PROJECTS WE'RE BIDDING ON? THE NEW ENERGY FACILITY PERHAPS?
DING
PLEASE, AFTER YOU, MISS...
OH, YES. THANK YOU...

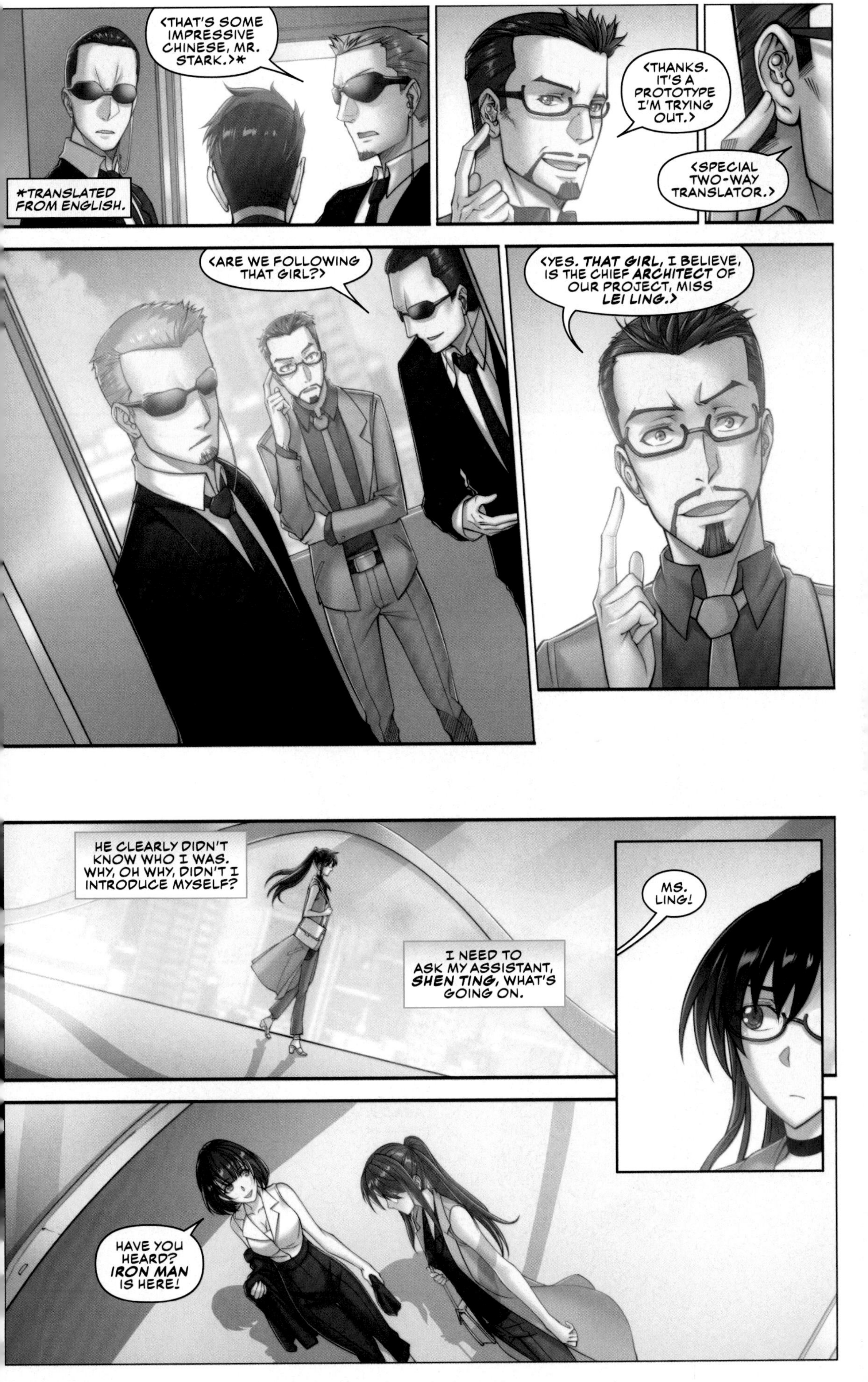
<THAT'S SOME IMPRESSIVE CHINESE, MR. STARK.>*
*TRANSLATED FROM ENGLISH.
<THANKS. IT'S A PROTOTYPE I'M TRYING OUT.>
<SPECIAL TWO-WAY TRANSLATOR.>
<ARE WE FOLLOWING THAT GIRL?>
<YES. THAT GIRL, I BELIEVE, IS THE CHIEF ARCHITECT OF OUR PROJECT, MISS LEI LING.>
HE CLEARLY DIDN'T KNOW WHO I WAS. WHY, OH WHY, DIDN'T I INTRODUCE MYSELF?
I NEED TO ASK MY ASSISTANT, SHEN TING, WHAT'S GOING ON.
MS. LING!
HAVE YOU HEARD? IRON MAN IS HERE!

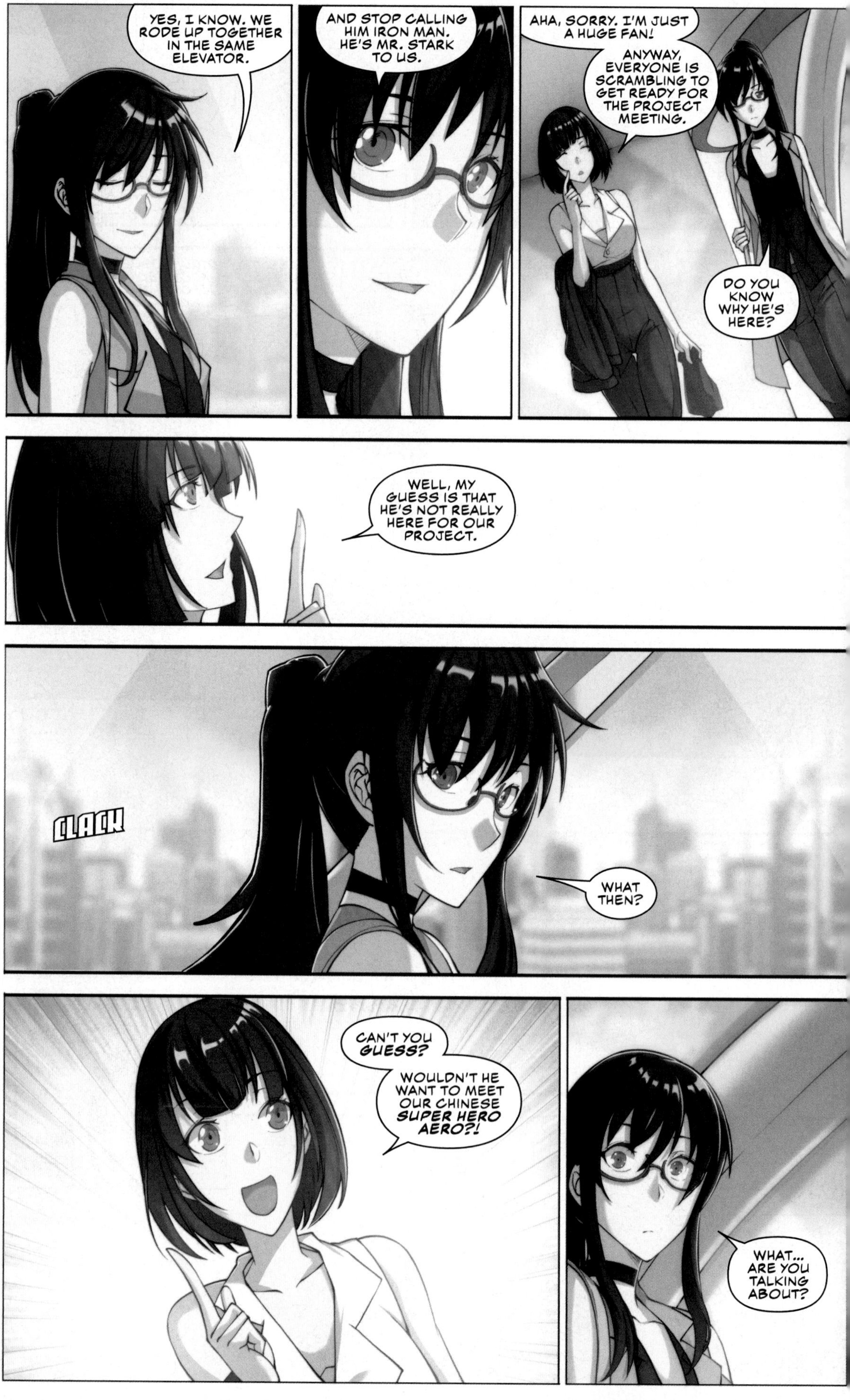
YES, I KNOW. WE RODE UP TOGETHER IN THE SAME ELEVATOR.
AND STOP CALLING HIM IRON MAN. HE'S MR. STARK TO US.
AHA, SORRY. I'M JUST A HUGE FAN!
ANYWAY, EVERYONE IS SCRAMBLING TO GET READY FOR THE PROJECT MEETING.
DO YOU KNOW WHY HE'S HERE?
WELL, MY GUESS IS THAT HE'S NOT REALLY HERE FOR OUR PROJECT.
CLACK
WHAT THEN?
CAN'T YOU GUESS?
WOULDN'T HE WANT TO MEET OUR CHINESE SUPER HERO AERO?!
WHAT... ARE YOU TALKING ABOUT?

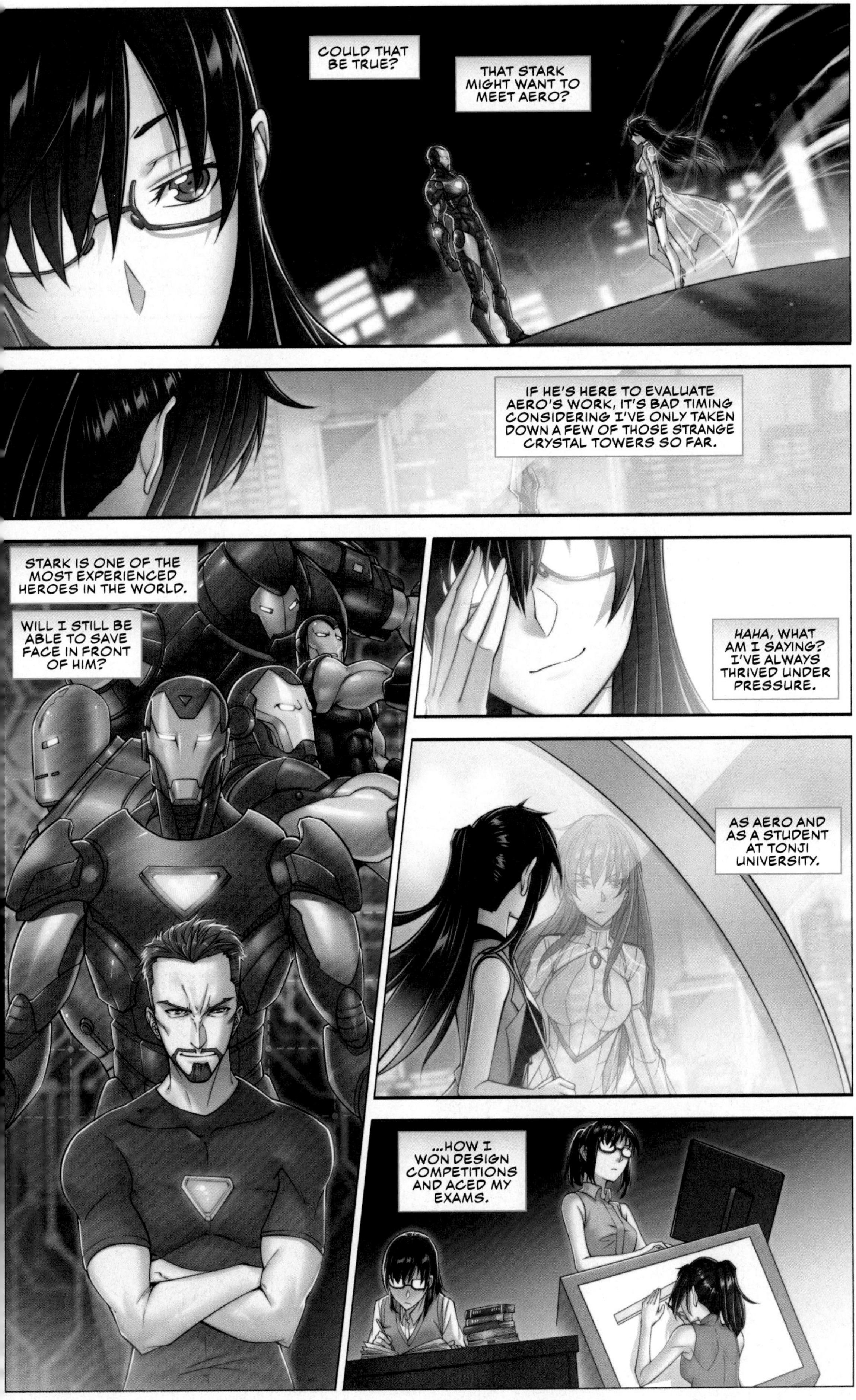
COULD THAT BE TRUE?
THAT STARK MIGHT WANT TO MEET AERO?
IF HE'S HERE TO EVALUATE AERO'S WORK, IT'S BAD TIMING CONSIDERING I'VE ONLY TAKEN DOWN A FEW OF THOSE STRANGE CRYSTAL TOWERS SO FAR.
STARK IS ONE OF THE MOST EXPERIENCED HEROES IN THE WORLD.
WILL I STILL BE ABLE TO SAVE FACE IN FRONT OF HIM?
HAHA, WHAT AM I SAYING? I'VE ALWAYS THRIVED UNDER PRESSURE.
AS AERO AND AS A STUDENT AT TONJI UNIVERSITY.
...HOW I WON DESIGN COMPETITIONS AND ACED MY EXAMS.

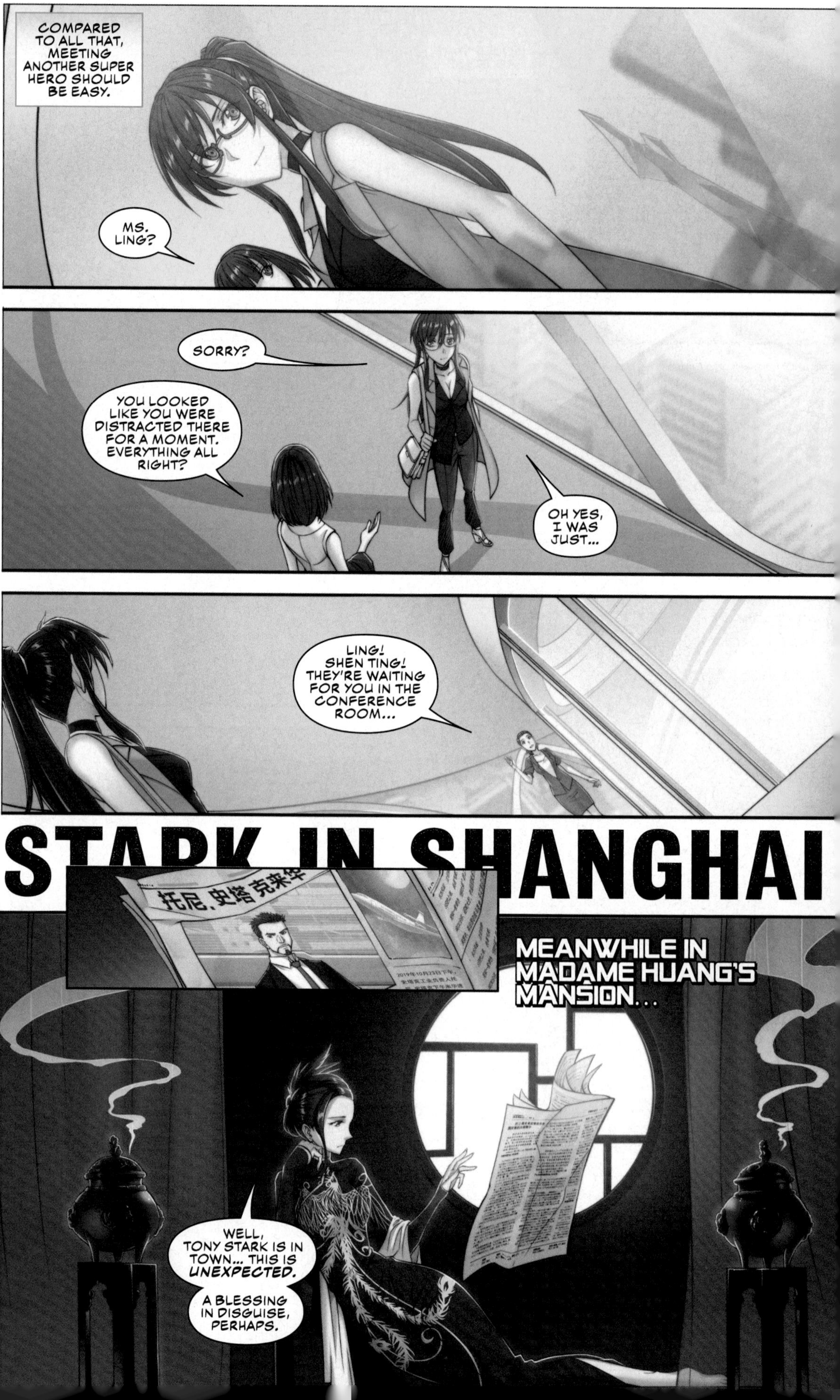
COMPARED TO ALL THAT, MEETING ANOTHER SUPER HERO SHOULD BE EASY.
MS. LING?
SORRY?
YOU LOOKED LIKE YOU WERE DISTRACTED THERE FOR A MOMENT. EVERYTHING ALL RIGHT?
OH YES, I WAS JUST...
LING! SHEN TING! THEY'RE WAITING FOR YOU IN THE CONFERENCE ROOM...
STARK IN SHANGHAI
托尼·史塔克来华
MEANWHILE IN MADAME HUANG'S MANSION...
WELL, TONY STARK IS IN TOWN... THIS IS UNEXPECTED.
A BLESSING IN DISGUISE, PERHAPS.

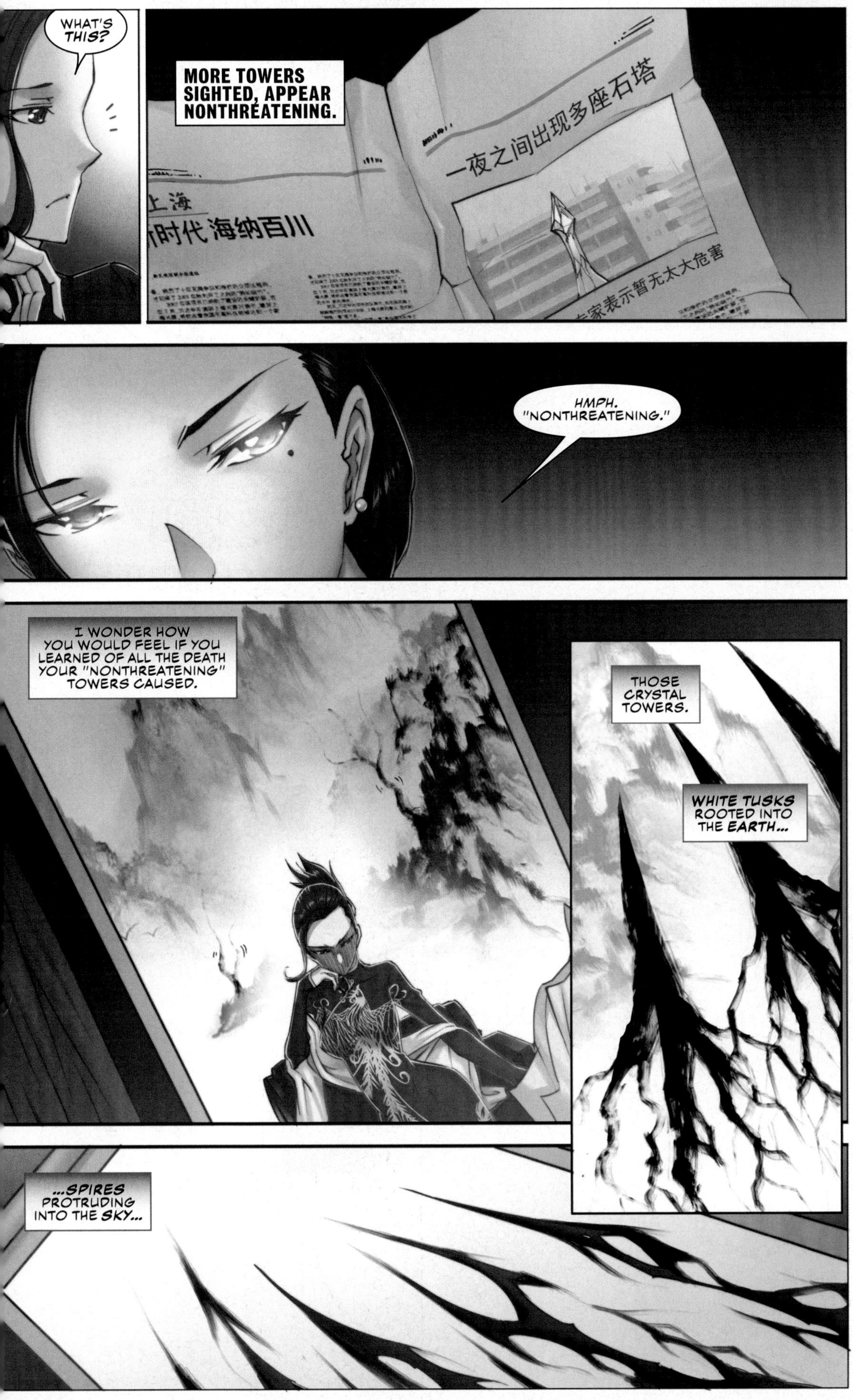
WHAT'S THIS?
MORE TOWERS SIGHTED, APPEAR NONTHREATENING.
上海
时代 海纳百川
一夜之间出现多座石塔
家表示暂无太大危害
HMPH. "NONTHREATENING."
I WONDER HOW YOU WOULD FEEL IF YOU LEARNED OF ALL THE DEATH YOUR "NONTHREATENING" TOWERS CAUSED.
THOSE CRYSTAL TOWERS.
WHITE TUSKS ROOTED INTO THE EARTH...
...SPIRES PROTRUDING INTO THE SKY...

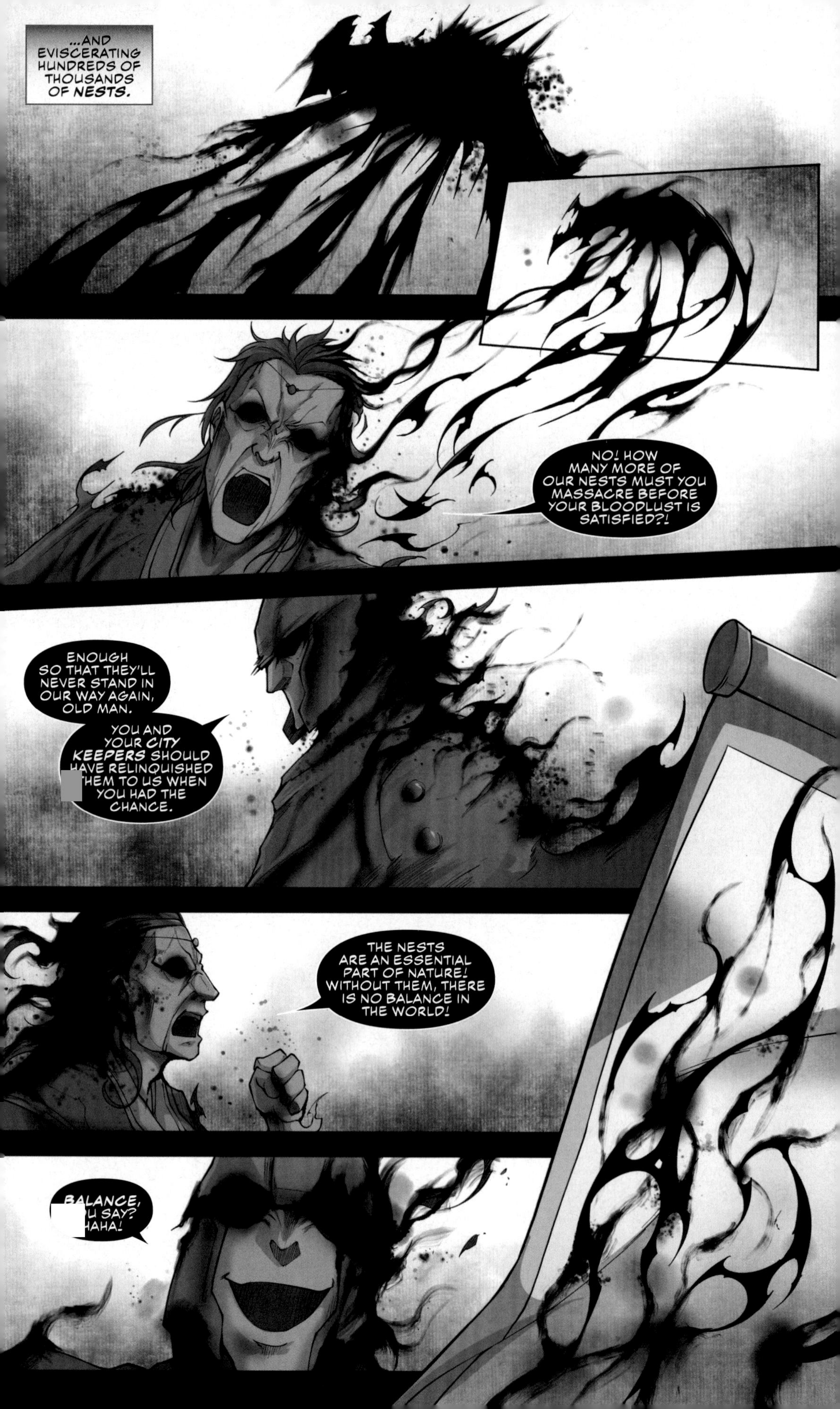
...AND EVISCERATING HUNDREDS OF THOUSANDS OF NESTS.
NO! HOW MANY MORE OF OUR NESTS MUST YOU MASSACRE BEFORE YOUR BLOODLUST IS SATISFIED?!
ENOUGH SO THAT THEY'LL NEVER STAND IN OUR WAY AGAIN, OLD MAN.
YOU AND YOUR CITY KEEPERS SHOULD AVE RELINQUISHED HEM TO US WHEN YOU HAD THE CHANCE.
THE NESTS ARE AN ESSENTIAL PART OF NATURE! WITHOUT THEM, THERE IS NO BALANCE IN THE WORLD!
BALANCE, U SAY? HAHA!

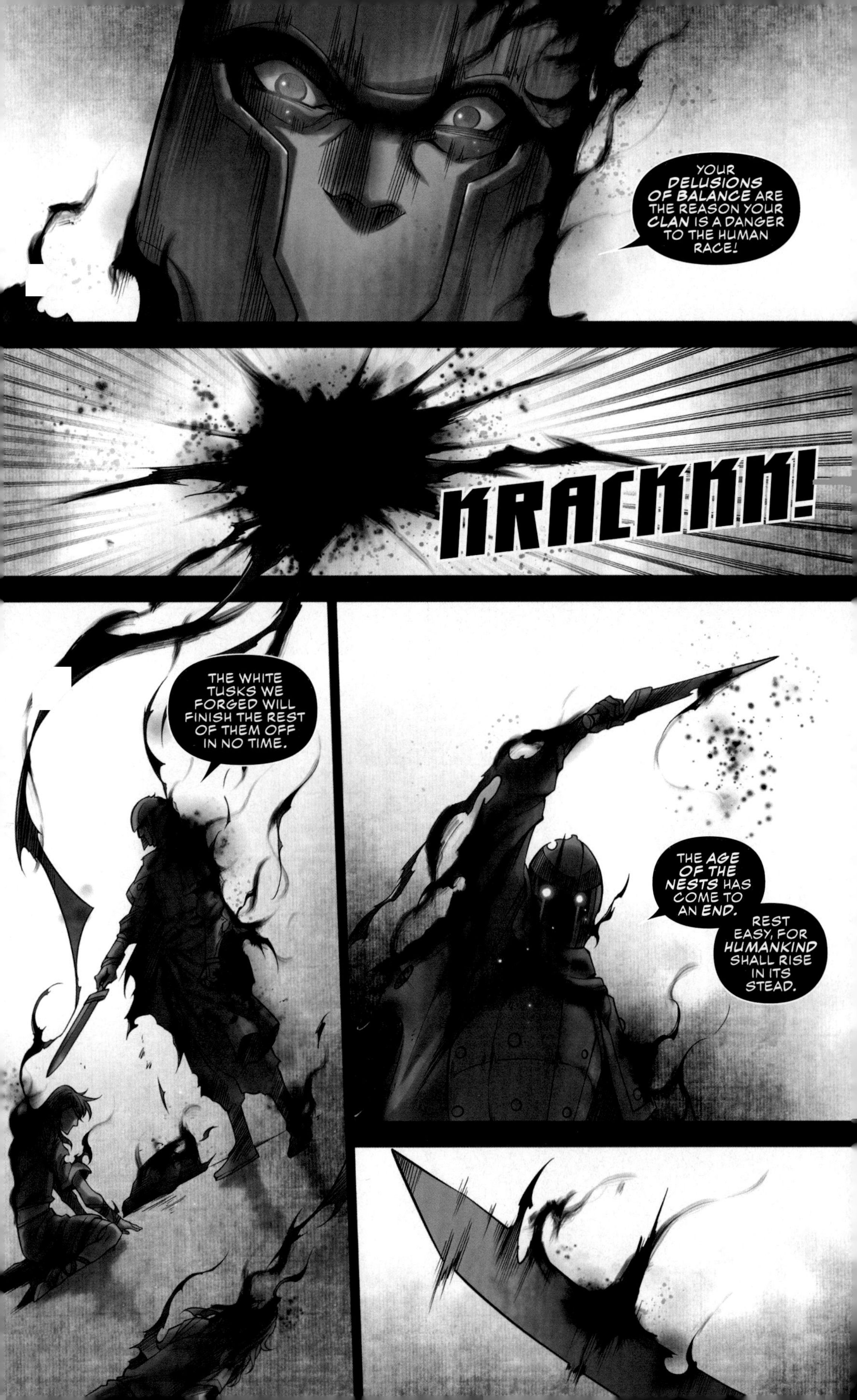
YOUR DELUSIONS OF BALANCE ARE THE REASON YOUR CLAN IS A DANGER TO THE HUMAN RACE!
KRACKKK!
THE WHITE TUSKS WE FORGED WILL FINISH THE REST OF THEM OFF IN NO TIME.
THE AGE OF THE NESTS HAS COME TO AN END.
REST EASY, FOR HUMANKIND SHALL RISE IN ITS STEAD.

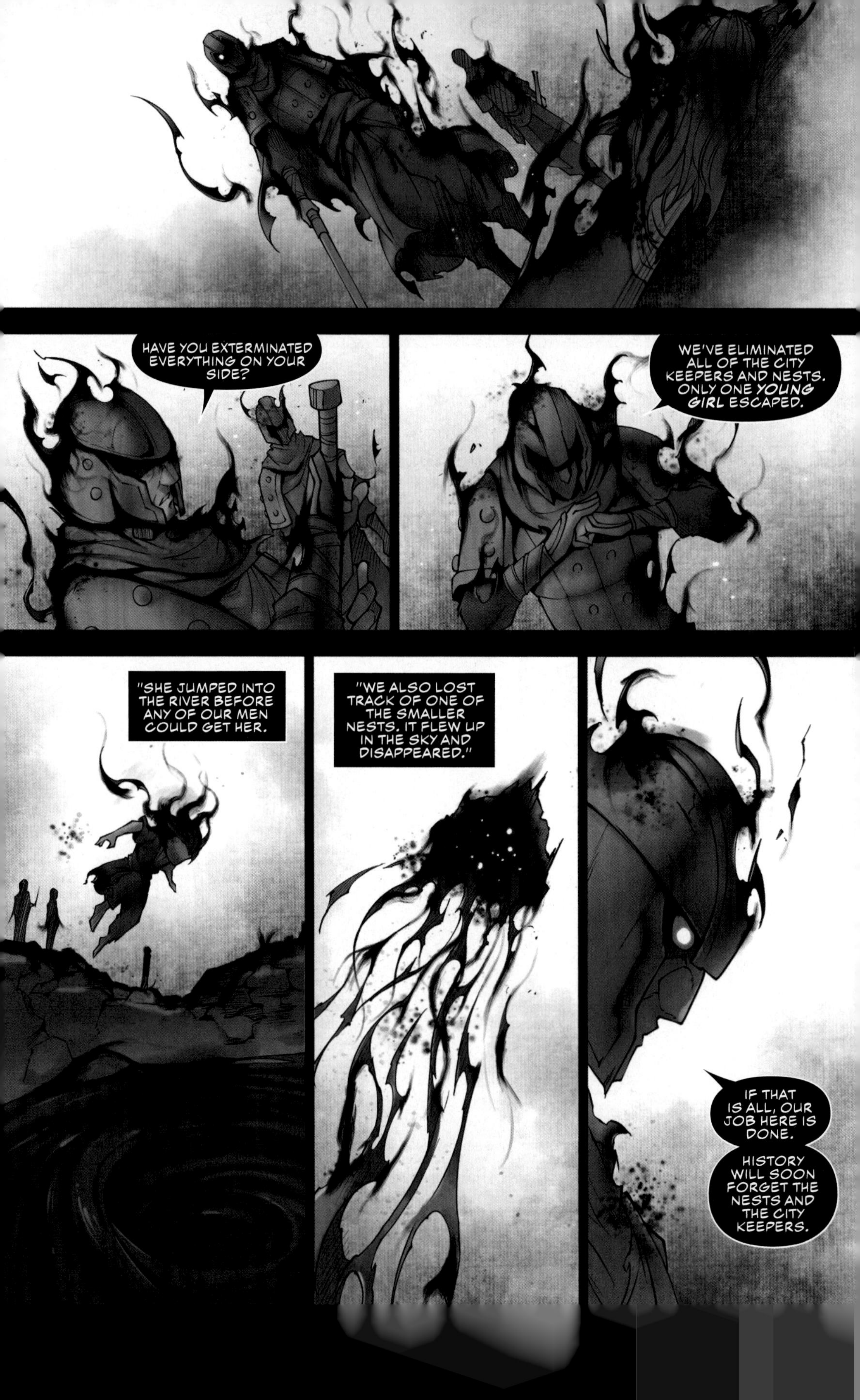
HAVE YOU EXTERMINATED EVERYTHING ON YOUR SIDE?
WE'VE ELIMINATED ALL OF THE CITY KEEPERS AND NESTS. ONLY ONE *YOUNG GIRL* ESCAPED.
"SHE JUMPED INTO THE RIVER BEFORE ANY OF OUR MEN COULD GET HER.
"WE ALSO LOST TRACK OF ONE OF THE SMALLER NESTS. IT FLEW UP IN THE SKY AND DISAPPEARED."
IF THAT IS ALL, OUR JOB HERE IS DONE.
HISTORY WILL SOON FORGET THE NESTS AND THE CITY KEEPERS.

HE WAS WRONG. I WAS THAT LITTLE GIRL, AND I *LIVED*.

FROM THAT DAY FORWARD, I WAS THE *LAST* OF THE CITY KEEPERS.

AS I ESCAPED, I FOUND A NEST, NEARLY DEAD.

WE BONDED TOGETHER. THE NEST ENVELOPED ME AND HID UNDERGROUND. THERE WE SLEPT FOR THOUSANDS OF YEARS.

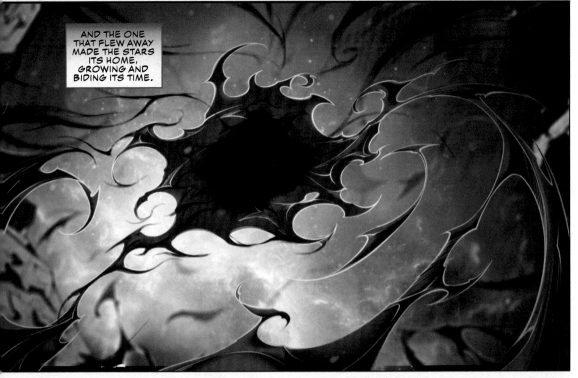

AND THE ONE THAT FLEW AWAY MADE THE STARS ITS HOME, GROWING AND BIDING ITS TIME.

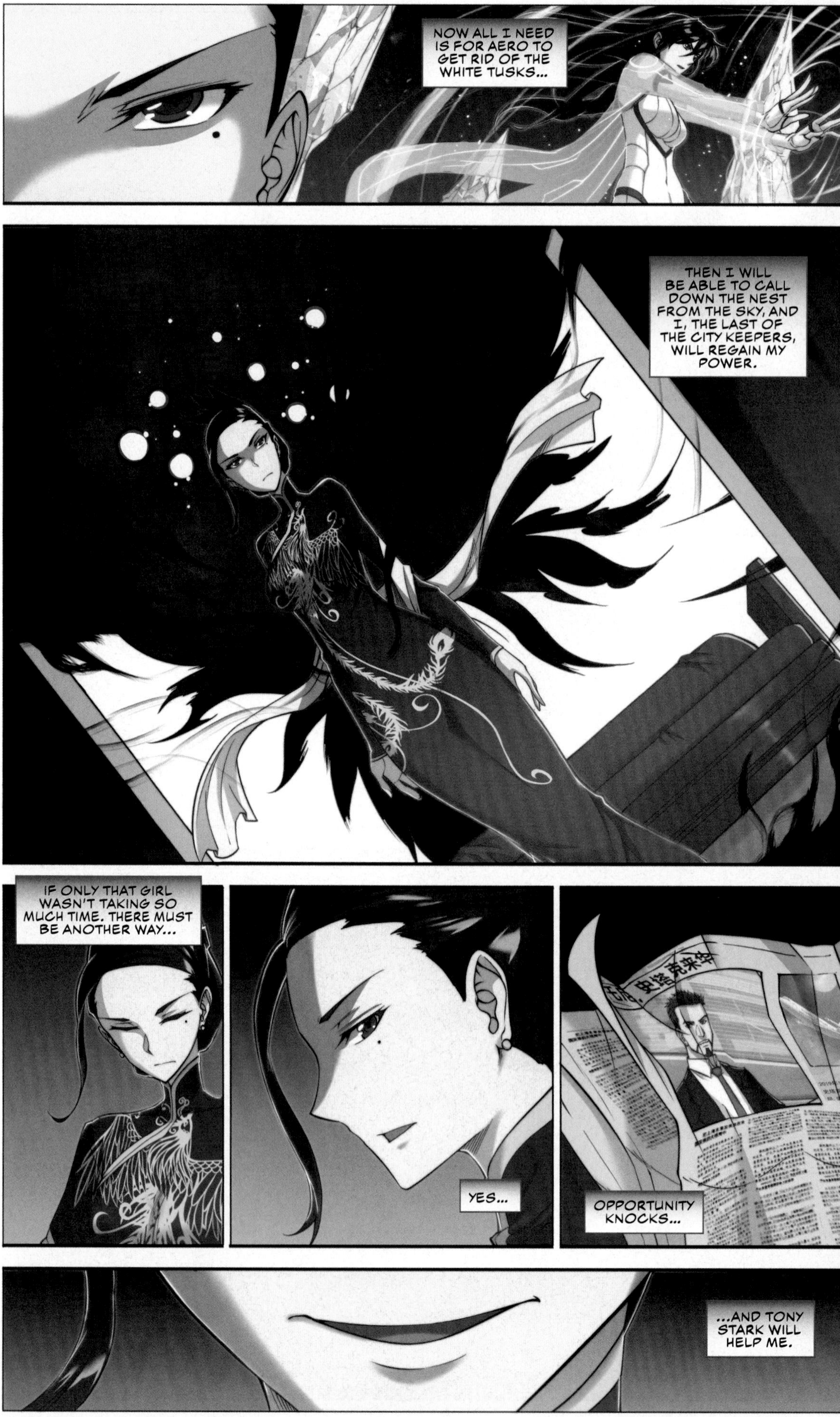
NOW ALL I NEED IS FOR AERO TO GET RID OF THE WHITE TUSKS...
THEN I WILL BE ABLE TO CALL DOWN THE NEST FROM THE SKY, AND I, THE LAST OF THE CITY KEEPERS, WILL REGAIN MY POWER.
IF ONLY THAT GIRL WASN'T TAKING SO MUCH TIME. THERE MUST BE ANOTHER WAY...
YES...
OPPORTUNITY KNOCKS...
...AND TONY STARK WILL HELP ME.

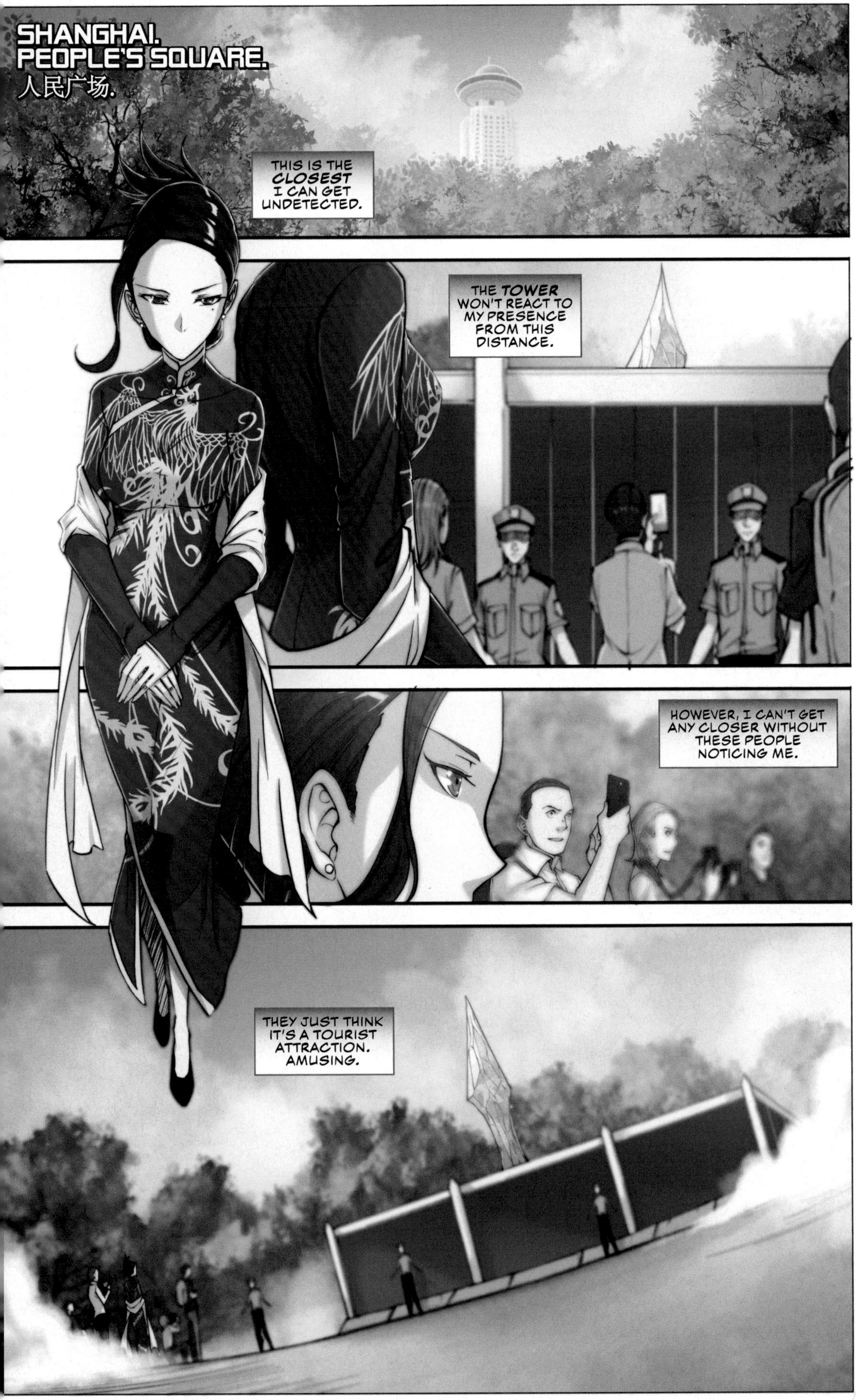
SHANGHAI. PEOPLE'S SQUARE.
人民广场.
THIS IS THE CLOSEST I CAN GET UNDETECTED.
THE TOWER WON'T REACT TO MY PRESENCE FROM THIS DISTANCE.
HOWEVER, I CAN'T GET ANY CLOSER WITHOUT THESE PEOPLE NOTICING ME.
THEY JUST THINK IT'S A TOURIST ATTRACTION. AMUSING.

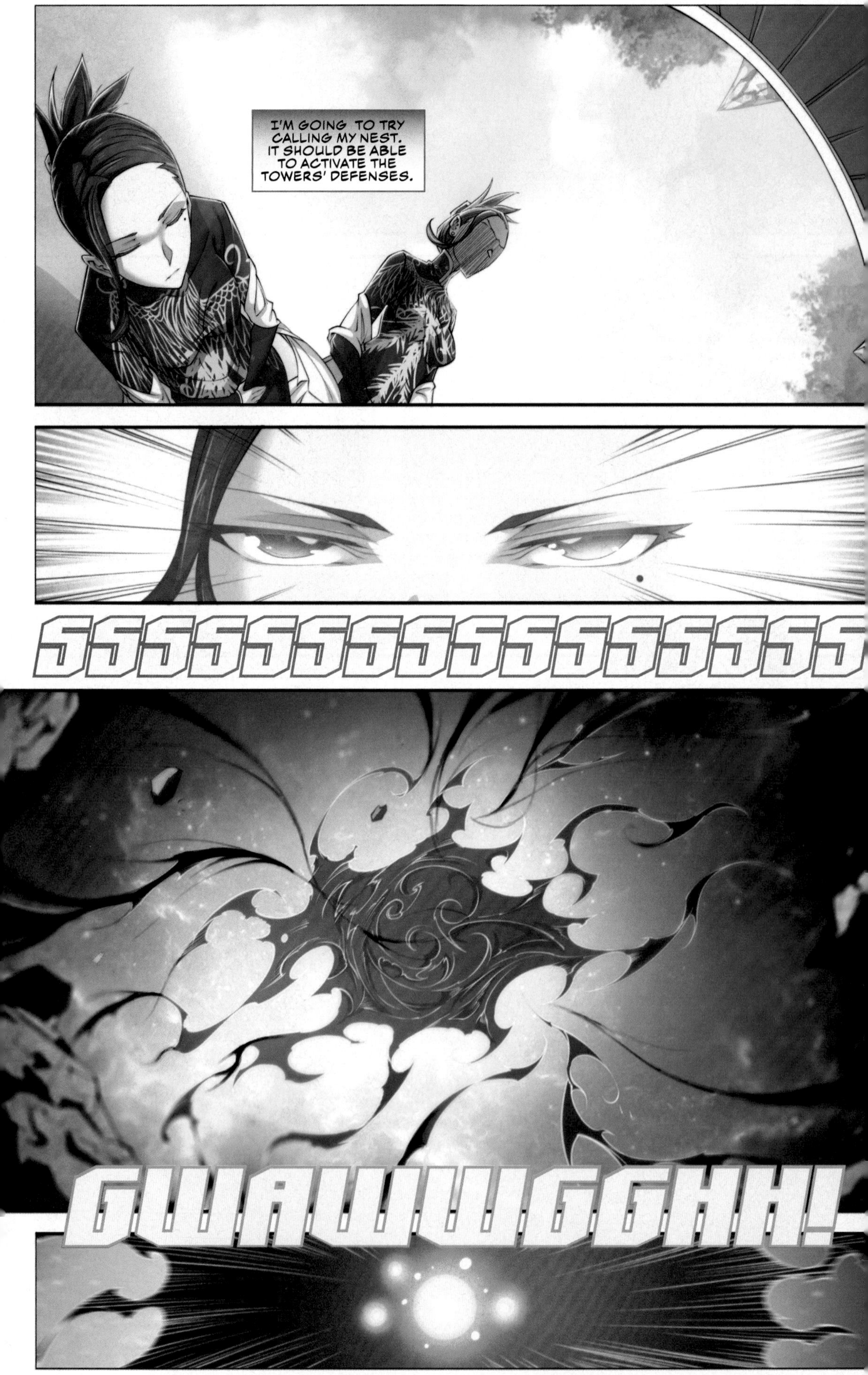
I'M GOING TO TRY CALLING MY NEST. IT SHOULD BE ABLE TO ACTIVATE THE TOWERS' DEFENSES.
SSSSSSSSSSSSSSSS
GWAWWGGHH!

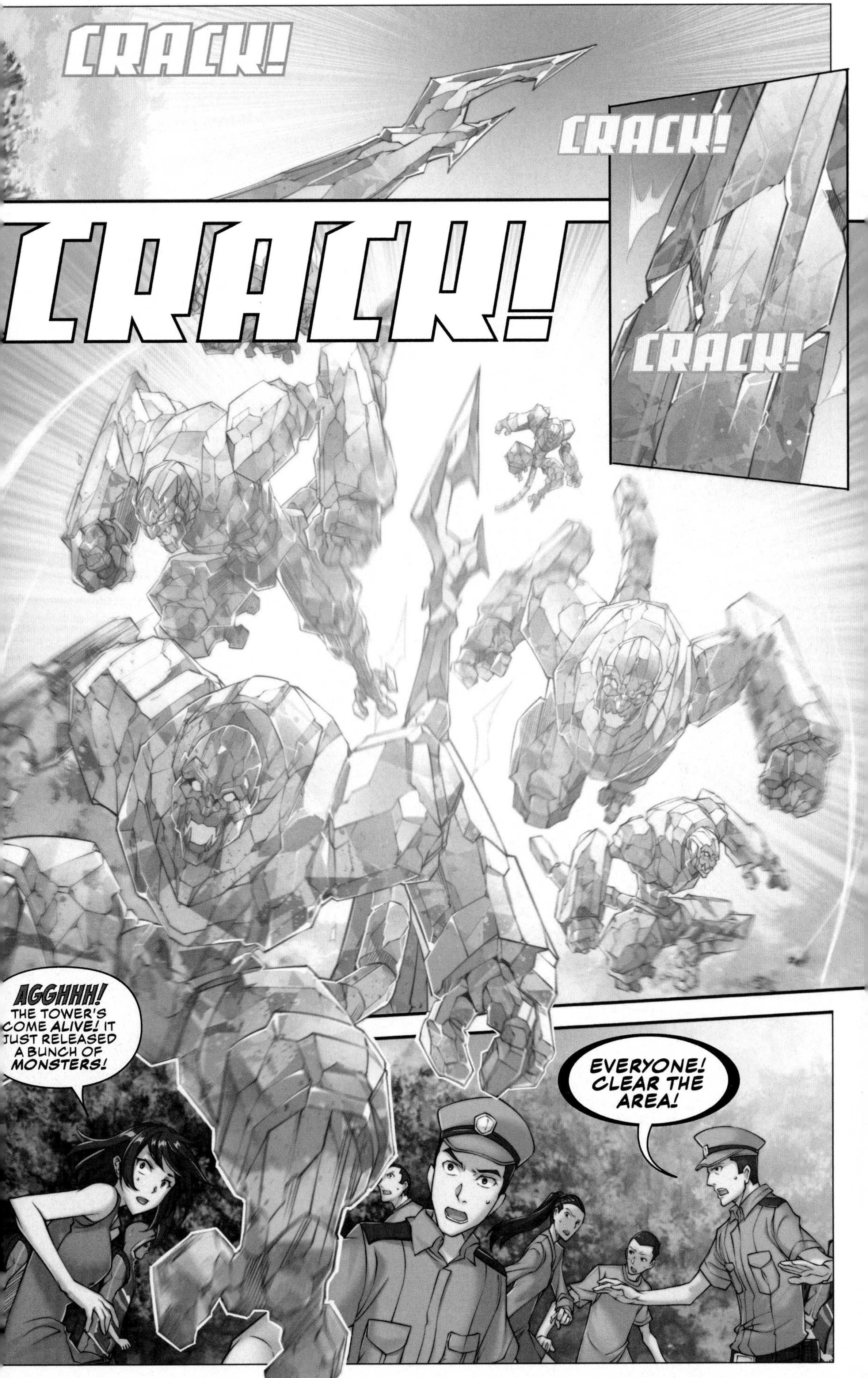

CRACK!
CRACK!
CRACK!
CRACK!
AGGHHH! THE TOWER'S COME ALIVE! IT JUST RELEASED A BUNCH OF MONSTERS!
EVERYONE! CLEAR THE AREA!

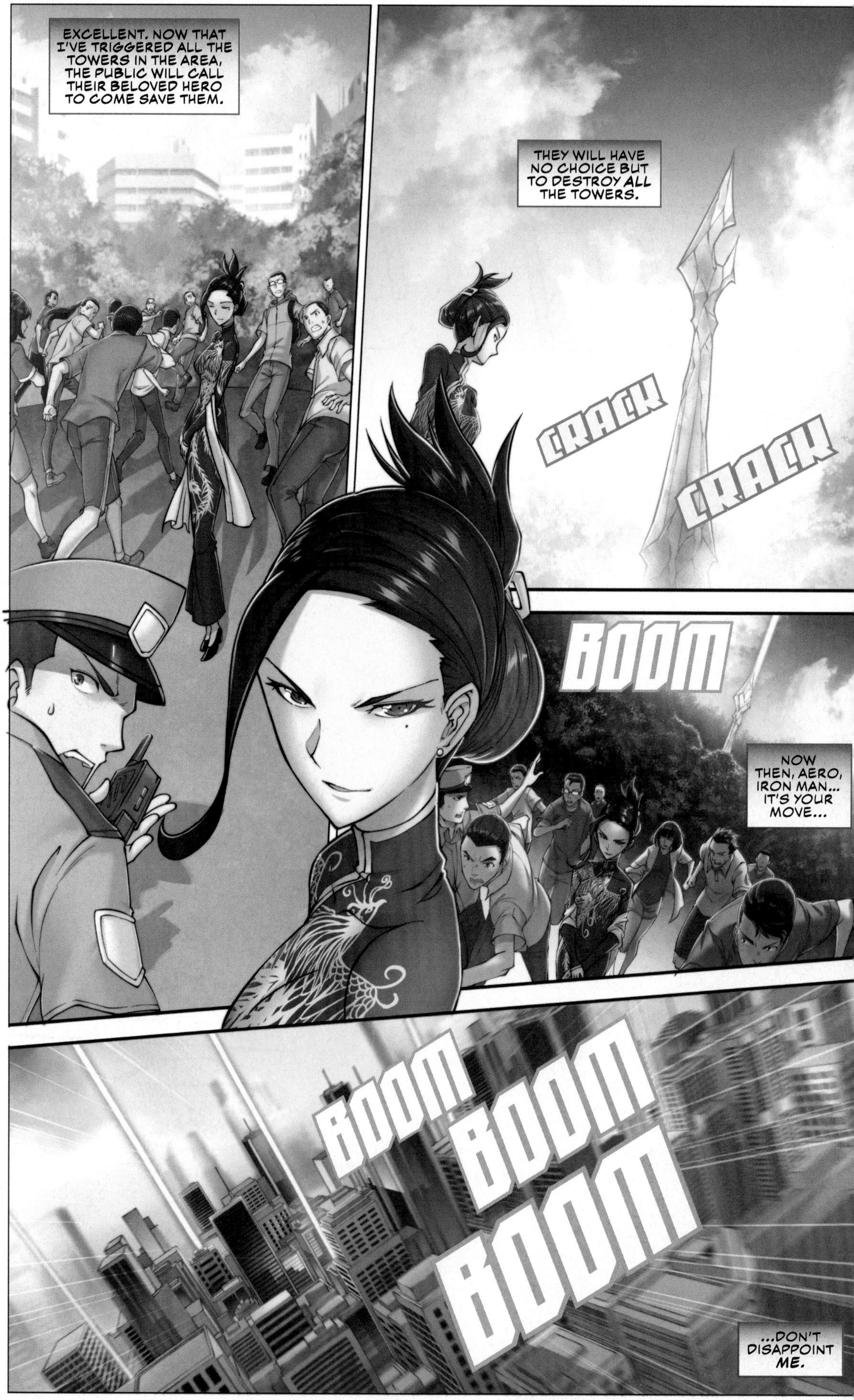
EXCELLENT. NOW THAT I'VE TRIGGERED ALL THE TOWERS IN THE AREA, THE PUBLIC WILL CALL THEIR BELOVED HERO TO COME SAVE THEM.
THEY WILL HAVE NO CHOICE BUT TO DESTROY ALL THE TOWERS.
CRACK
CRACK
BOOM
NOW THEN, AERO, IRON MAN... IT'S YOUR MOVE...
BOOM
BOOM
BOOM
...DON'T DISAPPOINT ME.

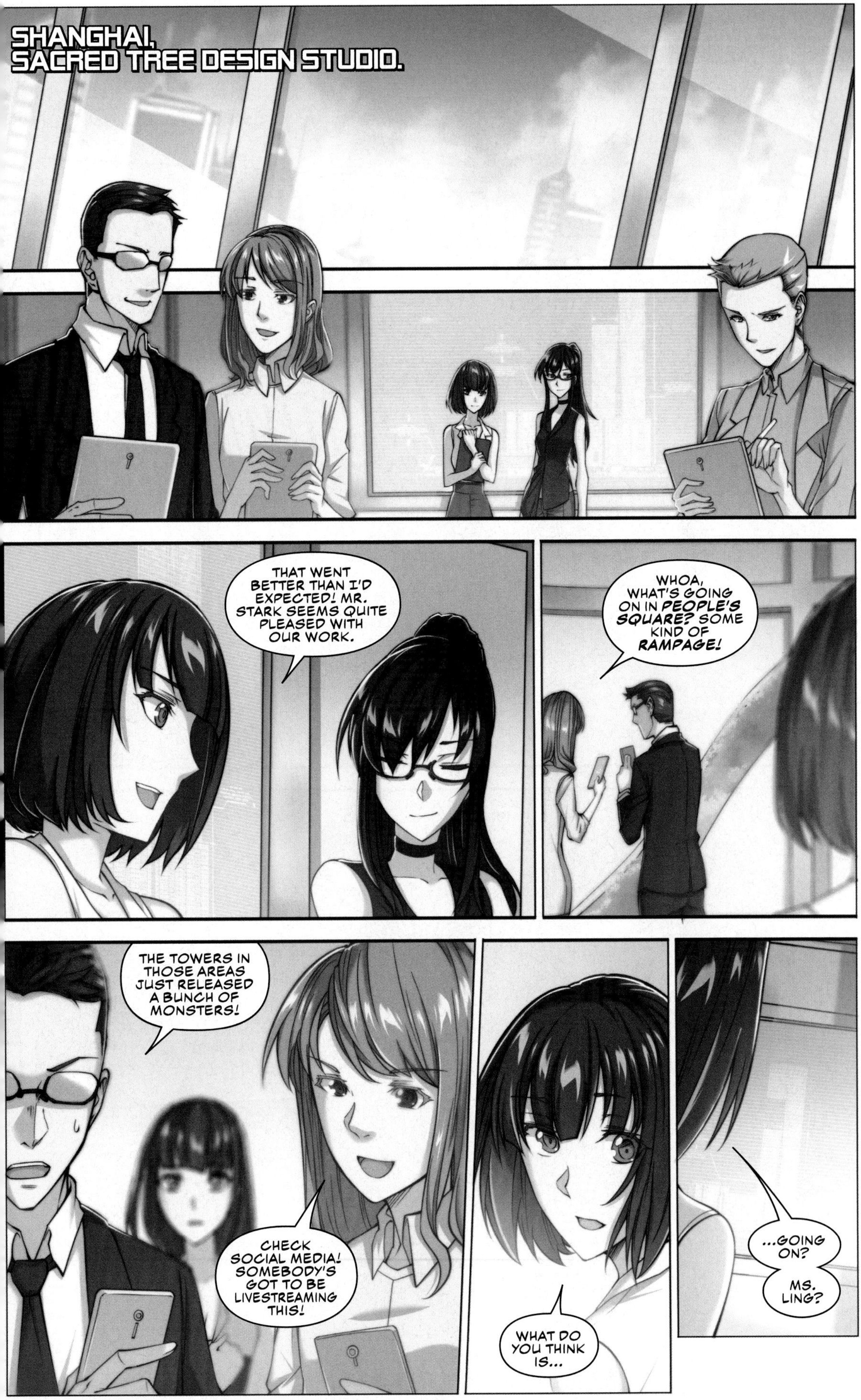
SHANGHAI, SACRED TREE DESIGN STUDIO.
THAT WENT BETTER THAN I'D EXPECTED! MR. STARK SEEMS QUITE PLEASED WITH OUR WORK.
WHOA, WHAT'S GOING ON IN PEOPLE'S SQUARE? SOME KIND OF RAMPAGE!
THE TOWERS IN THOSE AREAS JUST RELEASED A BUNCH OF MONSTERS!
CHECK SOCIAL MEDIA! SOMEBODY'S GOT TO BE LIVESTREAMING THIS!
WHAT DO YOU THINK IS...
...GOING ON?
MS. LING?

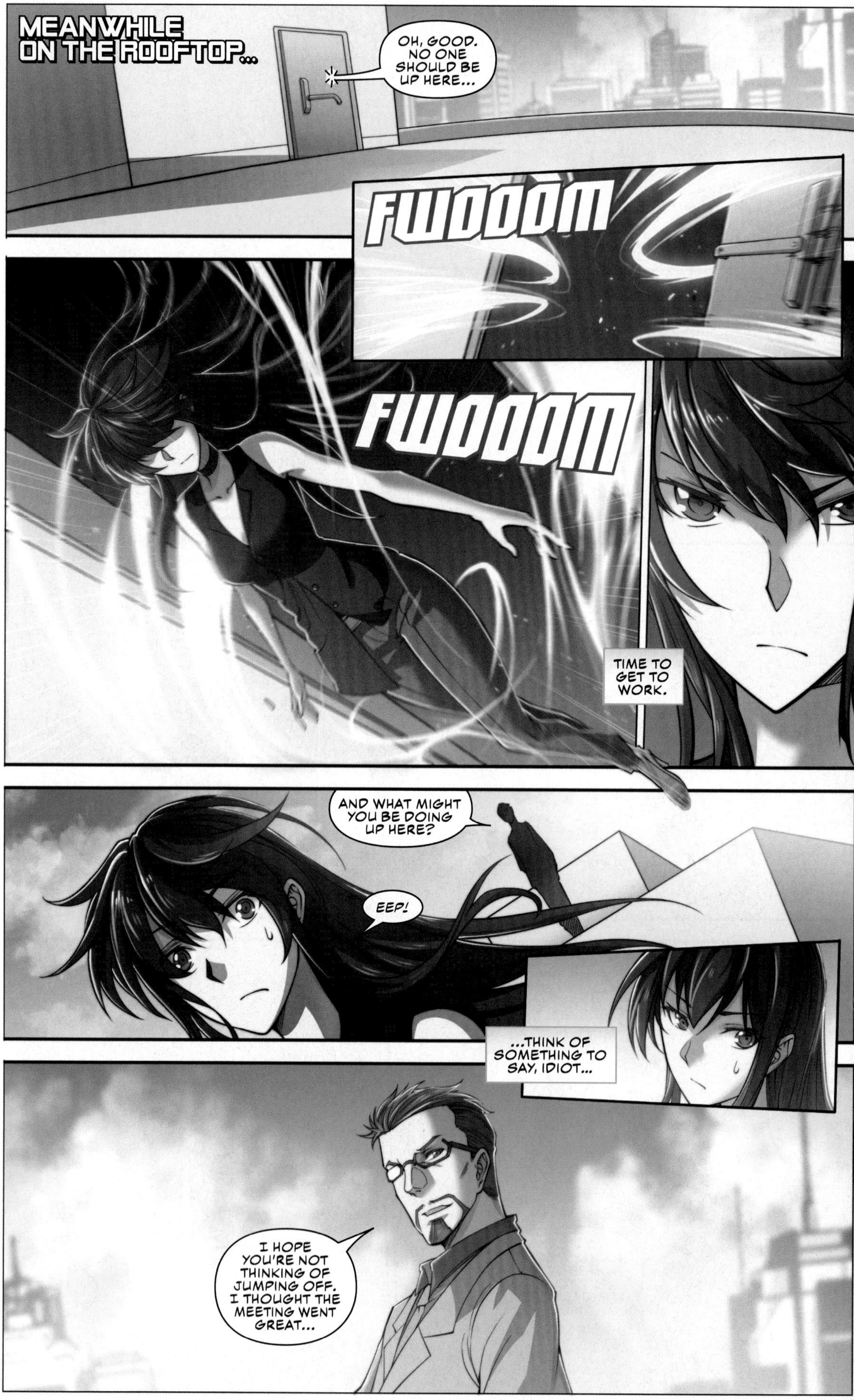
MEANWHILE ON THE ROOFTOP...
OH, GOOD. NO ONE SHOULD BE UP HERE...
FWOOOM
FWOOOM
TIME TO GET TO WORK.
AND WHAT MIGHT YOU BE DOING UP HERE?
EEP!
...THINK OF SOMETHING TO SAY, IDIOT...
I HOPE YOU'RE NOT THINKING OF JUMPING OFF. I THOUGHT THE MEETING WENT GREAT...

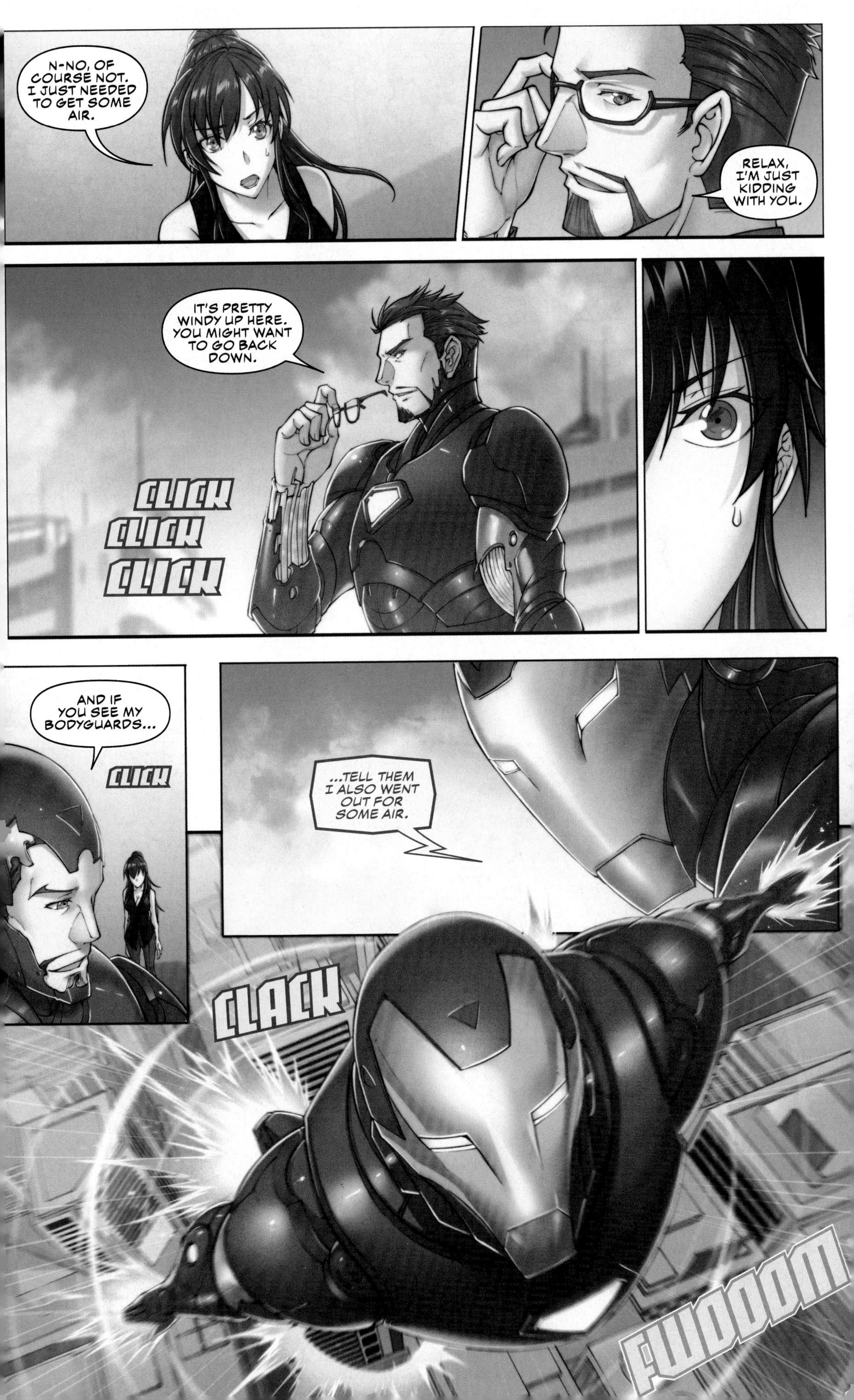

N-NO, OF COURSE NOT. I JUST NEEDED TO GET SOME AIR.
RELAX, I'M JUST KIDDING WITH YOU.
IT'S PRETTY WINDY UP HERE. YOU MIGHT WANT TO GO BACK DOWN.
CLICK
CLICK
CLICK
AND IF YOU SEE MY BODYGUARDS...
CLICK
...TELL THEM I ALSO WENT OUT FOR SOME AIR.
CLACK
FWOOOM

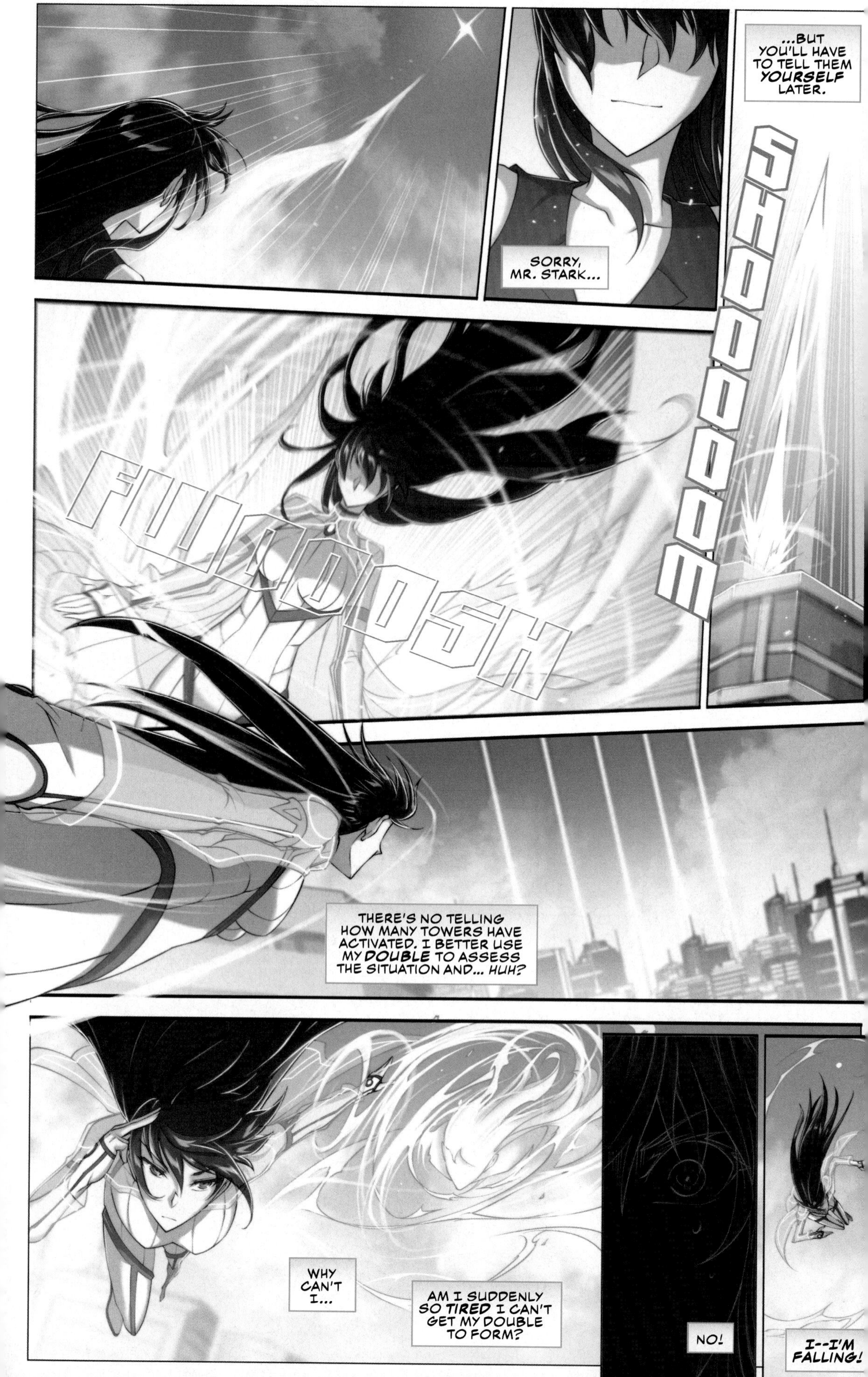
SORRY, MR. STARK...
...BUT YOU'LL HAVE TO TELL THEM YOURSELF LATER.
SHOOOOOOM
FWOOOSH
THERE'S NO TELLING HOW MANY TOWERS HAVE ACTIVATED. I BETTER USE MY DOUBLE TO ASSESS THE SITUATION AND... HUH?
WHY CAN'T I...
AM I SUDDENLY SO TIRED I CAN'T GET MY DOUBLE TO FORM?
NO!
I--I'M FALLING!

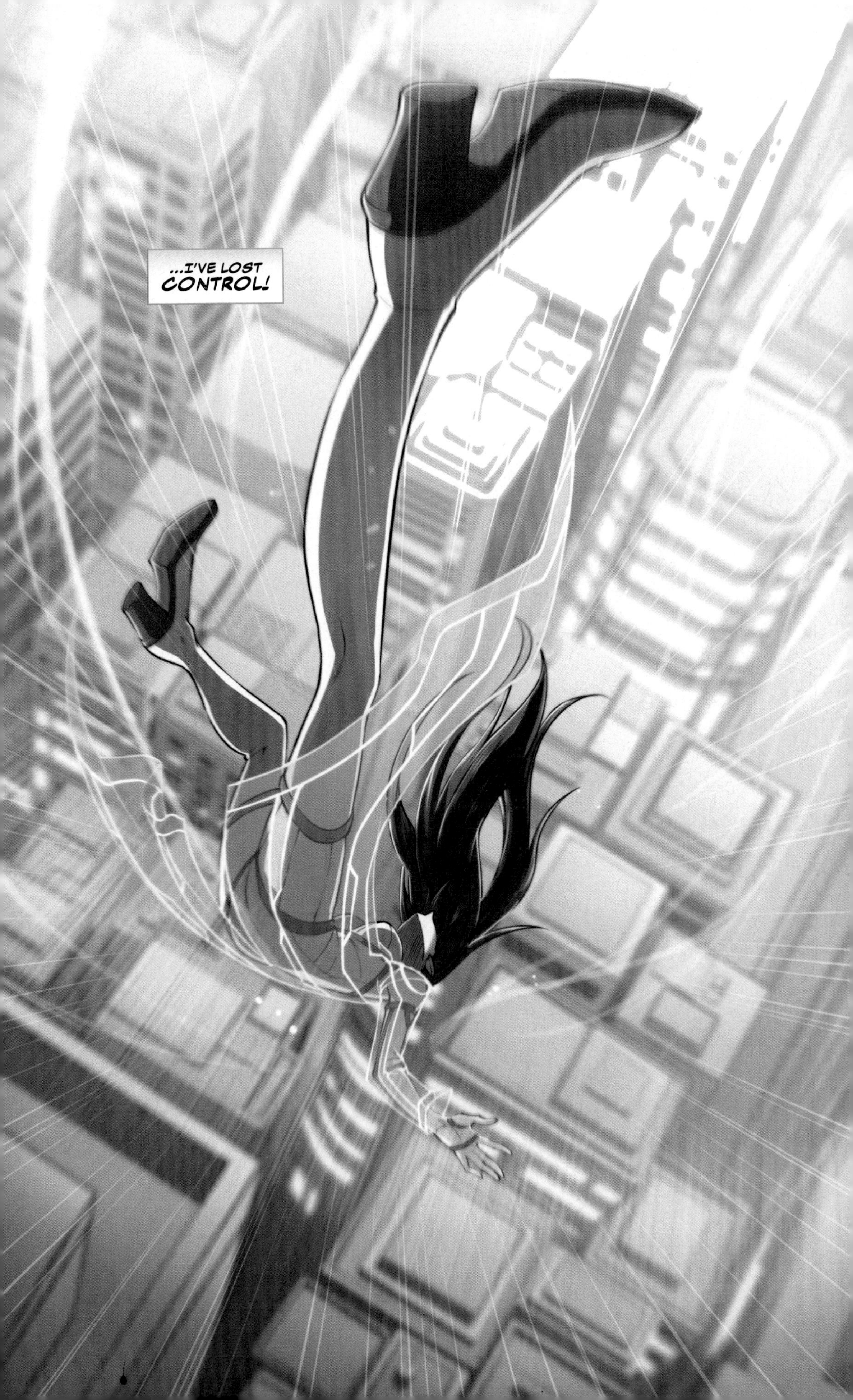
...I'VE LOST CONTROL!

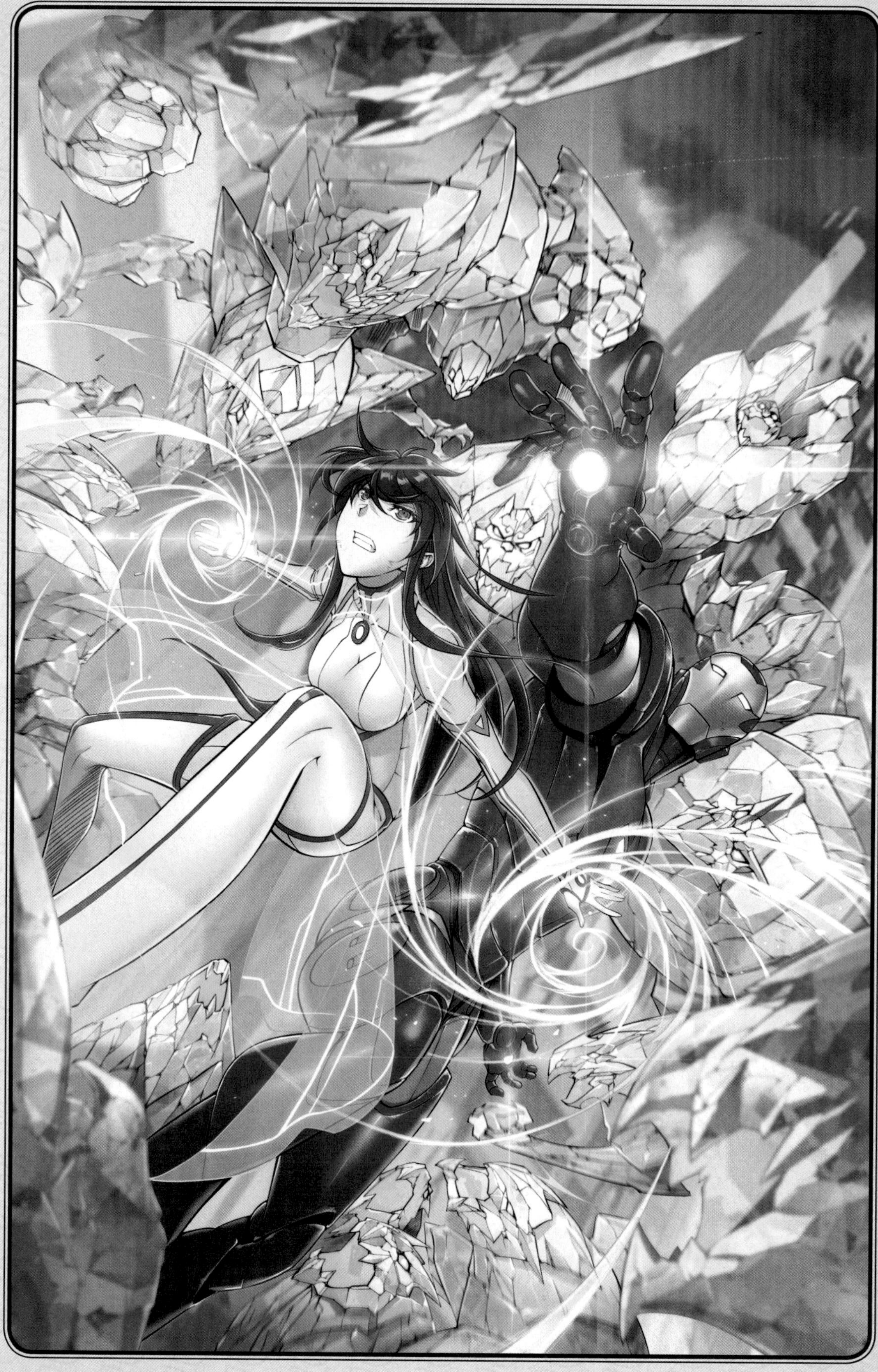

11 It Takes Two

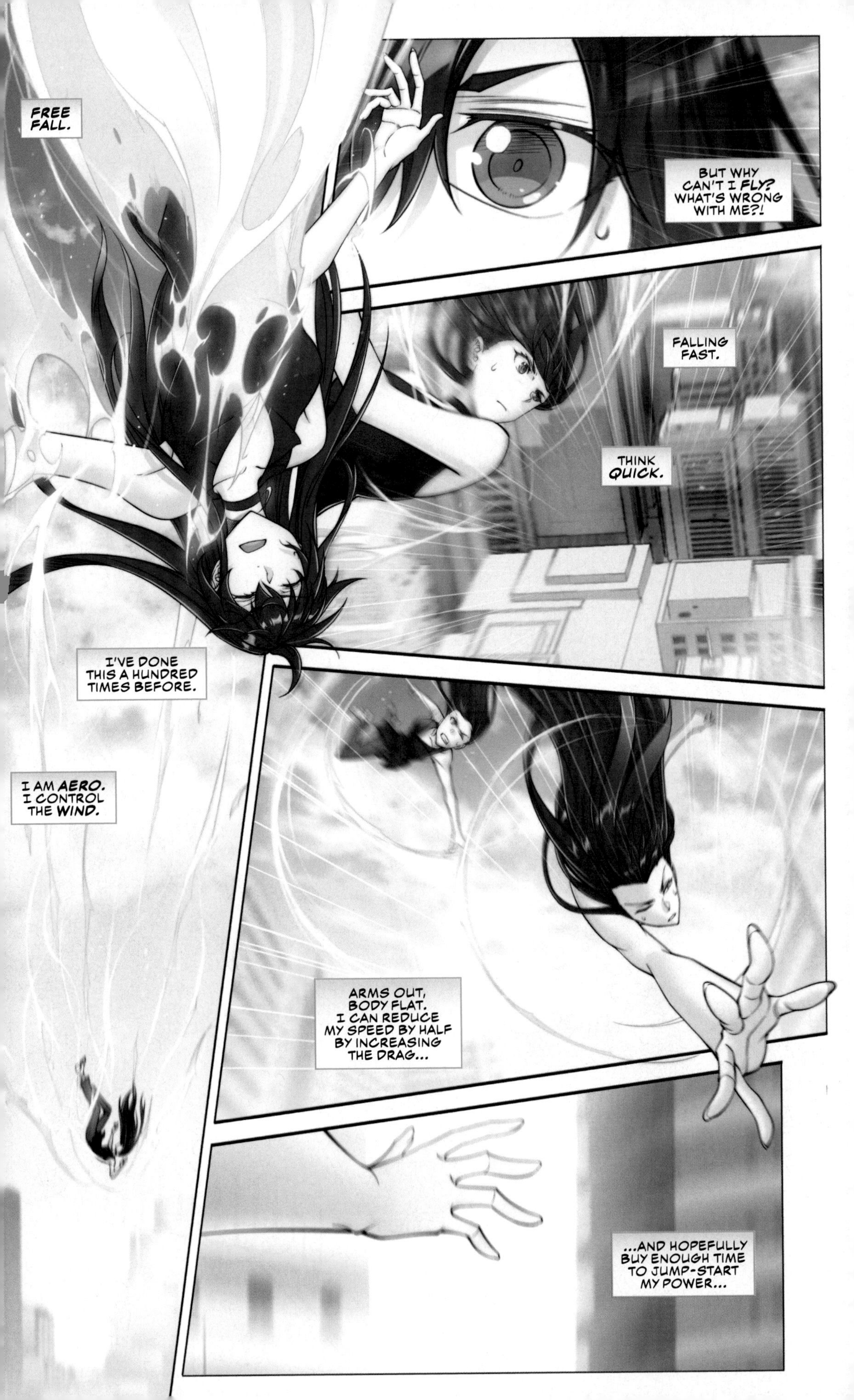
FREE FALL.
BUT WHY CAN'T I FLY? WHAT'S WRONG WITH ME?!
FALLING FAST.
THINK QUICK.
I'VE DONE THIS A HUNDRED TIMES BEFORE.
I AM AERO. I CONTROL THE WIND.
ARMS OUT, BODY FLAT. I CAN REDUCE MY SPEED BY HALF BY INCREASING THE DRAG...
...AND HOPEFULLY BUY ENOUGH TIME TO JUMP-START MY POWER...

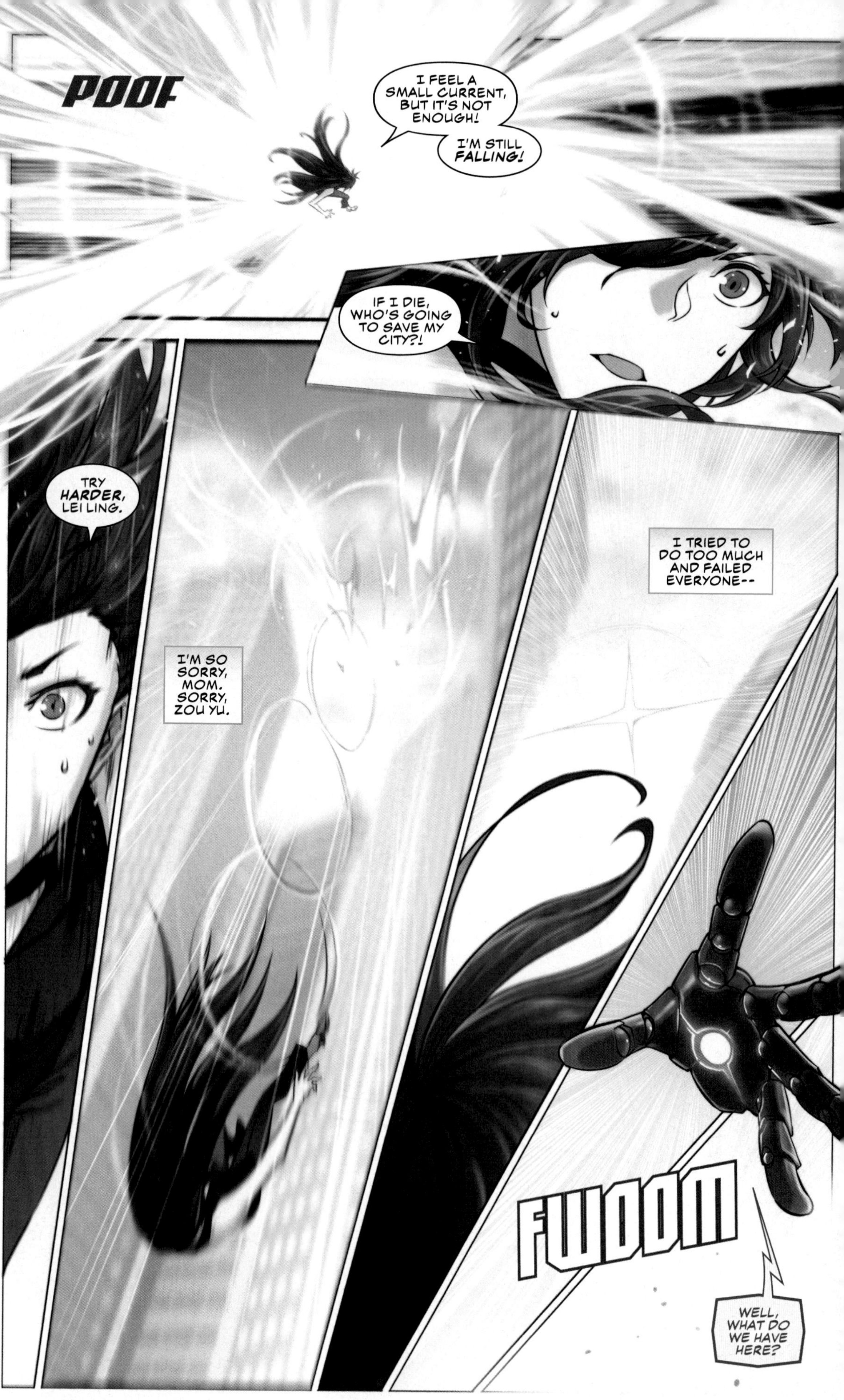
POOF
I FEEL A SMALL CURRENT, BUT IT'S NOT ENOUGH!
I'M STILL FALLING!
IF I DIE, WHO'S GOING TO SAVE MY CITY?!
TRY HARDER, LEI LING.
I'M SO SORRY, MOM. SORRY, ZOU YU.
I TRIED TO DO TOO MUCH AND FAILED EVERYONE--
FWOOM
WELL, WHAT DO WE HAVE HERE?

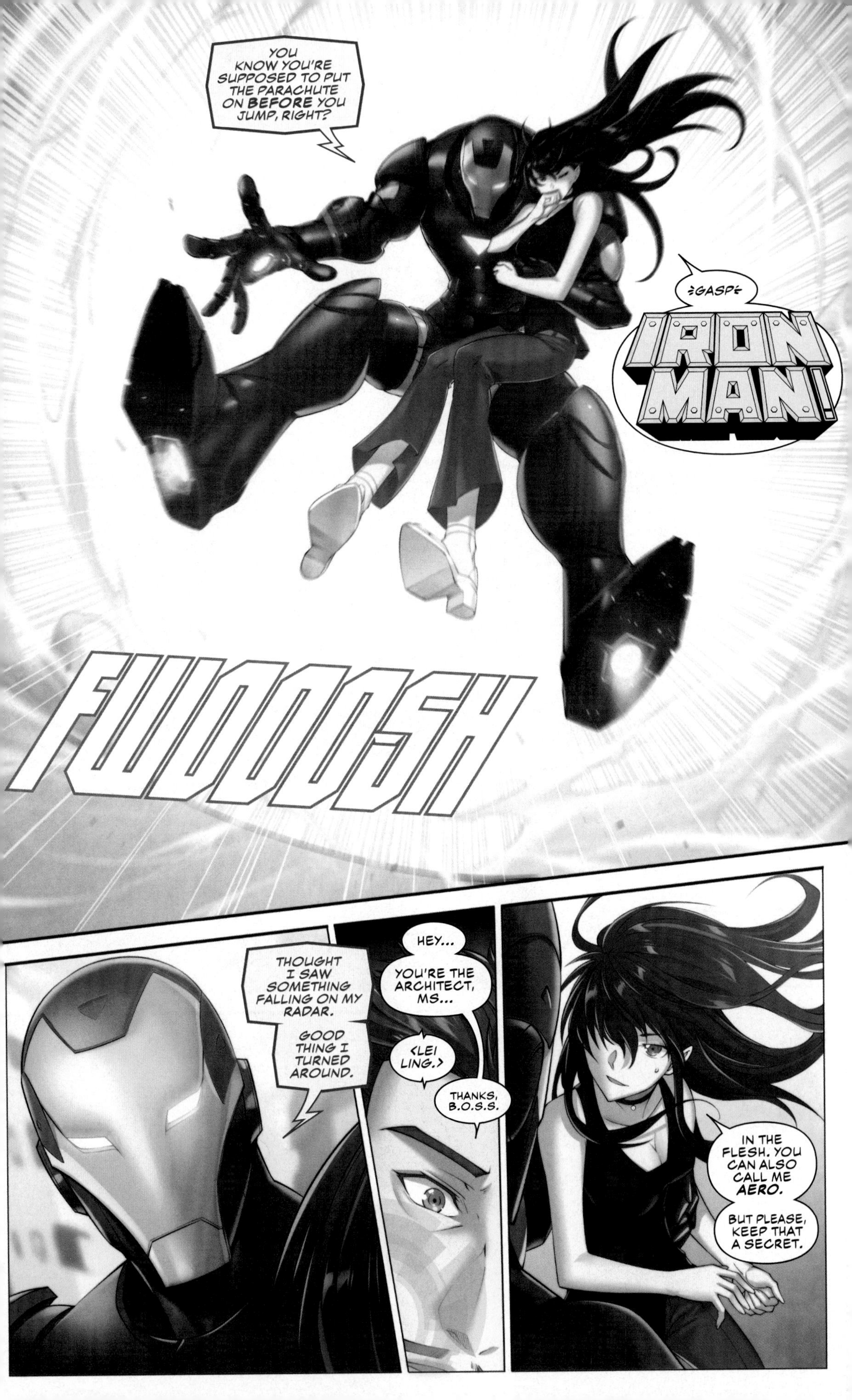
YOU KNOW YOU'RE SUPPOSED TO PUT THE PARACHUTE ON BEFORE YOU JUMP, RIGHT?
GASP
IRON MAN!
FWOOOSH
THOUGHT I SAW SOMETHING FALLING ON MY RADAR.
GOOD THING I TURNED AROUND.
HEY...
YOU'RE THE ARCHITECT, MS...
<LEI LING.>
THANKS, B.O.S.S.
IN THE FLESH. YOU CAN ALSO CALL ME AERO.
BUT PLEASE, KEEP THAT A SECRET.

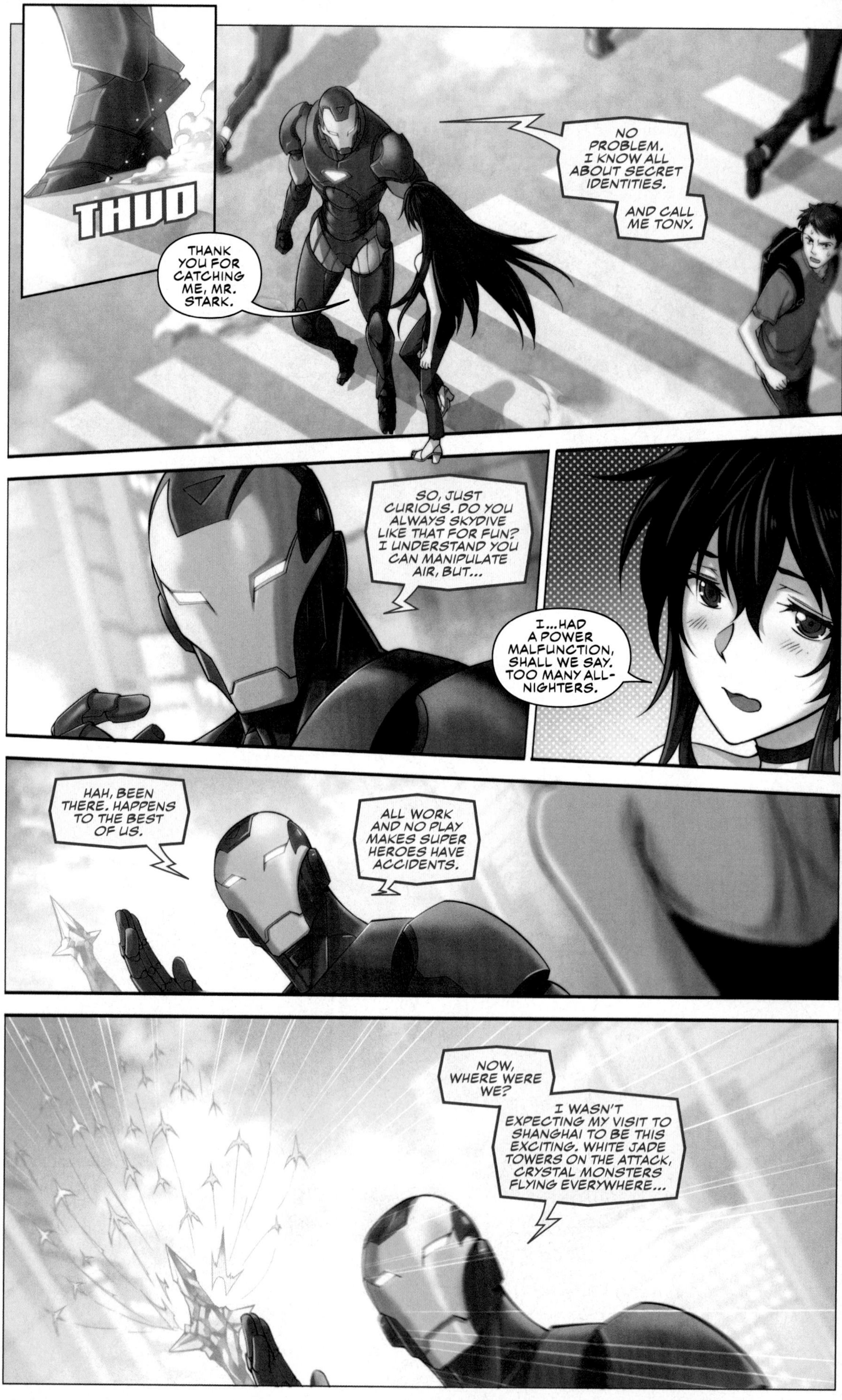
THUD
THANK YOU FOR CATCHING ME, MR. STARK.
NO PROBLEM. I KNOW ALL ABOUT SECRET IDENTITIES.
AND CALL ME TONY.
SO, JUST CURIOUS. DO YOU ALWAYS SKYDIVE LIKE THAT FOR FUN? I UNDERSTAND YOU CAN MANIPULATE AIR, BUT...
I...HAD A POWER MALFUNCTION, SHALL WE SAY. TOO MANY ALL-NIGHTERS.
HAH, BEEN THERE. HAPPENS TO THE BEST OF US.
ALL WORK AND NO PLAY MAKES SUPER HEROES HAVE ACCIDENTS.
NOW, WHERE WERE WE?
I WASN'T EXPECTING MY VISIT TO SHANGHAI TO BE THIS EXCITING. WHITE JADE TOWERS ON THE ATTACK, CRYSTAL MONSTERS FLYING EVERYWHERE...

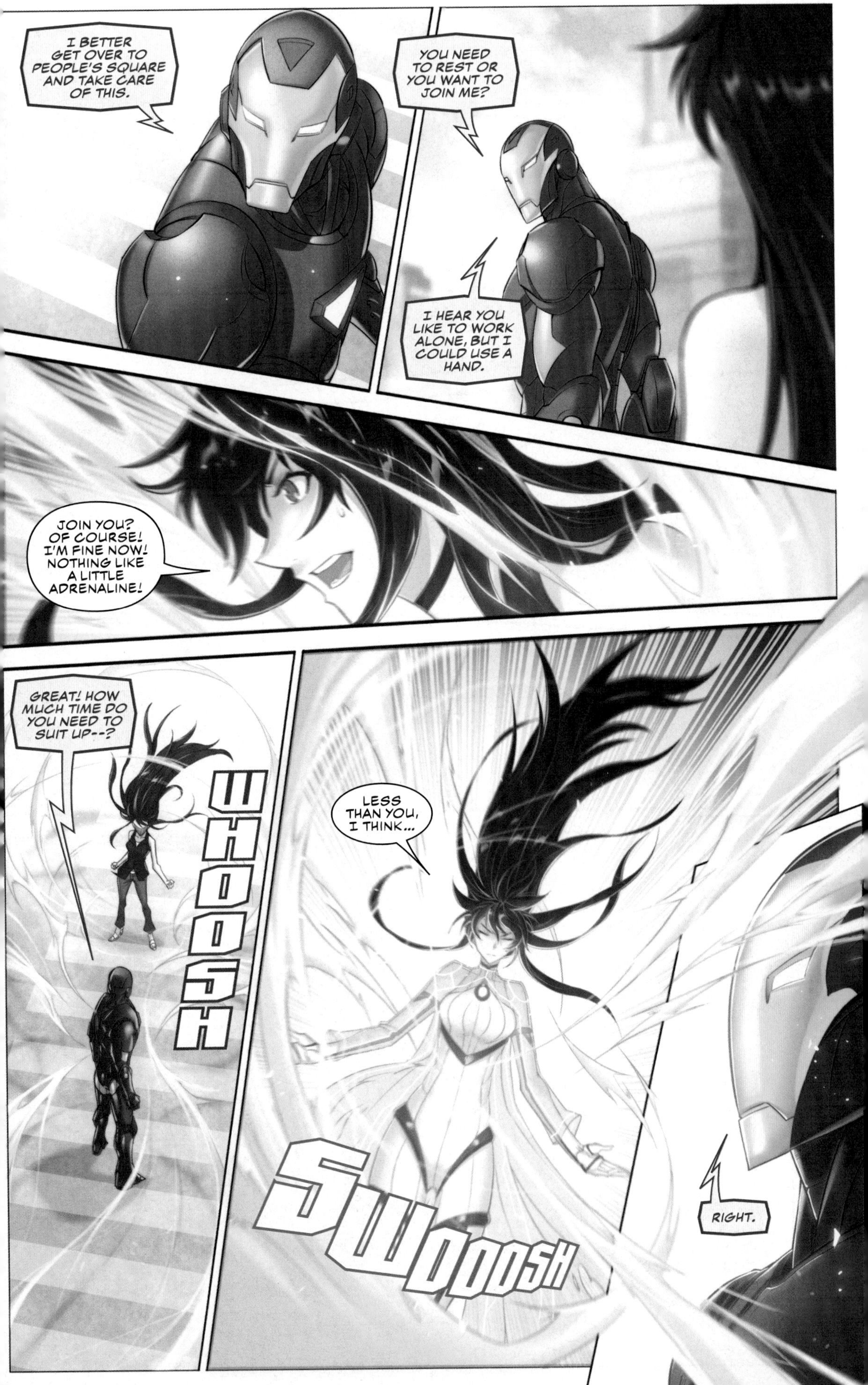
I BETTER GET OVER TO PEOPLE'S SQUARE AND TAKE CARE OF THIS.
YOU NEED TO REST OR YOU WANT TO JOIN ME?
I HEAR YOU LIKE TO WORK ALONE, BUT I COULD USE A HAND.
JOIN YOU? OF COURSE! I'M FINE NOW! NOTHING LIKE A LITTLE ADRENALINE!
GREAT! HOW MUCH TIME DO YOU NEED TO SUIT UP--?
WHOOOSH
LESS THAN YOU, I THINK...
SWOOOOSH
RIGHT.

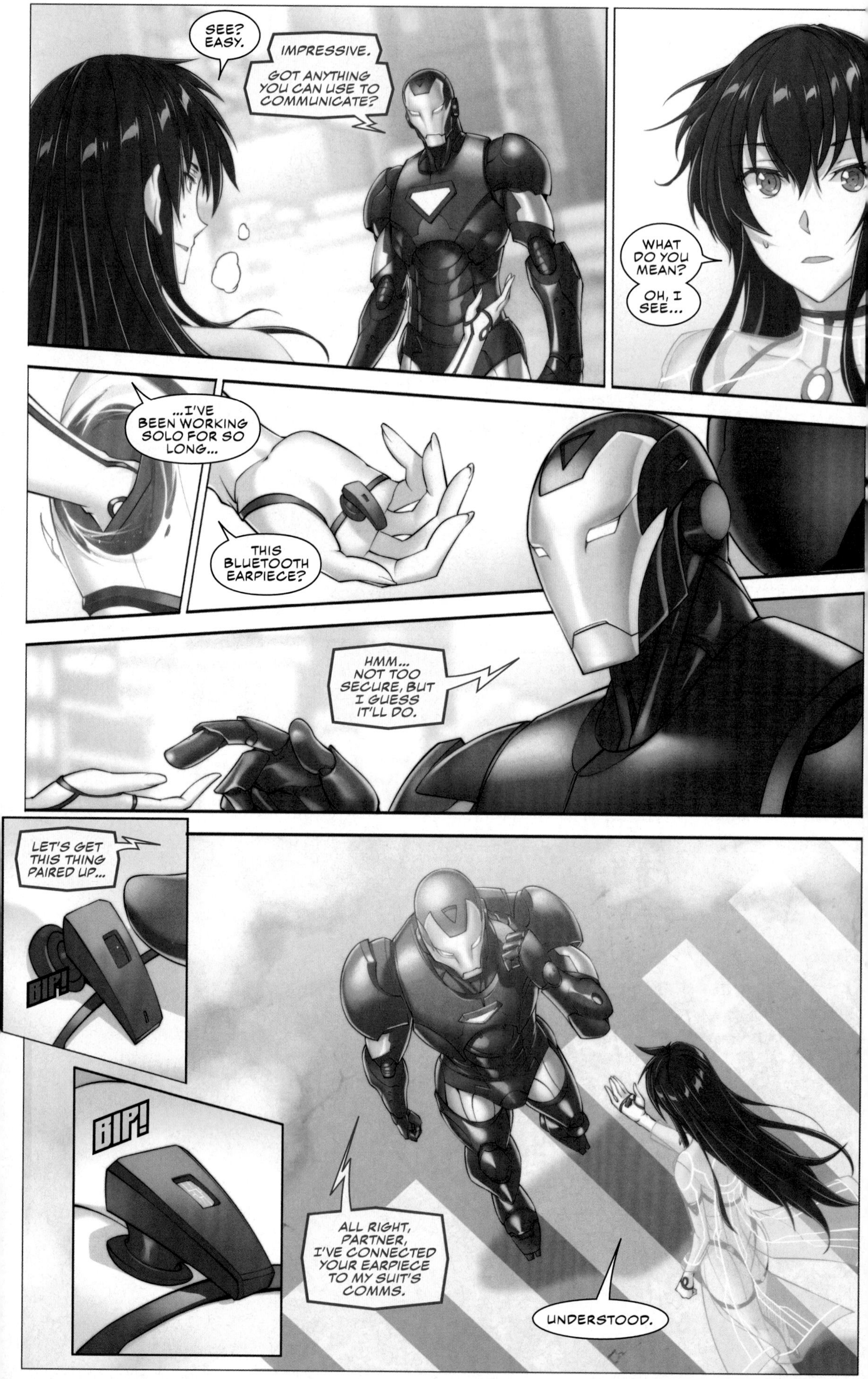
SEE? EASY.
IMPRESSIVE.
GOT ANYTHING YOU CAN USE TO COMMUNICATE?
WHAT DO YOU MEAN?
OH, I SEE...
...I'VE BEEN WORKING SOLO FOR SO LONG...
THIS BLUETOOTH EARPIECE?
HMM... NOT TOO SECURE, BUT I GUESS IT'LL DO.
LET'S GET THIS THING PAIRED UP...
BIP!
BIP!
ALL RIGHT, PARTNER, I'VE CONNECTED YOUR EARPIECE TO MY SUIT'S COMMS.
UNDERSTOOD.

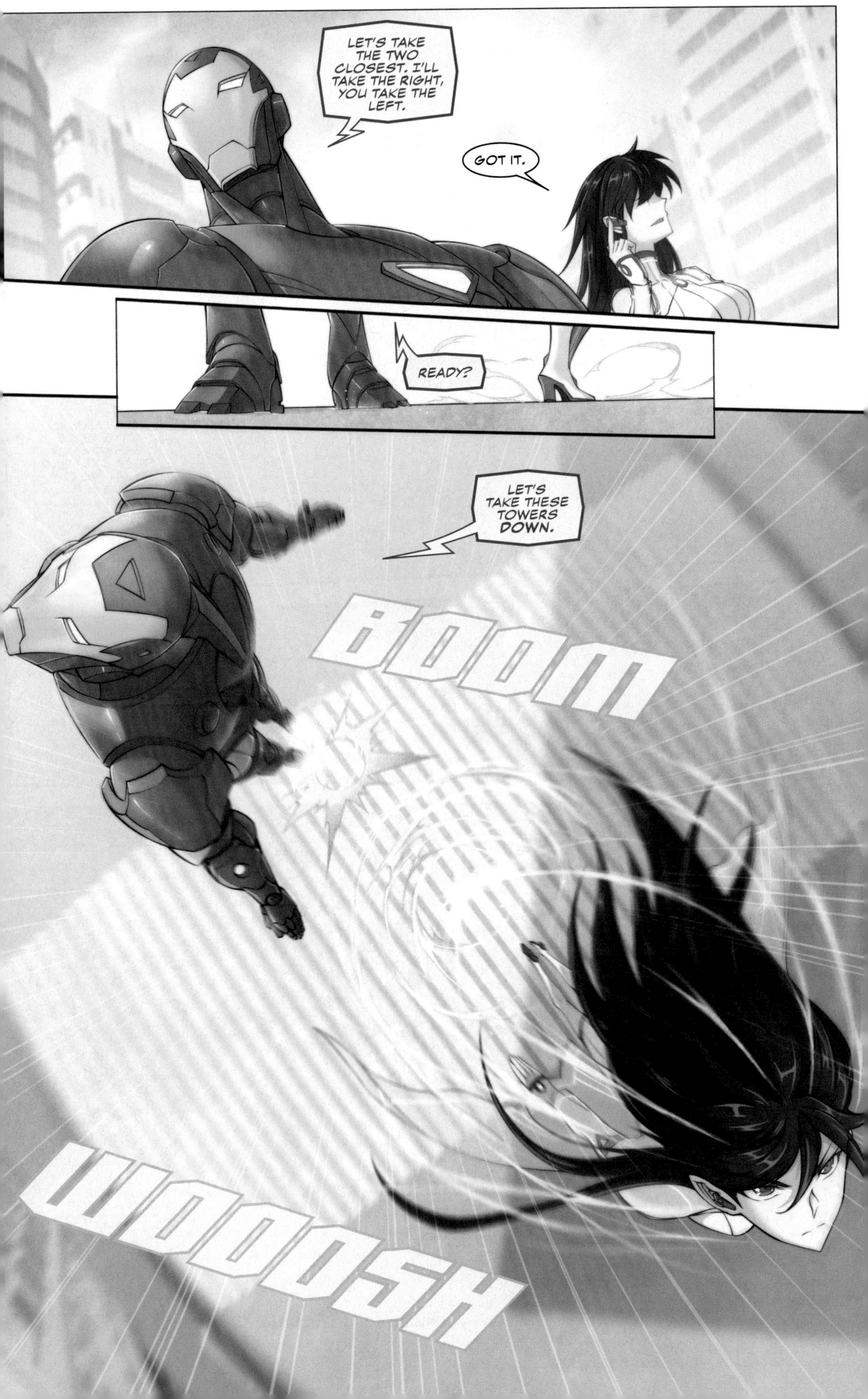
LET'S TAKE THE TWO CLOSEST. I'LL TAKE THE RIGHT, YOU TAKE THE LEFT.
GOT IT.
READY?
LET'S TAKE THESE TOWERS DOWN.
BOOM
WOOOSH

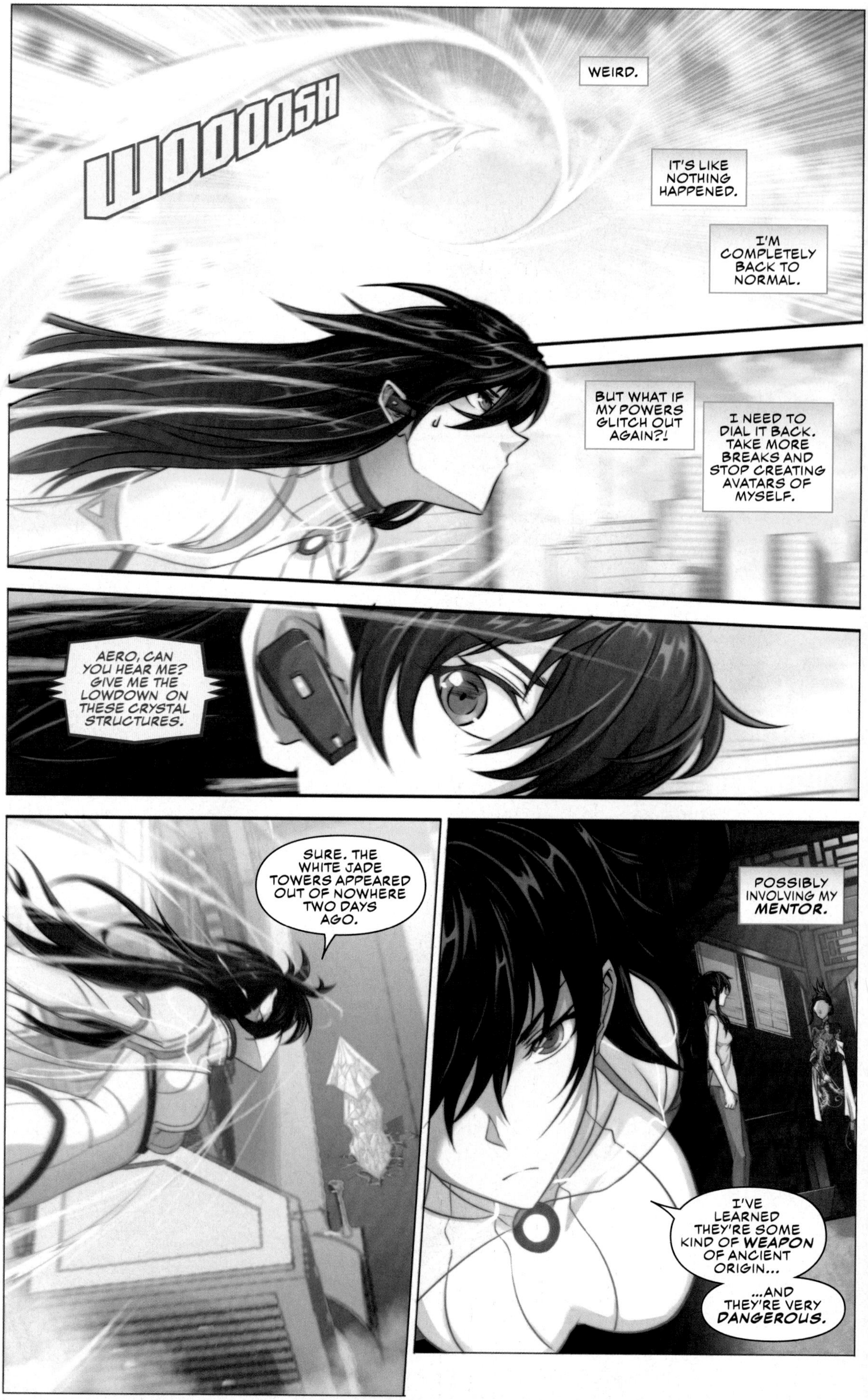
WOOOOSH
WEIRD.
IT'S LIKE NOTHING HAPPENED.
I'M COMPLETELY BACK TO NORMAL.
BUT WHAT IF MY POWERS GLITCH OUT AGAIN?!
I NEED TO DIAL IT BACK. TAKE MORE BREAKS AND STOP CREATING AVATARS OF MYSELF.
AERO, CAN YOU HEAR ME? GIVE ME THE LOWDOWN ON THESE CRYSTAL STRUCTURES.
SURE. THE WHITE JADE TOWERS APPEARED OUT OF NOWHERE TWO DAYS AGO.
POSSIBLY INVOLVING MY MENTOR.
I'VE LEARNED THEY'RE SOME KIND OF WEAPON OF ANCIENT ORIGIN...
...AND THEY'RE VERY DANGEROUS.

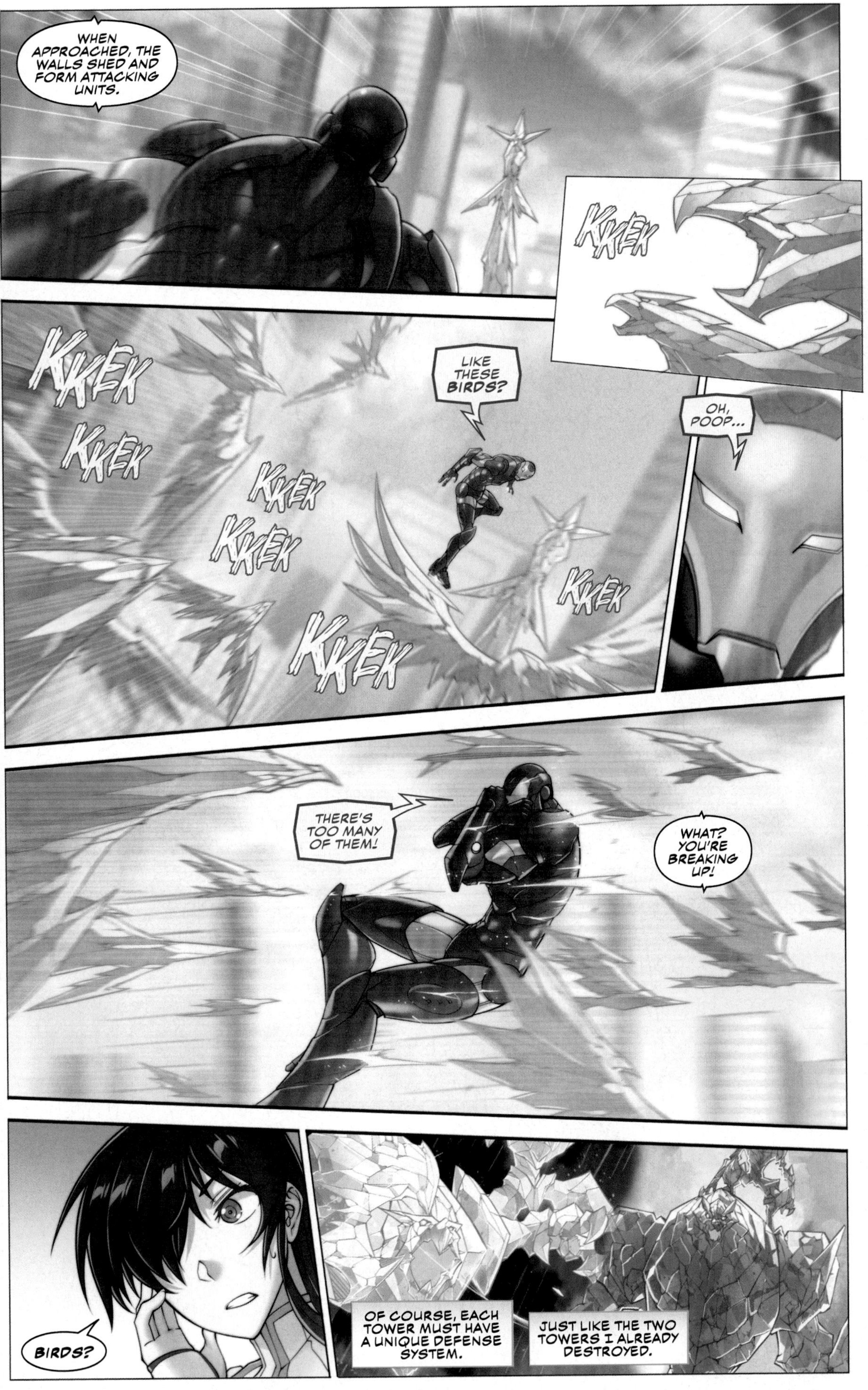

WHEN APPROACHED, THE WALLS SHED AND FORM ATTACKING UNITS.
KKKEK
KKKEK
LIKE THESE BIRDS?
KKKEK
KKKEK
KKKEK
KKKEK
KKKEK
KKKEK
OH, POOP...
THERE'S TOO MANY OF THEM!
WHAT? YOU'RE BREAKING UP!
BIRDS?
OF COURSE, EACH TOWER MUST HAVE A UNIQUE DEFENSE SYSTEM.
JUST LIKE THE TWO TOWERS I ALREADY DESTROYED.

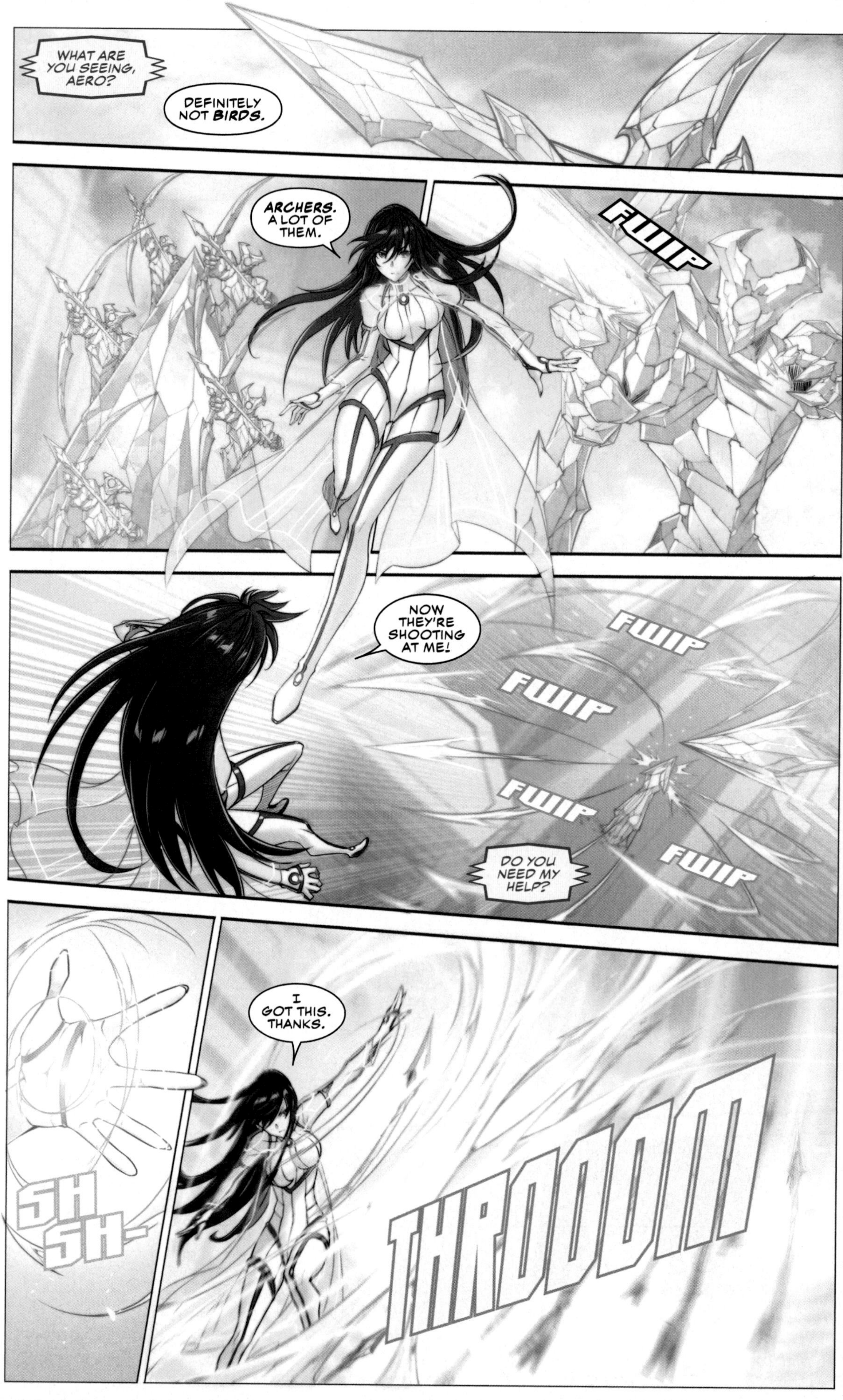
WHAT ARE YOU SEEING, AERO?
DEFINITELY NOT BIRDS.
ARCHERS. A LOT OF THEM.
FWIIP
NOW THEY'RE SHOOTING AT ME!
FWIP
FWIP
FWIP
FWIP
DO YOU NEED MY HELP?
I GOT THIS. THANKS.
SH SH-
THROOOM

ROGER THAT. DIFFERENT STROKES FOR DIFFERENT FOLKS. I'M ALMOST DONE BIRDING HERE.

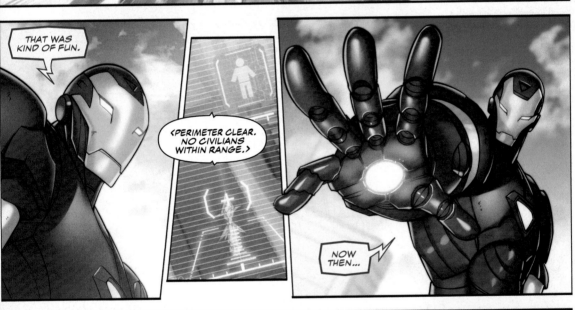

THAT WAS KIND OF FUN.

‹PERIMETER CLEAR. NO CIVILIANS WITHIN RANGE.›

NOW THEN...

LET'S TAKE CARE OF THE TOWER.

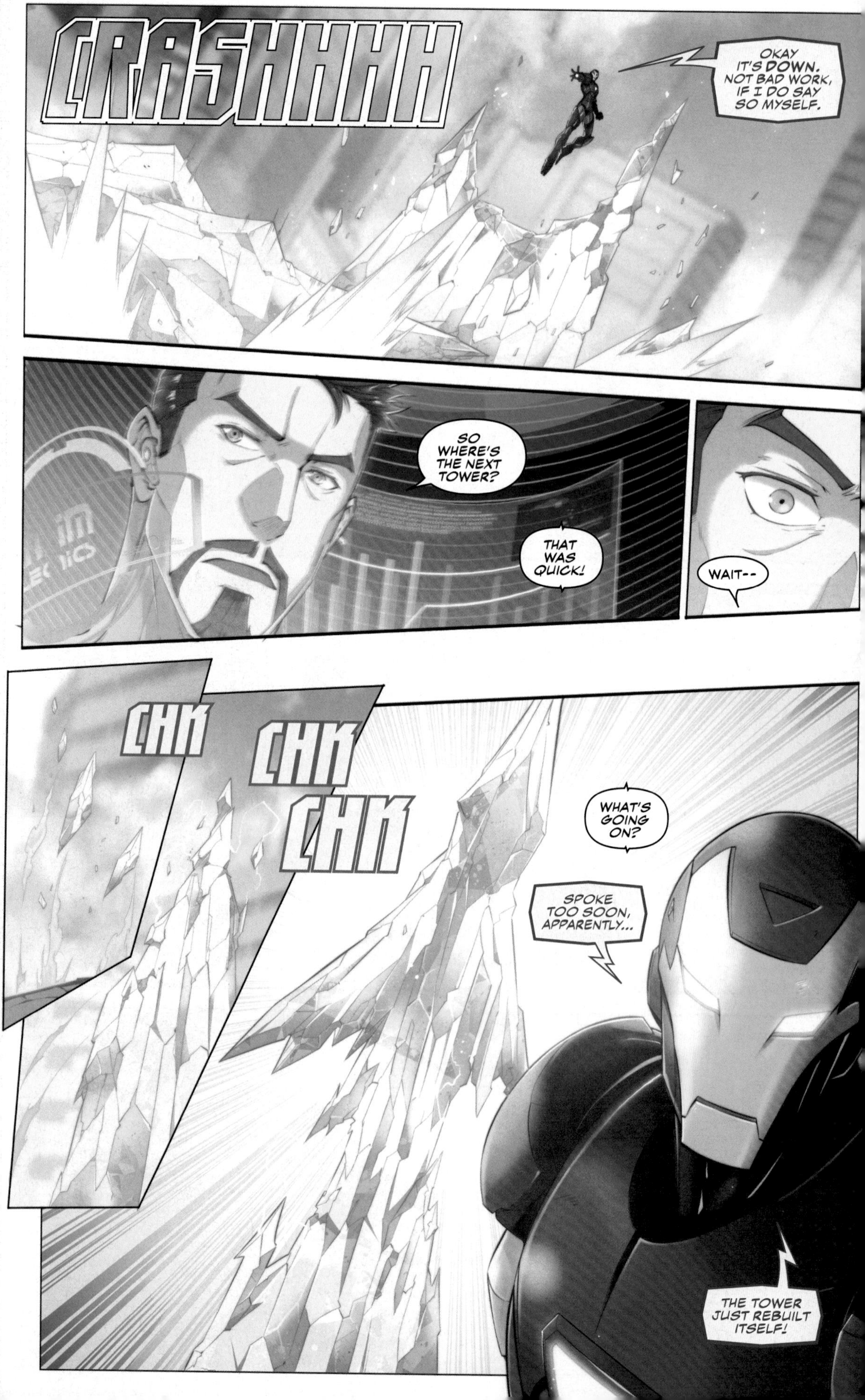
CRASHHHH
OKAY IT'S DOWN. NOT BAD WORK, IF I DO SAY SO MYSELF.
SO WHERE'S THE NEXT TOWER?
THAT WAS QUICK!
WAIT--
CHK
CHK
CHK
WHAT'S GOING ON?
SPOKE TOO SOON, APPARENTLY...
THE TOWER JUST REBUILT ITSELF!

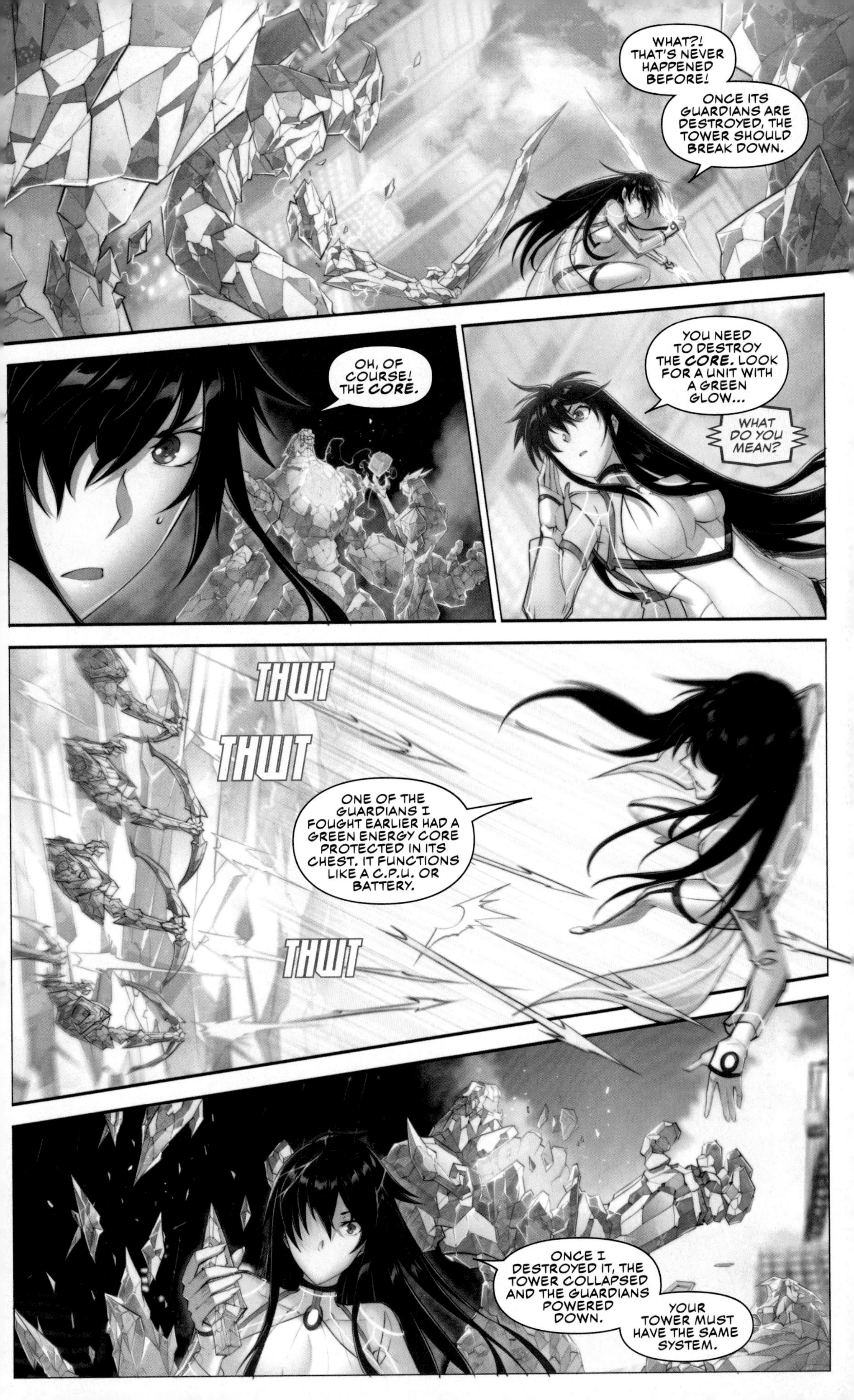
WHAT?! THAT'S NEVER HAPPENED BEFORE!
ONCE ITS GUARDIANS ARE DESTROYED, THE TOWER SHOULD BREAK DOWN.
OH, OF COURSE! THE CORE.
YOU NEED TO DESTROY THE CORE. LOOK FOR A UNIT WITH A GREEN GLOW...
WHAT DO YOU MEAN?
THWT
THWT
ONE OF THE GUARDIANS I FOUGHT EARLIER HAD A GREEN ENERGY CORE PROTECTED IN ITS CHEST. IT FUNCTIONS LIKE A C.P.U. OR BATTERY.
THWT
ONCE I DESTROYED IT, THE TOWER COLLAPSED AND THE GUARDIANS POWERED DOWN.
YOUR TOWER MUST HAVE THE SAME SYSTEM.

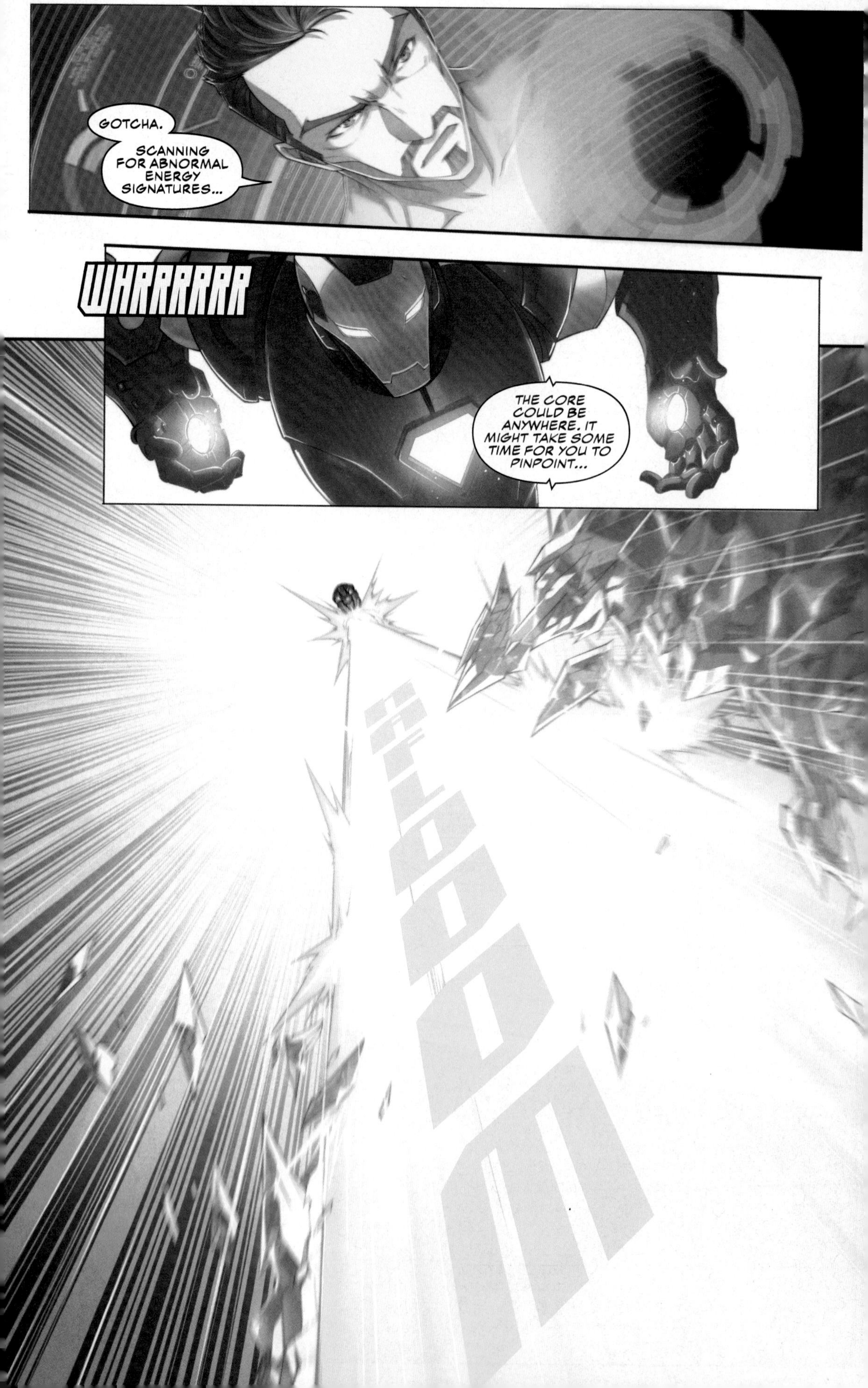
GOTCHA.
SCANNING FOR ABNORMAL ENERGY SIGNATURES...
WHRRRRRR
THE CORE COULD BE ANYWHERE. IT MIGHT TAKE SOME TIME FOR YOU TO PINPOINT...

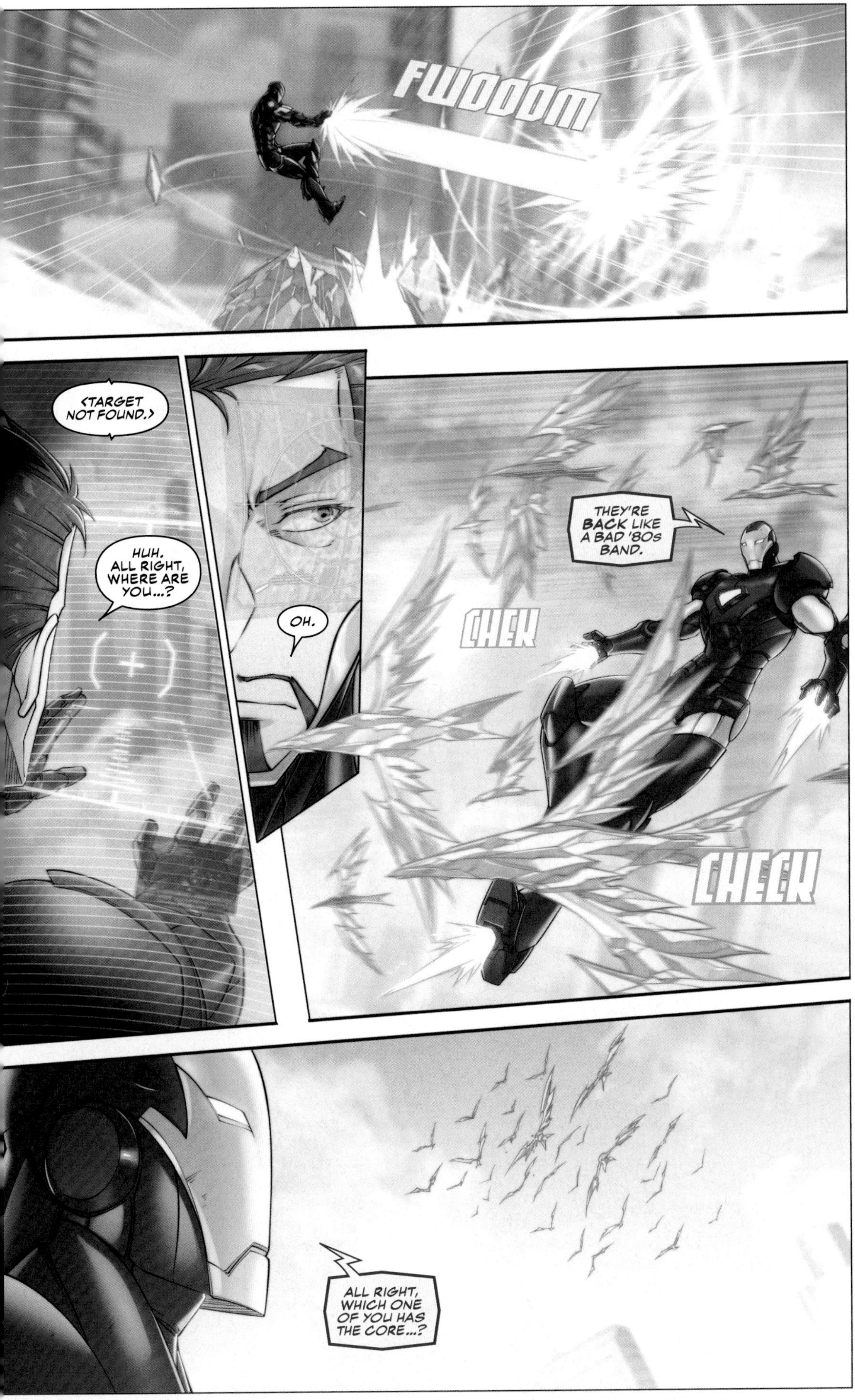
FWOOOM
<TARGET NOT FOUND.>
HUH. ALL RIGHT, WHERE ARE YOU...?
OH.
THEY'RE BACK LIKE A BAD '80s BAND.
CHEK
CHECK
ALL RIGHT, WHICH ONE OF YOU HAS THE CORE...?

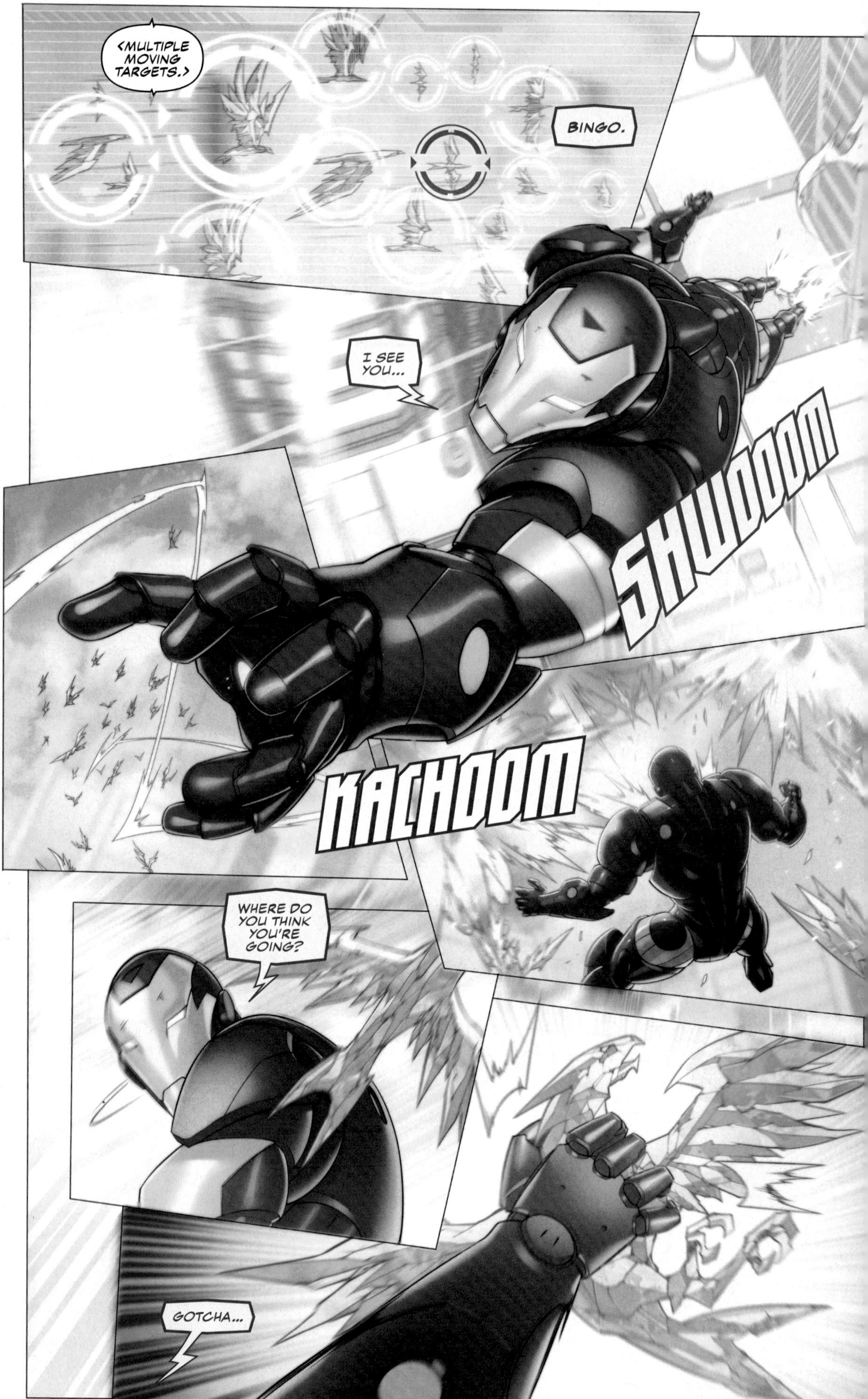
<MULTIPLE MOVING TARGETS.>
BINGO.
I SEE YOU...
SHWOOOM
KACHOOM
WHERE DO YOU THINK YOU'RE GOING?
GOTCHA...

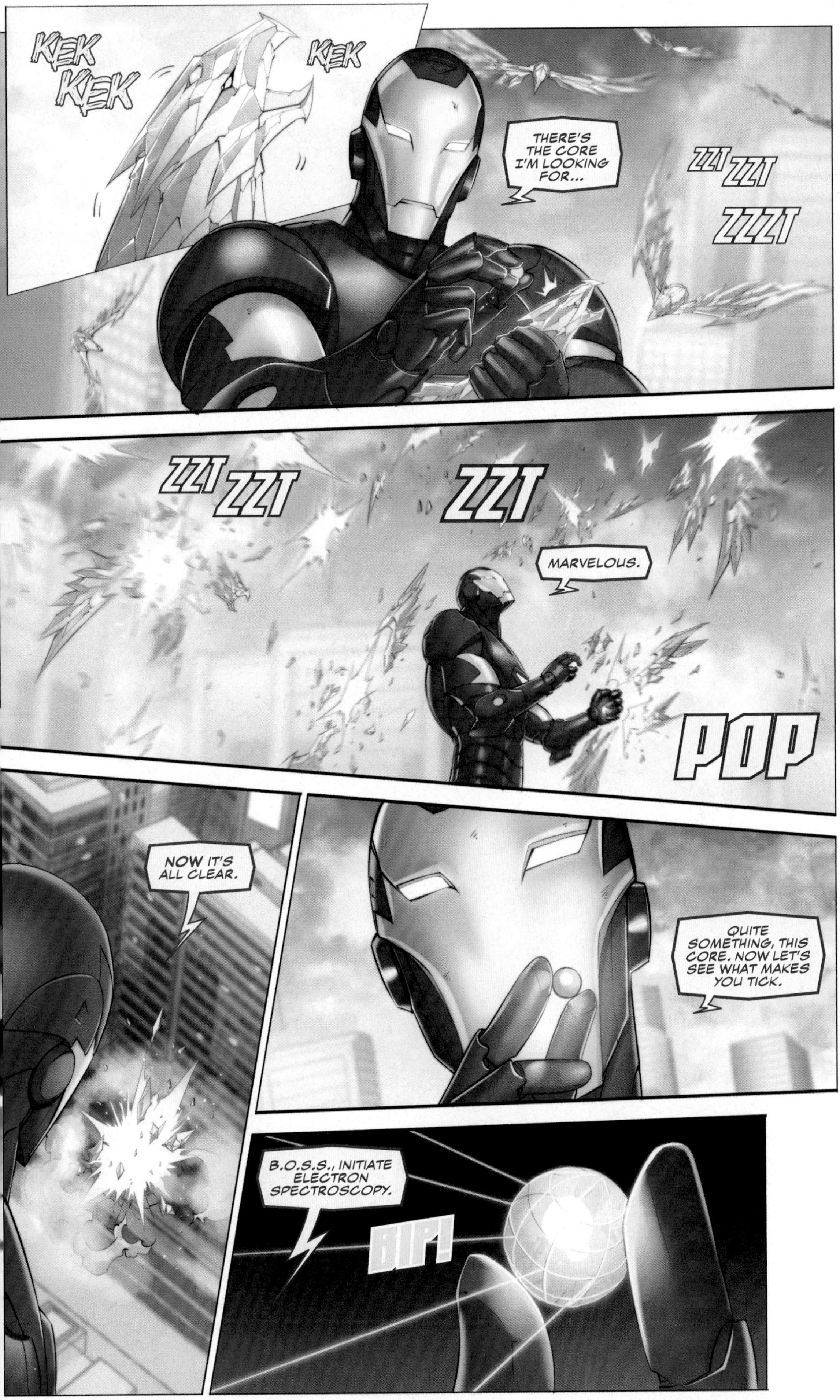
KEK KEK
KEK
THERE'S THE CORE I'M LOOKING FOR...
ZZT ZZT
ZZZT
ZZT ZZT
ZZT
MARVELOUS.
POP
NOW IT'S ALL CLEAR.
QUITE SOMETHING, THIS CORE. NOW LET'S SEE WHAT MAKES YOU TICK.
B.O.S.S., INITIATE ELECTRON SPECTROSCOPY.
BIP!

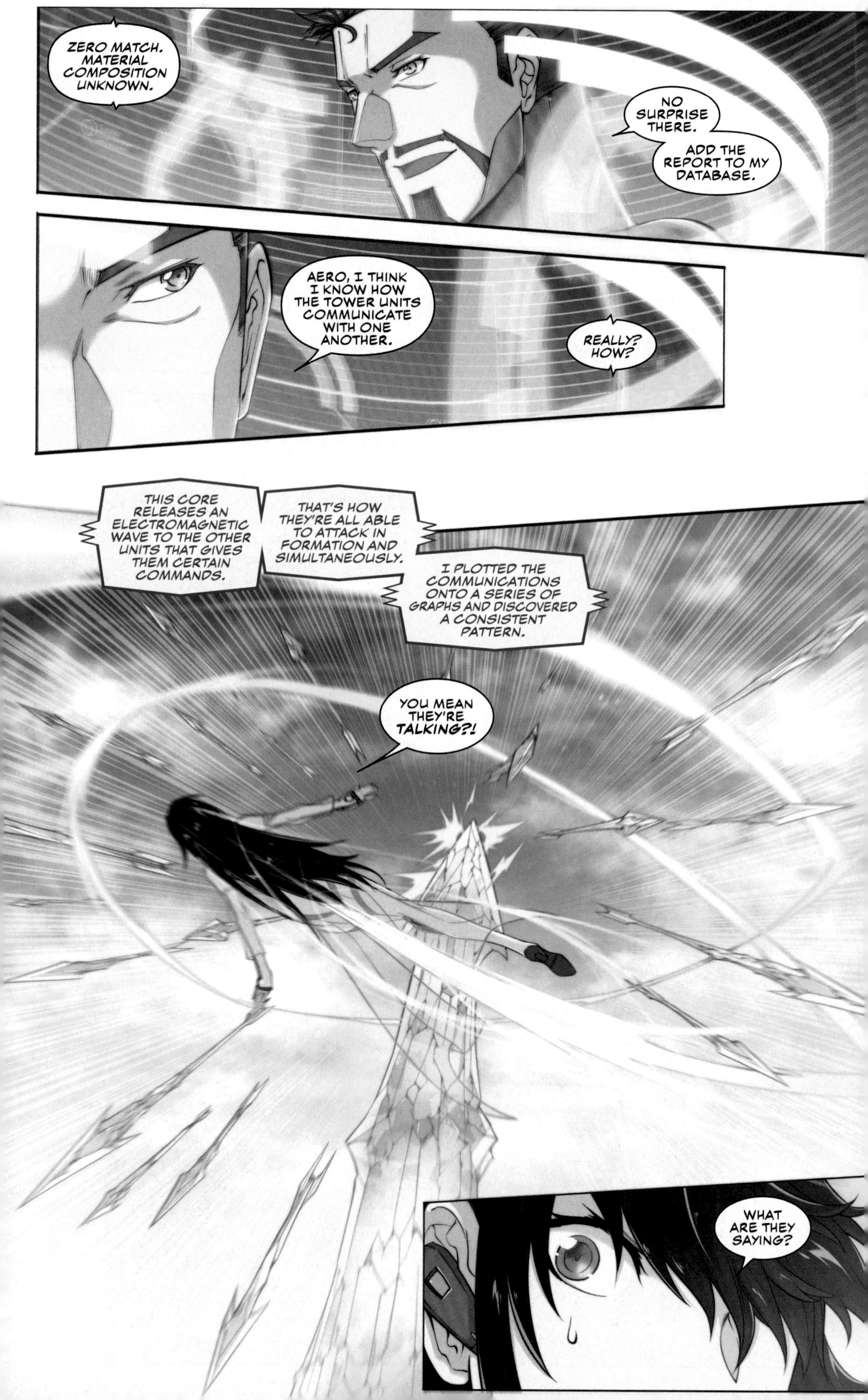

ZERO MATCH. MATERIAL COMPOSITION UNKNOWN.
NO SURPRISE THERE.
ADD THE REPORT TO MY DATABASE.
AERO, I THINK I KNOW HOW THE TOWER UNITS COMMUNICATE WITH ONE ANOTHER.
REALLY? HOW?
THIS CORE RELEASES AN ELECTROMAGNETIC WAVE TO THE OTHER UNITS THAT GIVES THEM CERTAIN COMMANDS.
THAT'S HOW THEY'RE ALL ABLE TO ATTACK IN FORMATION AND SIMULTANEOUSLY.
I PLOTTED THE COMMUNICATIONS ONTO A SERIES OF GRAPHS AND DISCOVERED A CONSISTENT PATTERN.
YOU MEAN THEY'RE *TALKING?!*
WHAT ARE THEY SAYING?

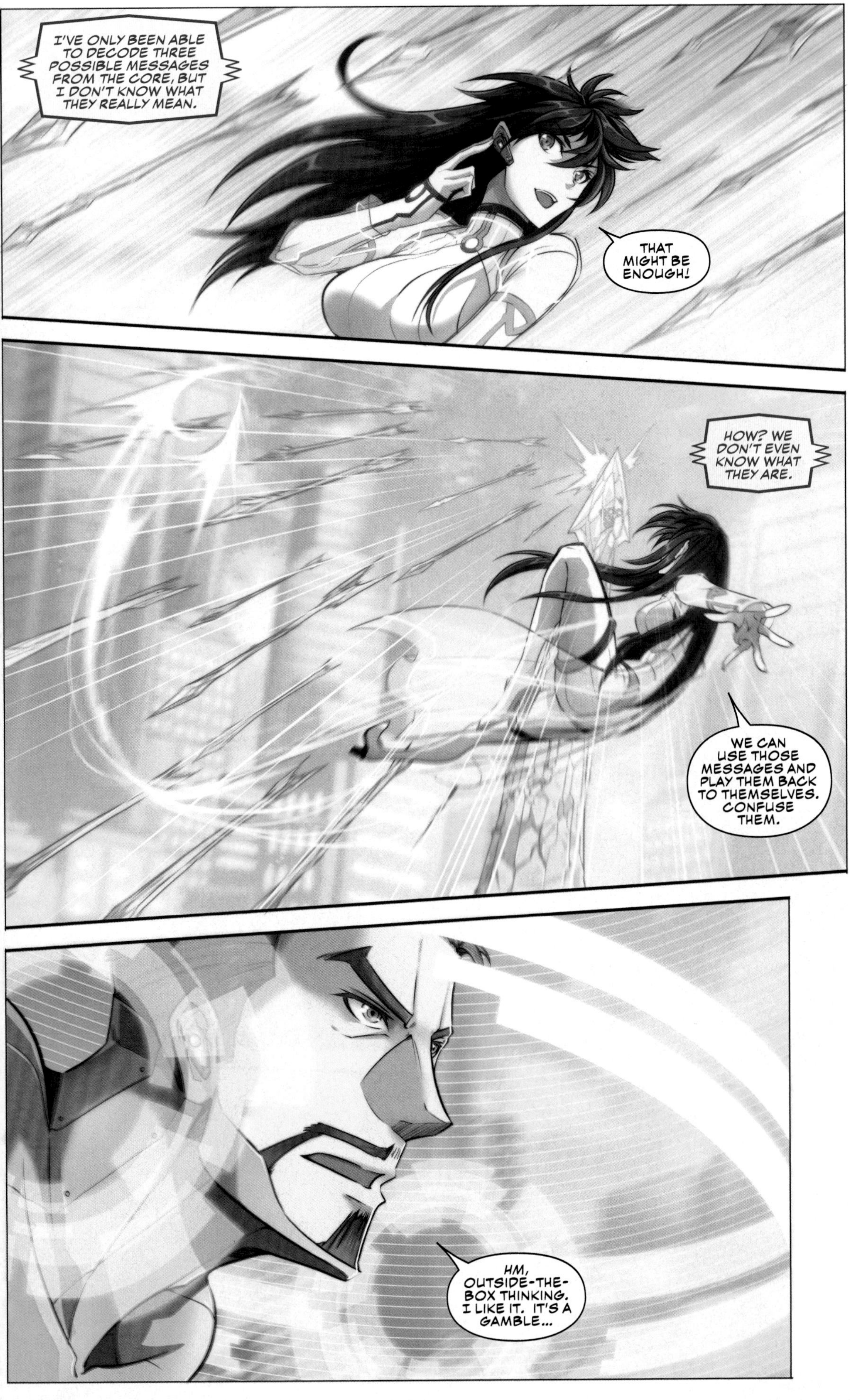
I'VE ONLY BEEN ABLE TO DECODE THREE POSSIBLE MESSAGES FROM THE CORE, BUT I DON'T KNOW WHAT THEY REALLY MEAN.
THAT MIGHT BE ENOUGH!
HOW? WE DON'T EVEN KNOW WHAT THEY ARE.
WE CAN USE THOSE MESSAGES AND PLAY THEM BACK TO THEMSELVES. CONFUSE THEM.
HM, OUTSIDE-THE-BOX THINKING. I LIKE IT. IT'S A GAMBLE...

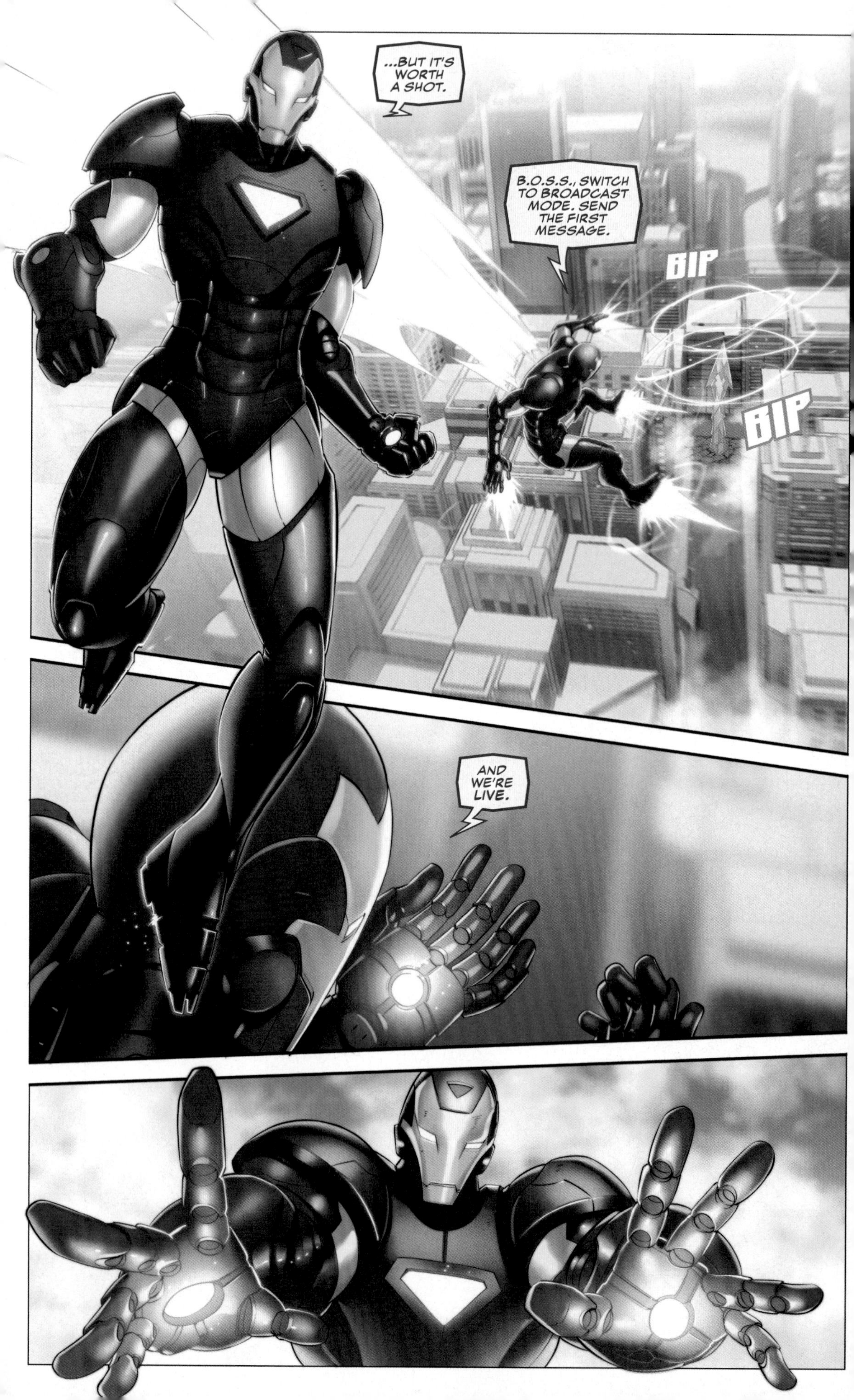
...BUT IT'S WORTH A SHOT.
B.O.S.S., SWITCH TO BROADCAST MODE. SEND THE FIRST MESSAGE.
BIP
BIP
AND WE'RE LIVE.

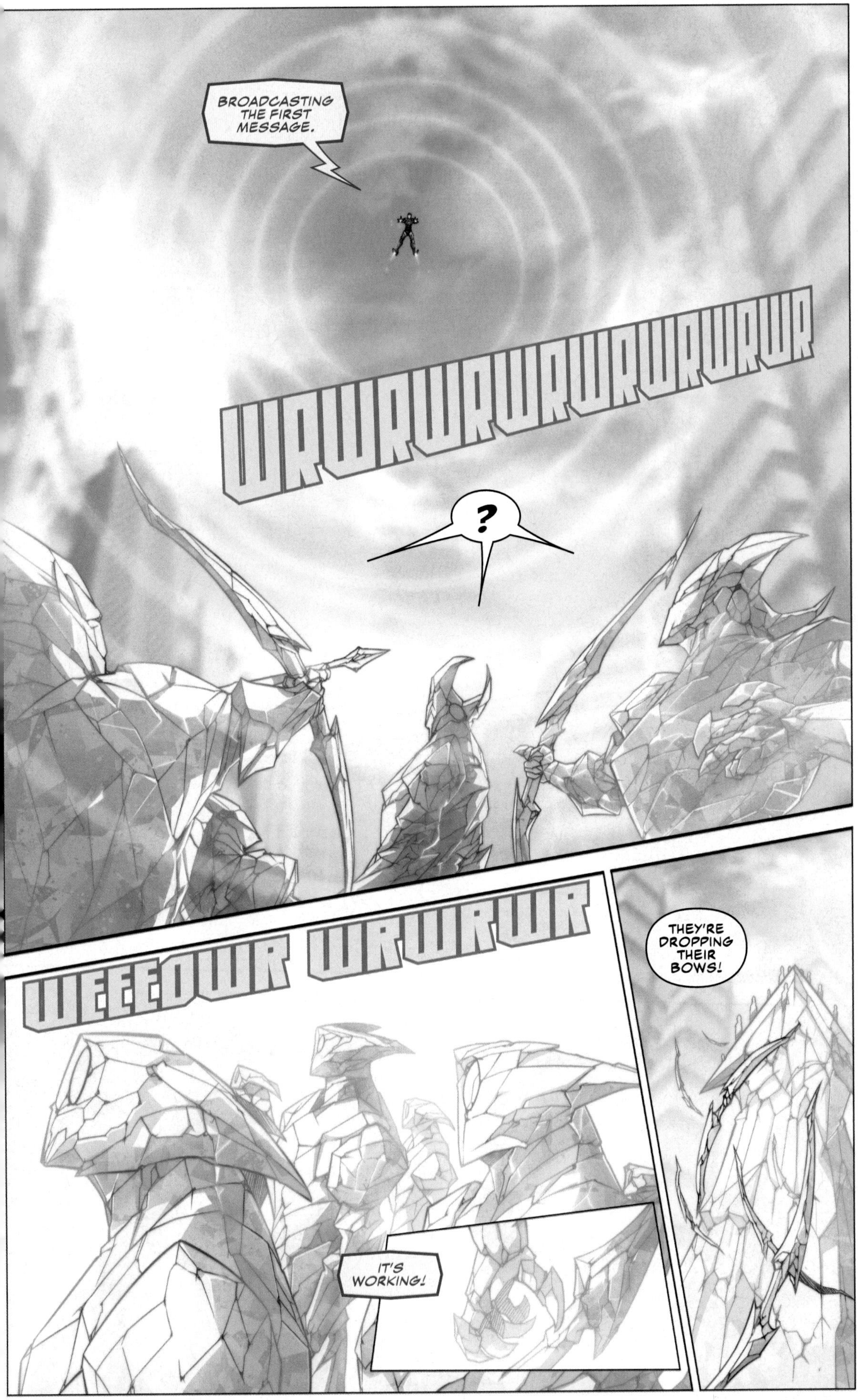
BROADCASTING THE FIRST MESSAGE.
WRWRWRWRWRWRWRWRWR
?
WEEEOWR WRWRWR
THEY'RE DROPPING THEIR BOWS!
IT'S WORKING!

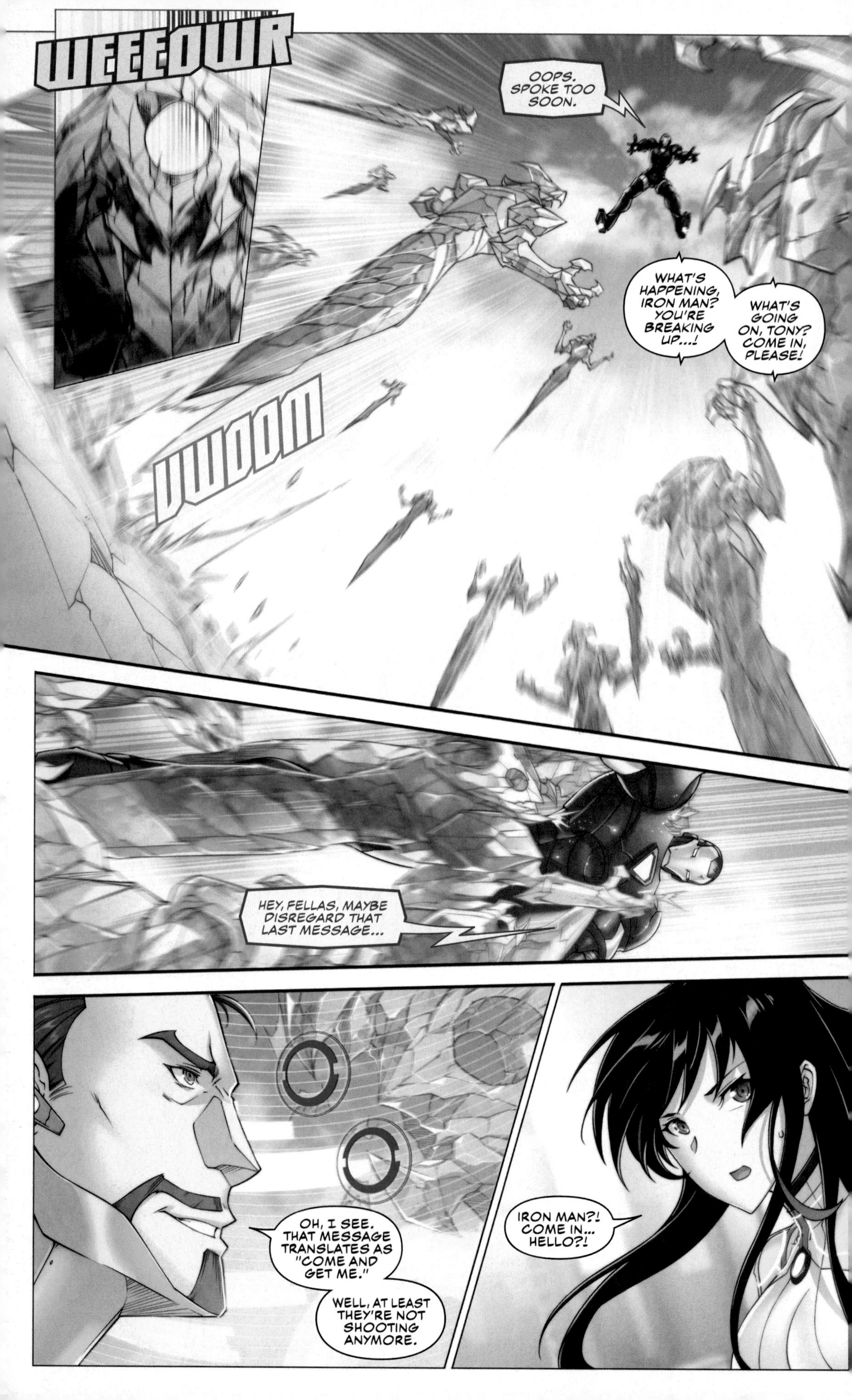
WEEEOWR
OOPS. SPOKE TOO SOON.
WHAT'S HAPPENING, IRON MAN? YOU'RE BREAKING UP...!
WHAT'S GOING ON, TONY? COME IN, PLEASE!
VWOOM
HEY, FELLAS, MAYBE DISREGARD THAT LAST MESSAGE...
OH, I SEE. THAT MESSAGE TRANSLATES AS "COME AND GET ME."
WELL, AT LEAST THEY'RE NOT SHOOTING ANYMORE.
IRON MAN?! COME IN... HELLO?!

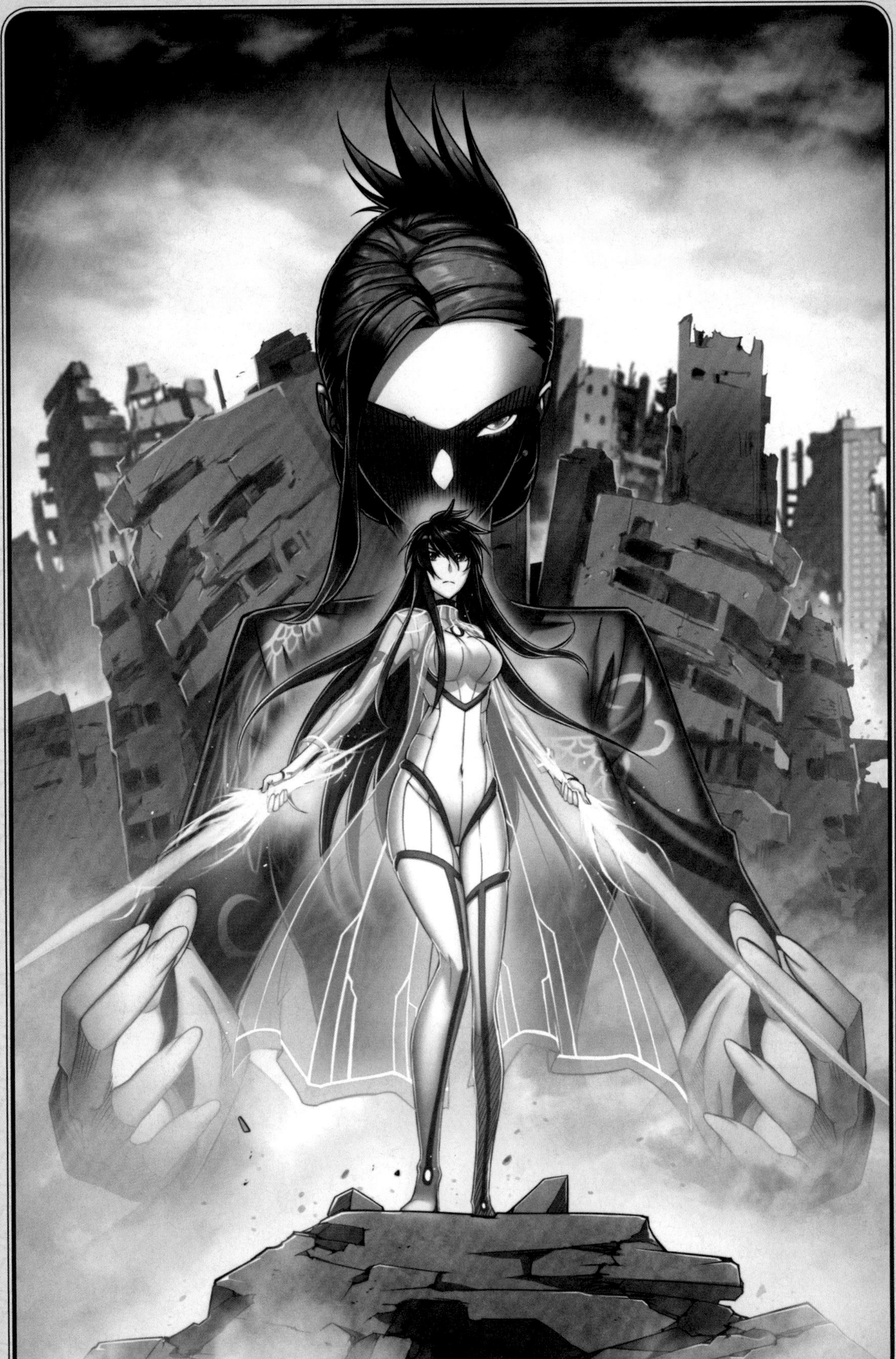

12 **Birds of a Feather**

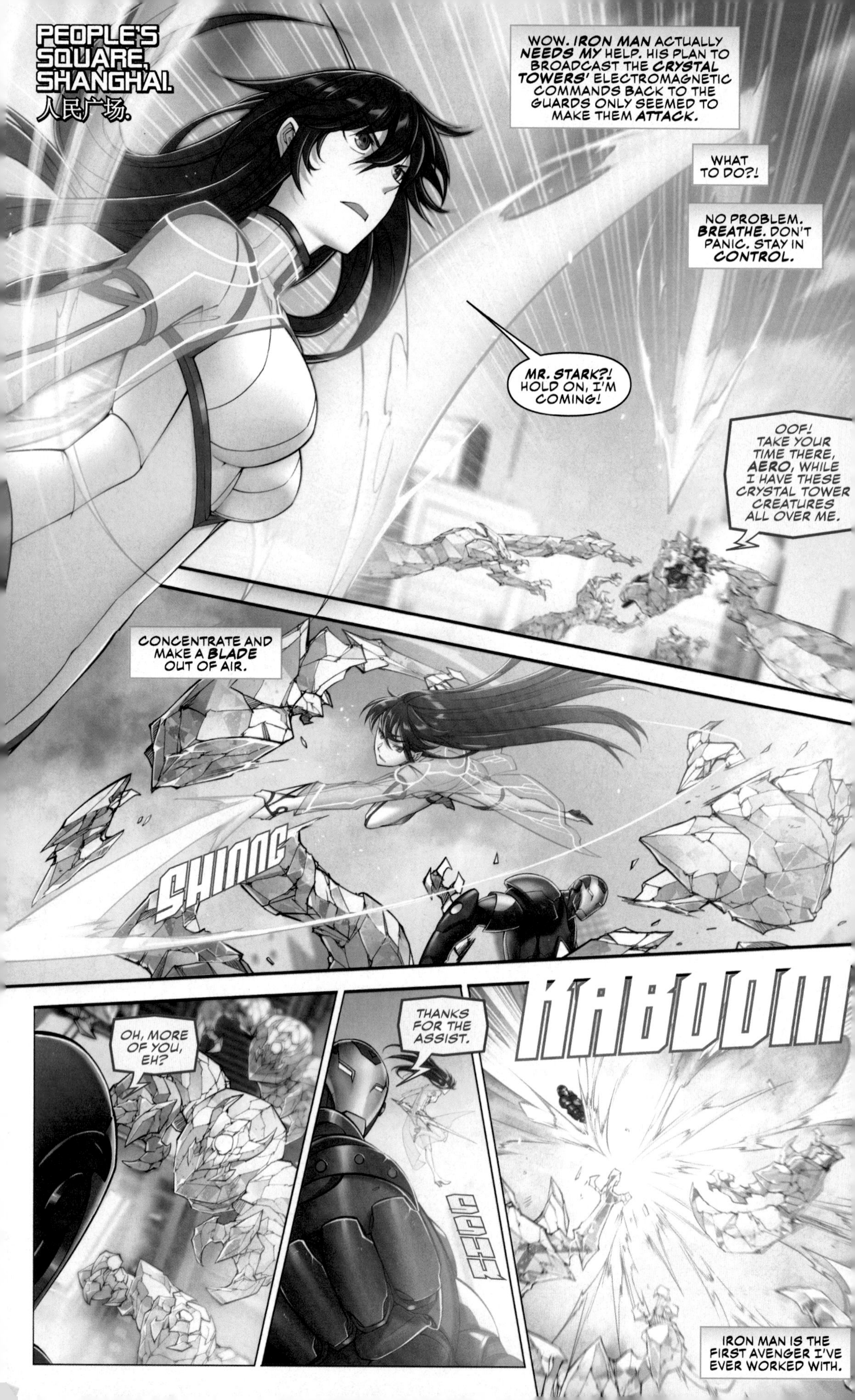

PEOPLE'S SQUARE, SHANGHAI.
人民广场.
WOW. IRON MAN ACTUALLY NEEDS MY HELP. HIS PLAN TO BROADCAST THE CRYSTAL TOWERS' ELECTROMAGNETIC COMMANDS BACK TO THE GUARDS ONLY SEEMED TO MAKE THEM ATTACK.
WHAT TO DO?!
NO PROBLEM. BREATHE. DON'T PANIC. STAY IN CONTROL.
MR. STARK?! HOLD ON, I'M COMING!
OOF! TAKE YOUR TIME THERE, AERO, WHILE I HAVE THESE CRYSTAL TOWER CREATURES ALL OVER ME.
CONCENTRATE AND MAKE A BLADE OUT OF AIR.
SHINNG
OH, MORE OF YOU, EH?
THANKS FOR THE ASSIST.
KABOOM
IRON MAN IS THE FIRST AVENGER I'VE EVER WORKED WITH.

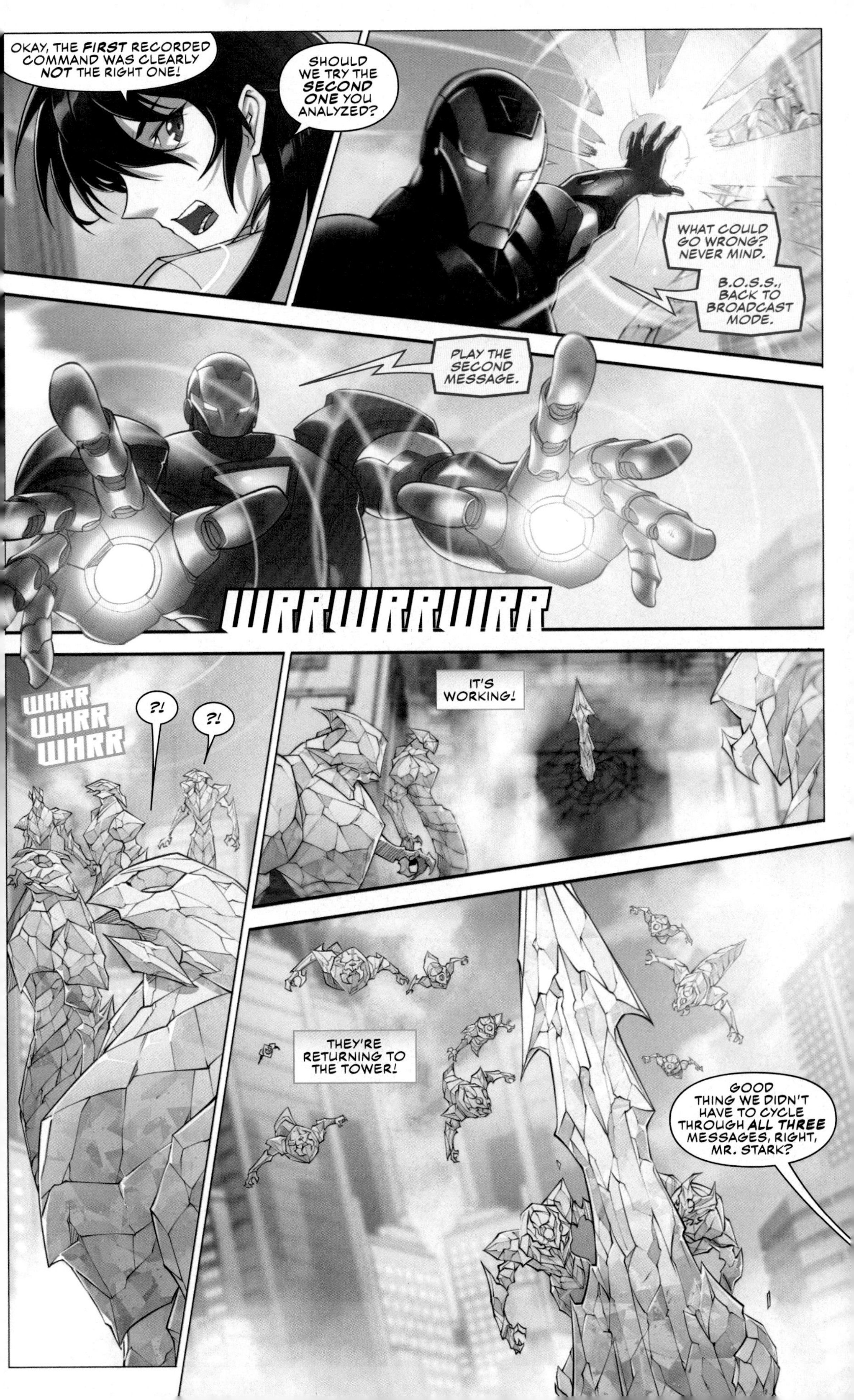
OKAY, THE FIRST RECORDED COMMAND WAS CLEARLY NOT THE RIGHT ONE!
SHOULD WE TRY THE SECOND ONE YOU ANALYZED?
WHAT COULD GO WRONG? NEVER MIND.
B.O.S.S., BACK TO BROADCAST MODE.
PLAY THE SECOND MESSAGE.
WRRWRRWRR
WHRR WHRR WHRR
?!
?!
IT'S WORKING!
THEY'RE RETURNING TO THE TOWER!
GOOD THING WE DIDN'T HAVE TO CYCLE THROUGH ALL THREE MESSAGES, RIGHT, MR. STARK?

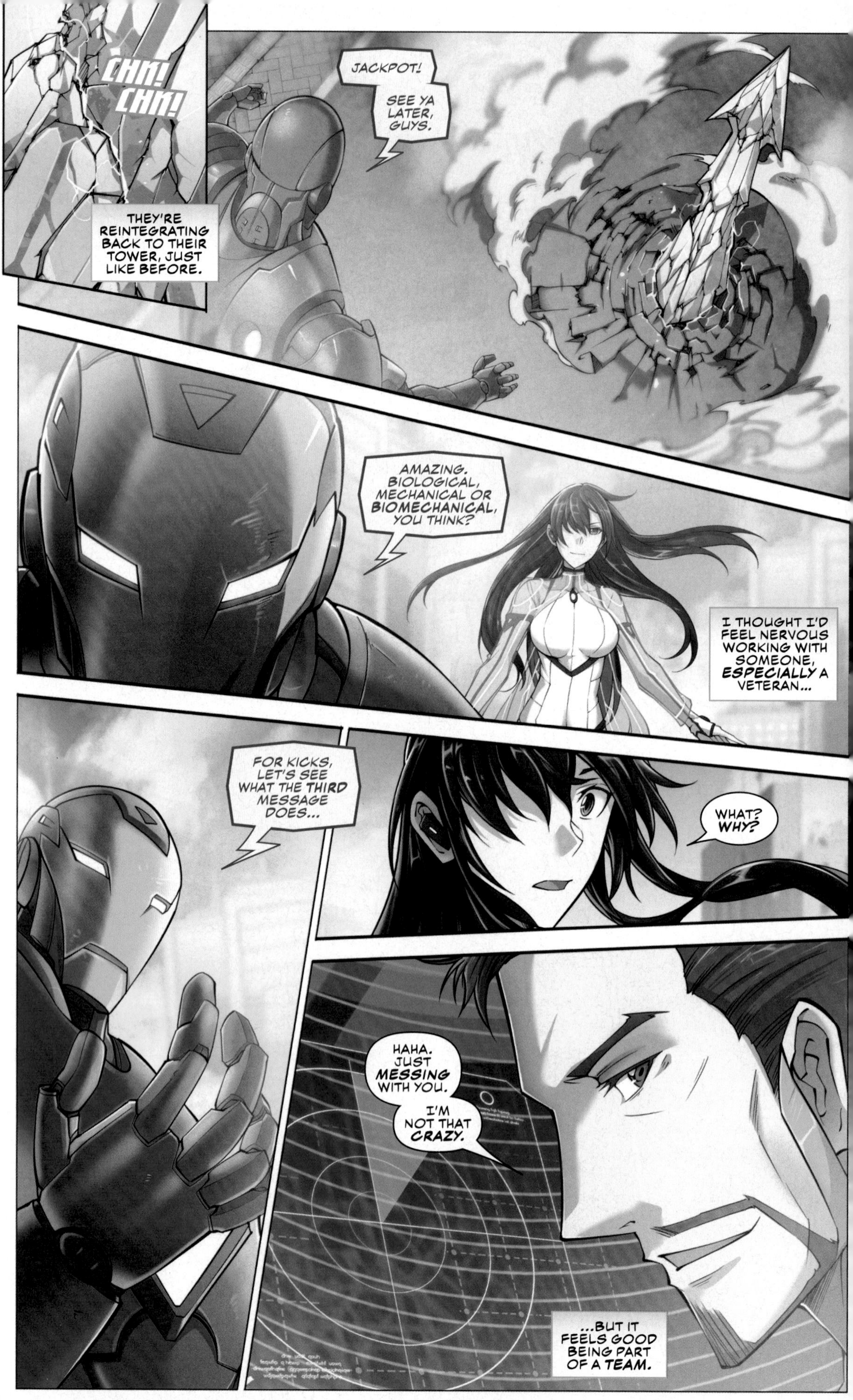
CHN! CHN!
THEY'RE REINTEGRATING BACK TO THEIR TOWER, JUST LIKE BEFORE.
JACKPOT!
SEE YA LATER, GUYS.
AMAZING. BIOLOGICAL, MECHANICAL OR BIOMECHANICAL, YOU THINK?
I THOUGHT I'D FEEL NERVOUS WORKING WITH SOMEONE, ESPECIALLY A VETERAN...
FOR KICKS, LET'S SEE WHAT THE THIRD MESSAGE DOES...
WHAT? WHY?
HAHA. JUST MESSING WITH YOU.
I'M NOT THAT CRAZY.
...BUT IT FEELS GOOD BEING PART OF A TEAM.

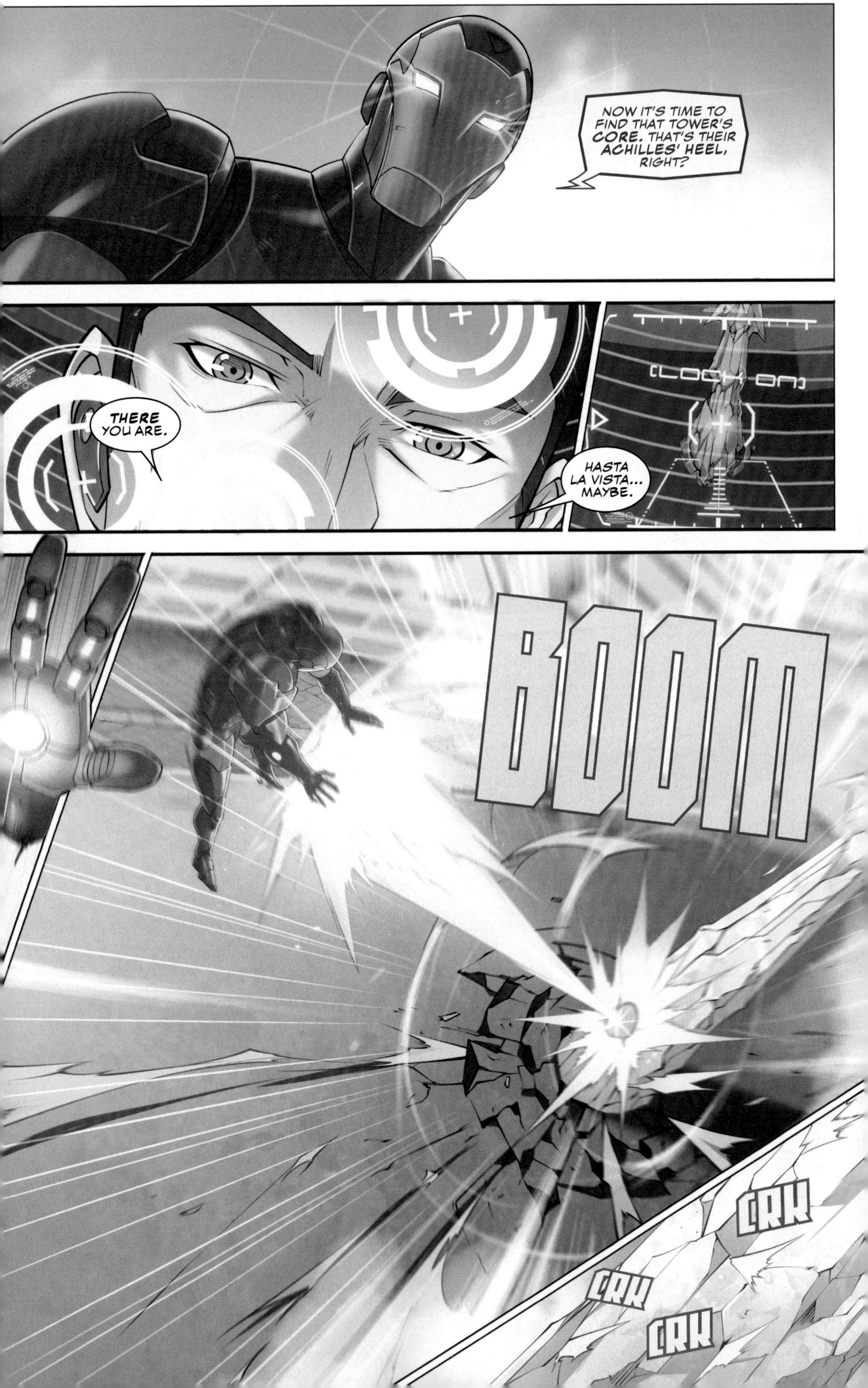
NOW IT'S TIME TO FIND THAT TOWER'S CORE. THAT'S THEIR ACHILLES' HEEL, RIGHT?
THERE YOU ARE.
[LOCK ON]
HASTA LA VISTA... MAYBE.
BOOM
CRK
CRK
CRK

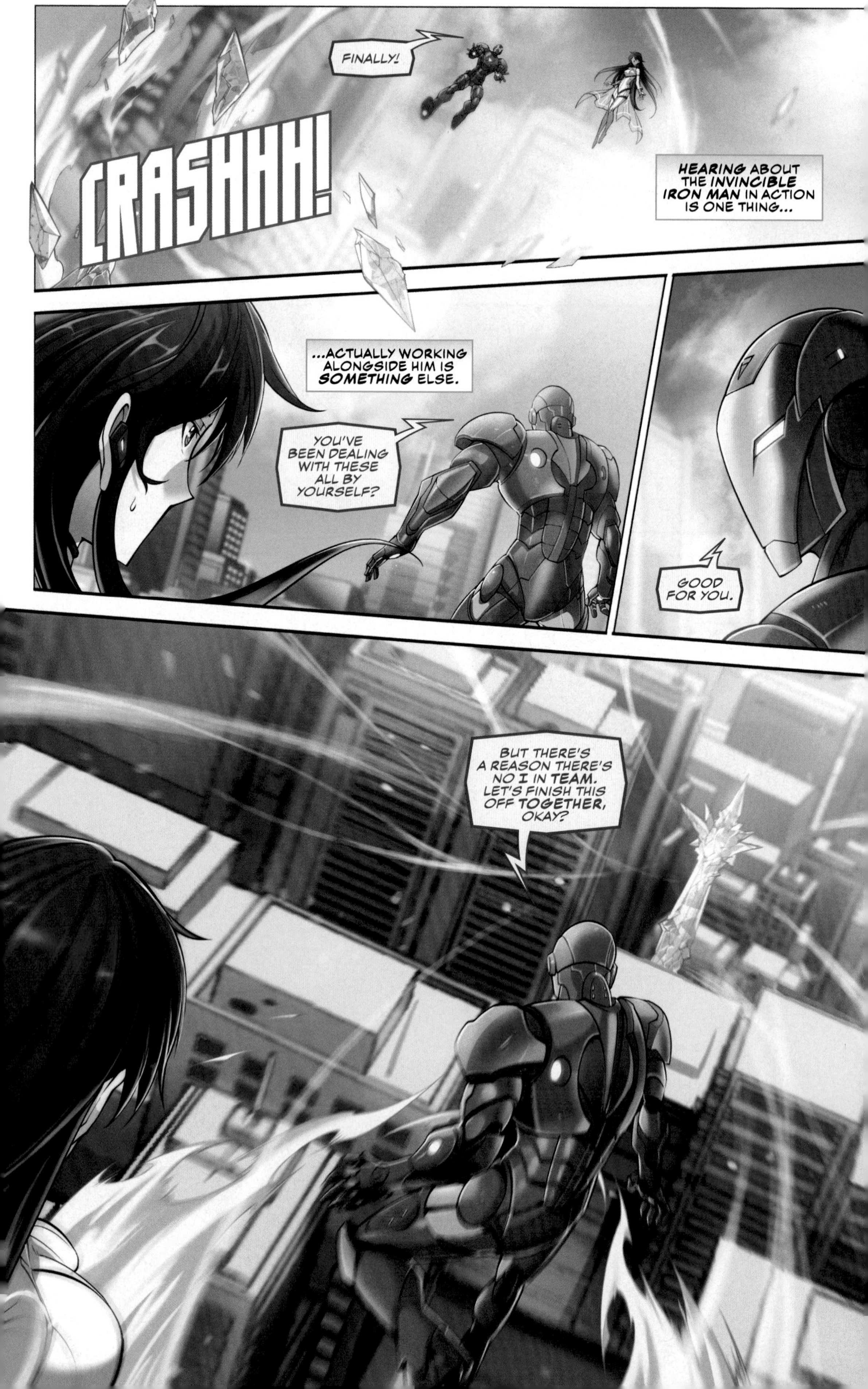
FINALLY!
CRASHHH!
HEARING ABOUT THE INVINCIBLE IRON MAN IN ACTION IS ONE THING...
...ACTUALLY WORKING ALONGSIDE HIM IS SOMETHING ELSE.
YOU'VE BEEN DEALING WITH THESE ALL BY YOURSELF?
GOOD FOR YOU.
BUT THERE'S A REASON THERE'S NO I IN TEAM. LET'S FINISH THIS OFF TOGETHER, OKAY?

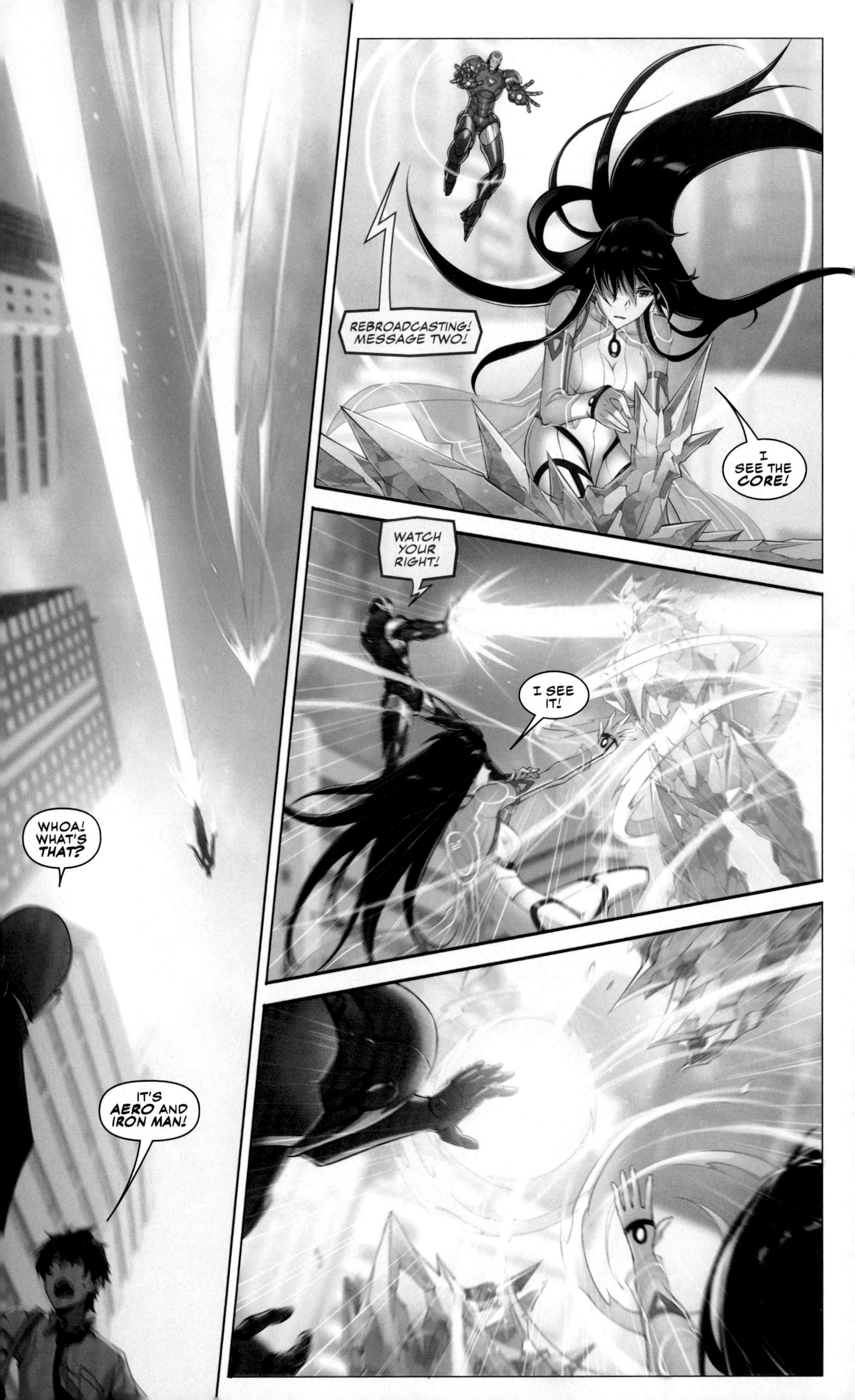
REBROADCASTING! MESSAGE TWO!
I SEE THE CORE!
WATCH YOUR RIGHT!
I SEE IT!
WHOA! WHAT'S THAT?
IT'S AERO AND IRON MAN!

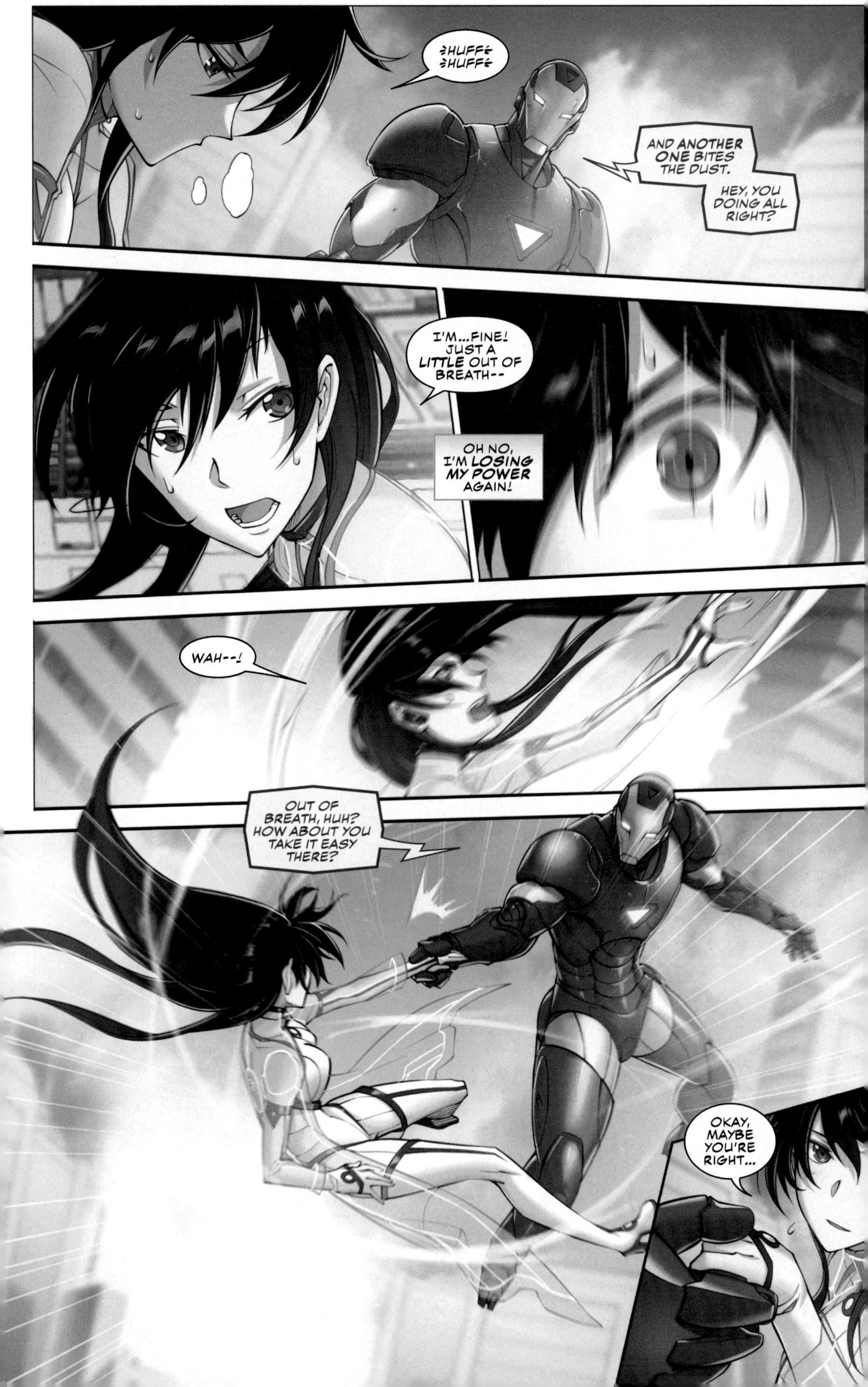
HUFF HUFF
AND ANOTHER ONE BITES THE DUST.
HEY, YOU DOING ALL RIGHT?
I'M...FINE! JUST A LITTLE OUT OF BREATH--
OH NO, I'M LOSING MY POWER AGAIN!
WAH--!
OUT OF BREATH, HUH? HOW ABOUT YOU TAKE IT EASY THERE?
OKAY, MAYBE YOU'RE RIGHT...

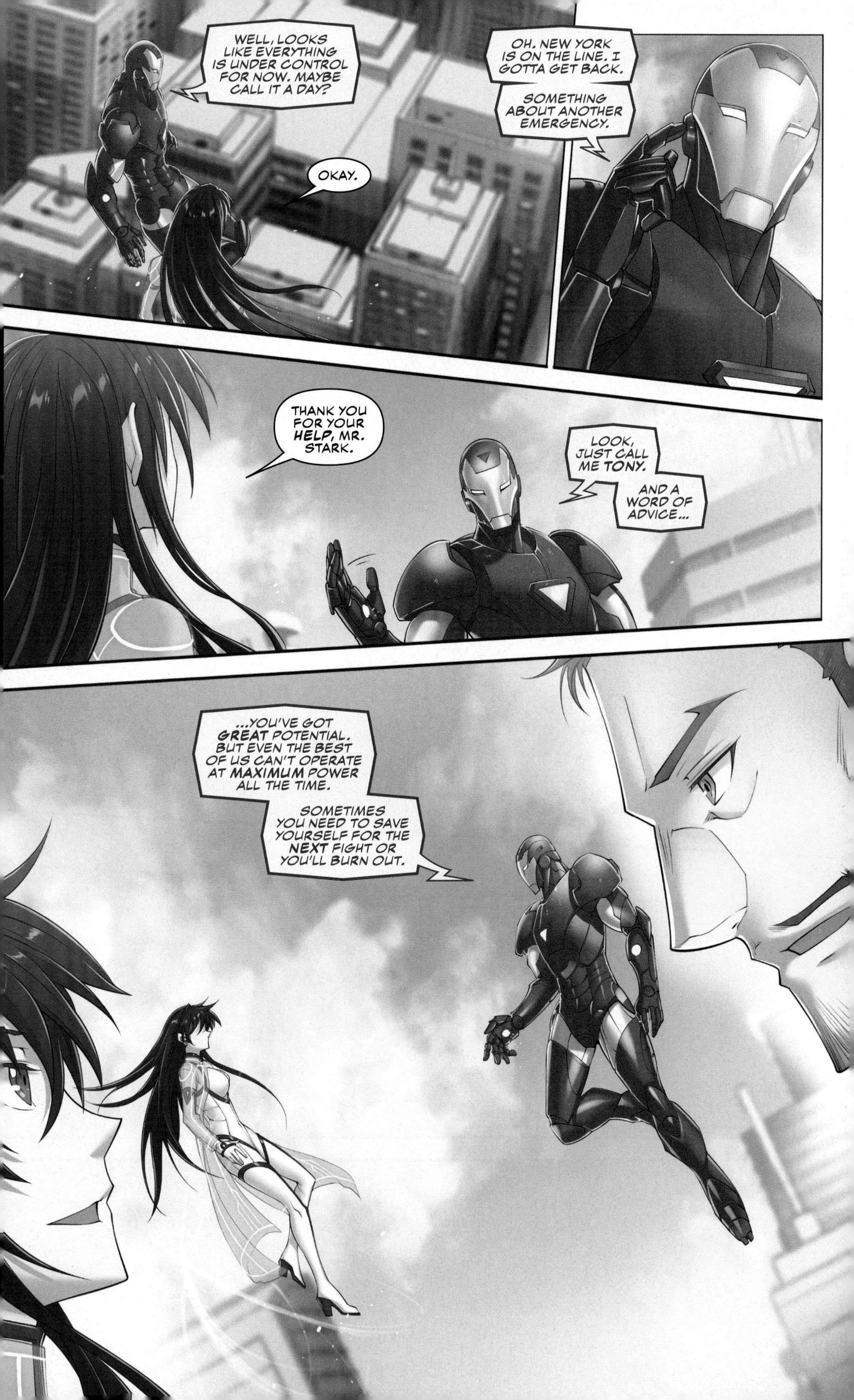
WELL, LOOKS LIKE EVERYTHING IS UNDER CONTROL FOR NOW. MAYBE CALL IT A DAY?
OKAY.
OH. NEW YORK IS ON THE LINE. I GOTTA GET BACK.
SOMETHING ABOUT ANOTHER EMERGENCY.
THANK YOU FOR YOUR HELP, MR. STARK.
LOOK, JUST CALL ME TONY.
AND A WORD OF ADVICE...
...YOU'VE GOT GREAT POTENTIAL. BUT EVEN THE BEST OF US CAN'T OPERATE AT MAXIMUM POWER ALL THE TIME.
SOMETIMES YOU NEED TO SAVE YOURSELF FOR THE NEXT FIGHT OR YOU'LL BURN OUT.

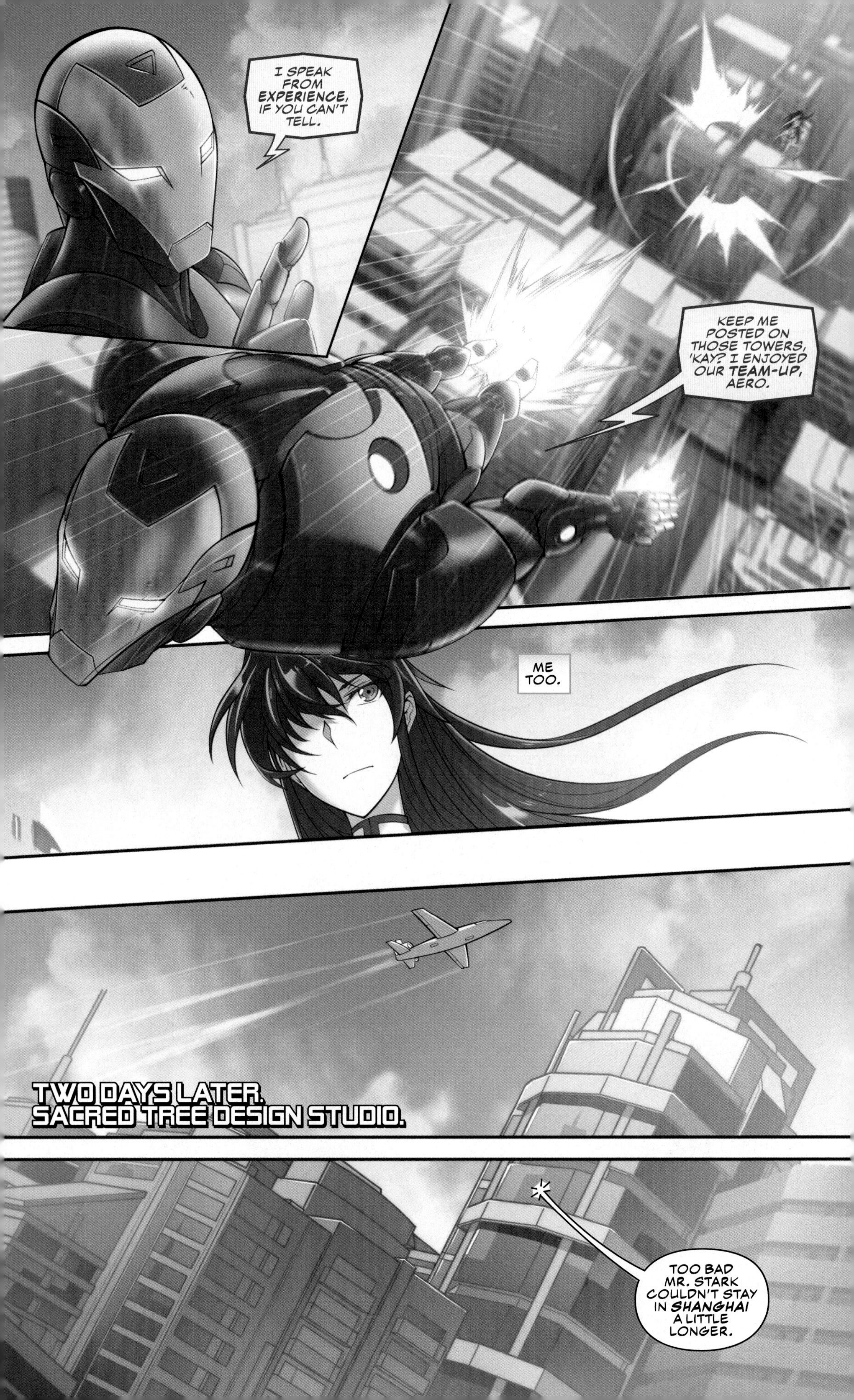

I SPEAK FROM EXPERIENCE, IF YOU CAN'T TELL.
KEEP ME POSTED ON THOSE TOWERS, 'KAY? I ENJOYED OUR TEAM-UP, AERO.
ME TOO.
TWO DAYS LATER. SACRED TREE DESIGN STUDIO.
TOO BAD MR. STARK COULDN'T STAY IN SHANGHAI A LITTLE LONGER.

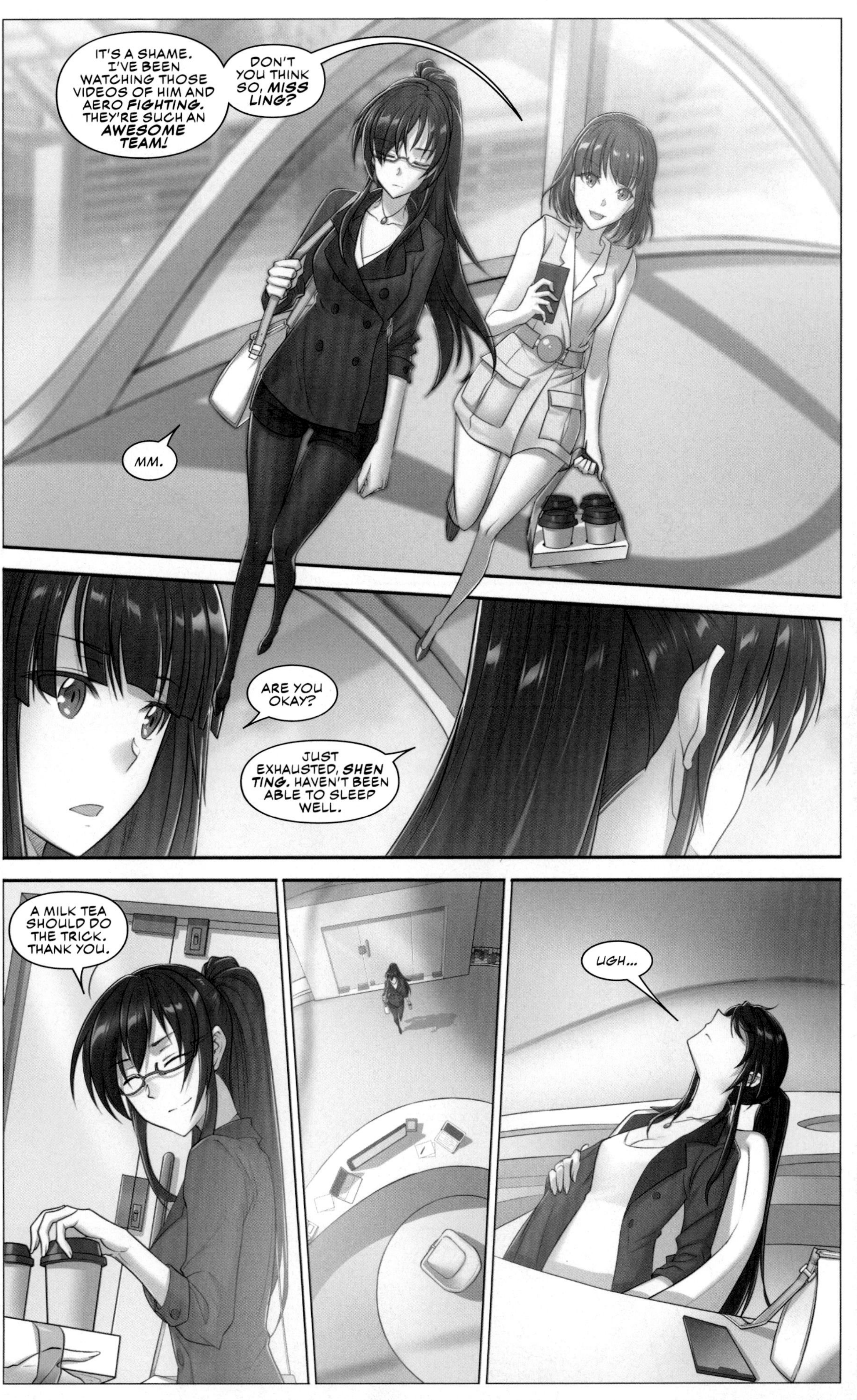
IT'S A SHAME. I'VE BEEN WATCHING THOSE VIDEOS OF HIM AND AERO FIGHTING. THEY'RE SUCH AN AWESOME TEAM!
DON'T YOU THINK SO, MISS LING?
MM.
ARE YOU OKAY?
JUST EXHAUSTED, SHEN TING. HAVEN'T BEEN ABLE TO SLEEP WELL.
A MILK TEA SHOULD DO THE TRICK. THANK YOU.
UGH...

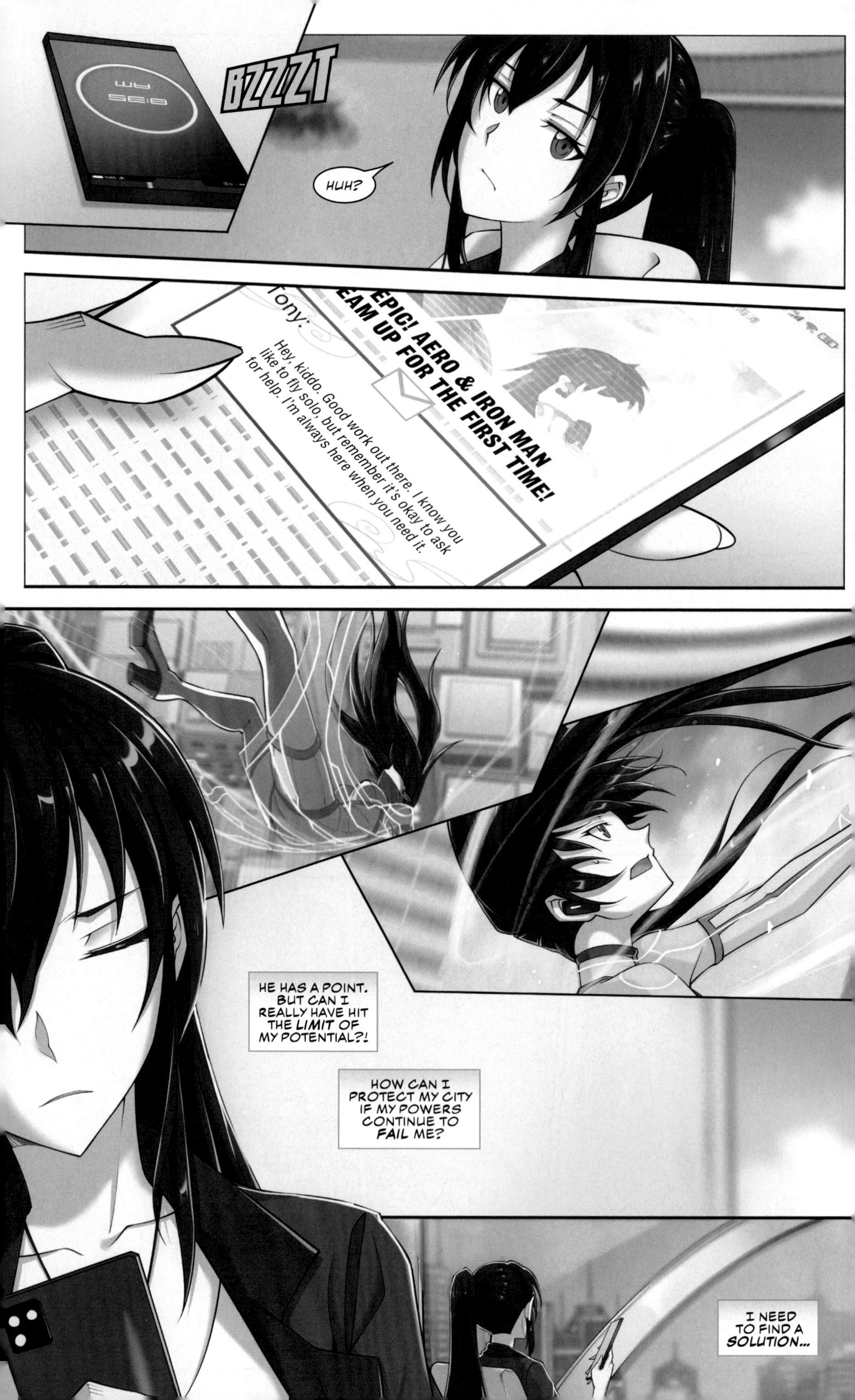
BZZZT
HUH?
EPIC! AERO & IRON MAN
TEAM UP FOR THE FIRST TIME!
Tony:
Hey, kiddo. Good work out there. I know you like to fly solo, but remember it's okay to ask for help. I'm always here when you need it.
HE HAS A POINT. BUT CAN I REALLY HAVE HIT THE LIMIT OF MY POTENTIAL?!
HOW CAN I PROTECT MY CITY IF MY POWERS CONTINUE TO FAIL ME?
I NEED TO FIND A SOLUTION...

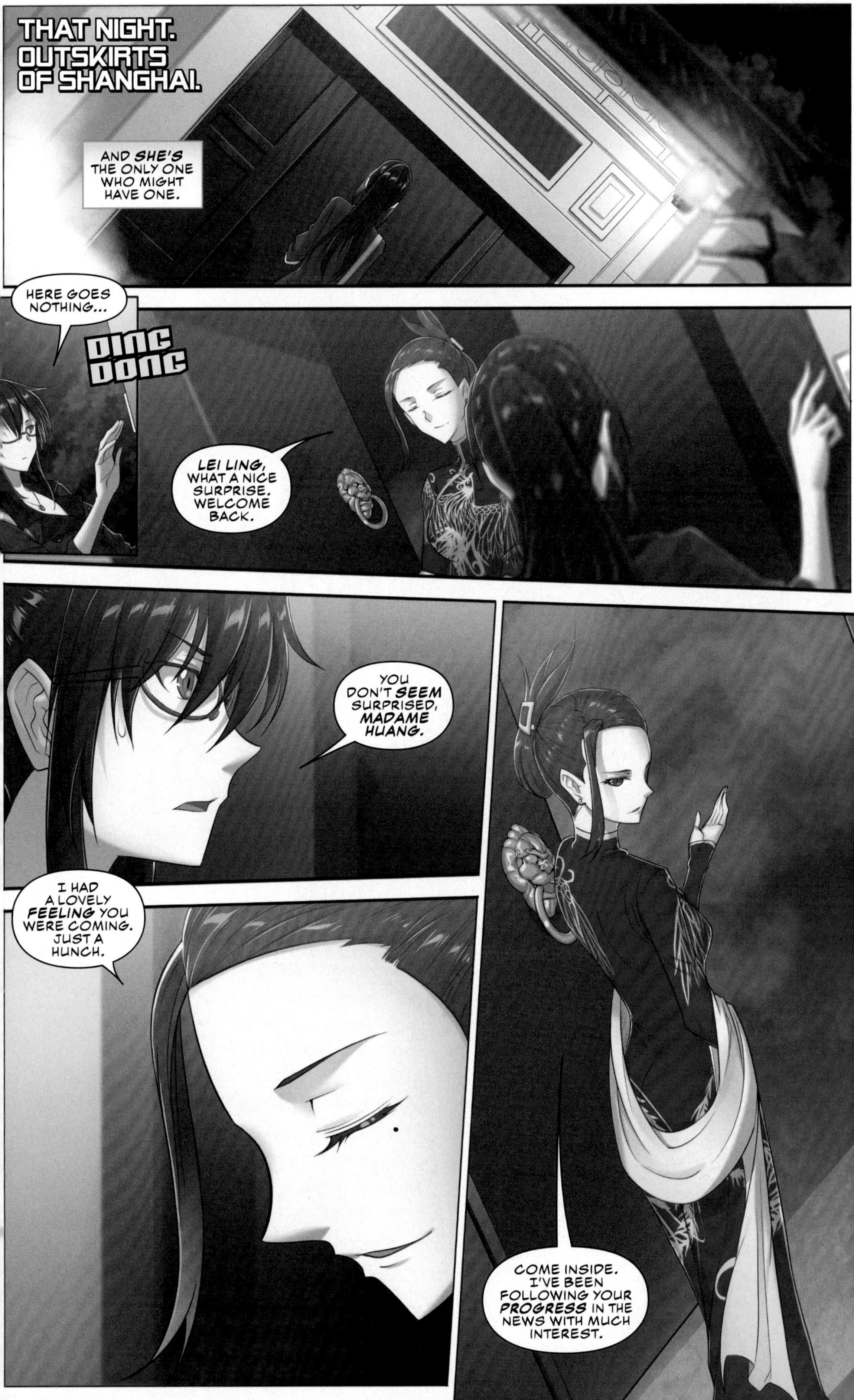
THAT NIGHT. OUTSKIRTS OF SHANGHAI.
AND SHE'S THE ONLY ONE WHO MIGHT HAVE ONE.
HERE GOES NOTHING...
DING DONG
LEI LING, WHAT A NICE SURPRISE. WELCOME BACK.
YOU DON'T SEEM SURPRISED, MADAME HUANG.
I HAD A LOVELY FEELING YOU WERE COMING. JUST A HUNCH.
COME INSIDE. I'VE BEEN FOLLOWING YOUR PROGRESS IN THE NEWS WITH MUCH INTEREST.

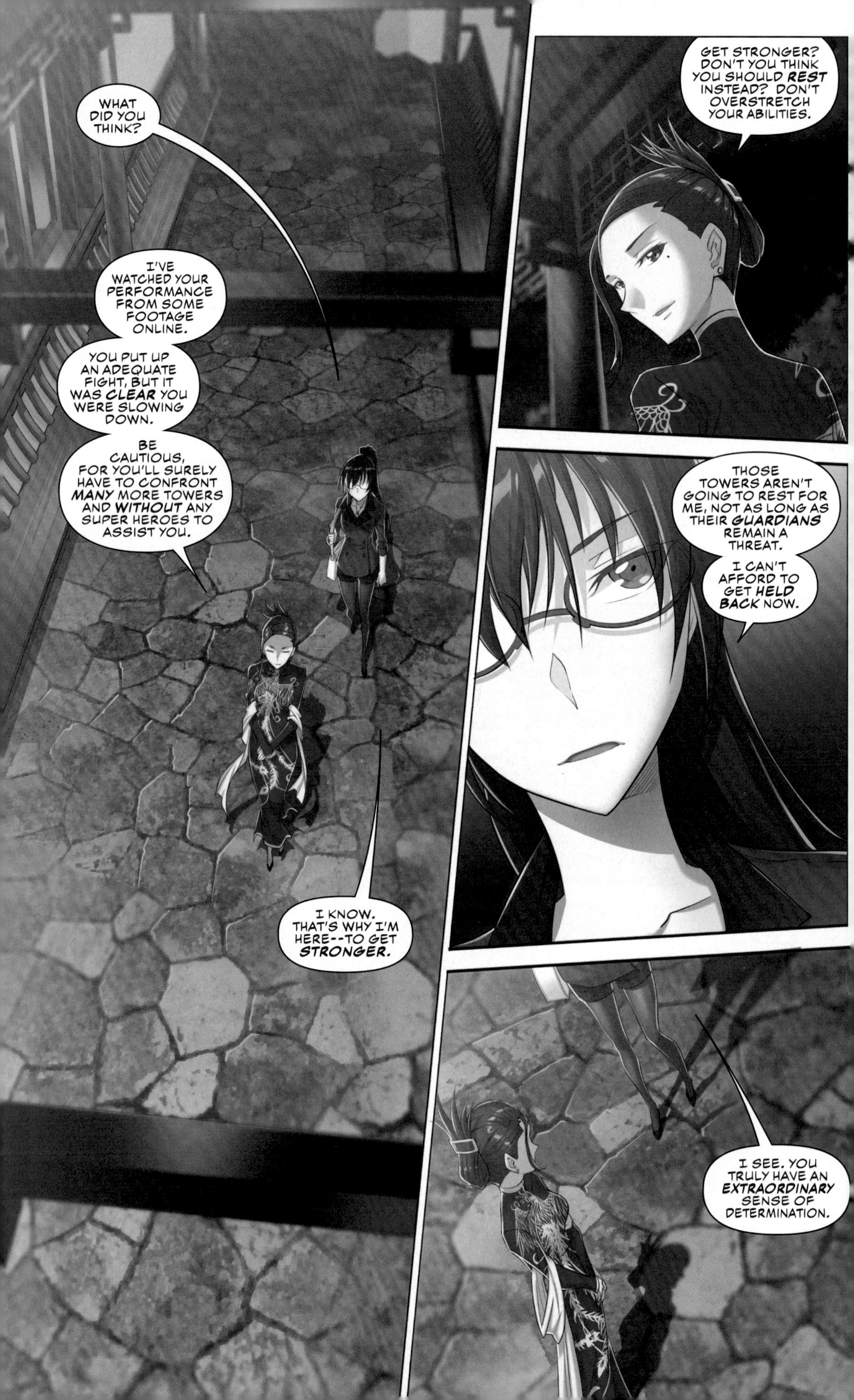
WHAT DID YOU THINK?
I'VE WATCHED YOUR PERFORMANCE FROM SOME FOOTAGE ONLINE.
YOU PUT UP AN ADEQUATE FIGHT, BUT IT WAS CLEAR YOU WERE SLOWING DOWN.
BE CAUTIOUS, FOR YOU'LL SURELY HAVE TO CONFRONT MANY MORE TOWERS AND WITHOUT ANY SUPER HEROES TO ASSIST YOU.
I KNOW. THAT'S WHY I'M HERE--TO GET STRONGER.
GET STRONGER? DON'T YOU THINK YOU SHOULD REST INSTEAD? DON'T OVERSTRETCH YOUR ABILITIES.
THOSE TOWERS AREN'T GOING TO REST FOR ME, NOT AS LONG AS THEIR GUARDIANS REMAIN A THREAT.
I CAN'T AFFORD TO GET HELD BACK NOW.
I SEE. YOU TRULY HAVE AN EXTRAORDINARY SENSE OF DETERMINATION.

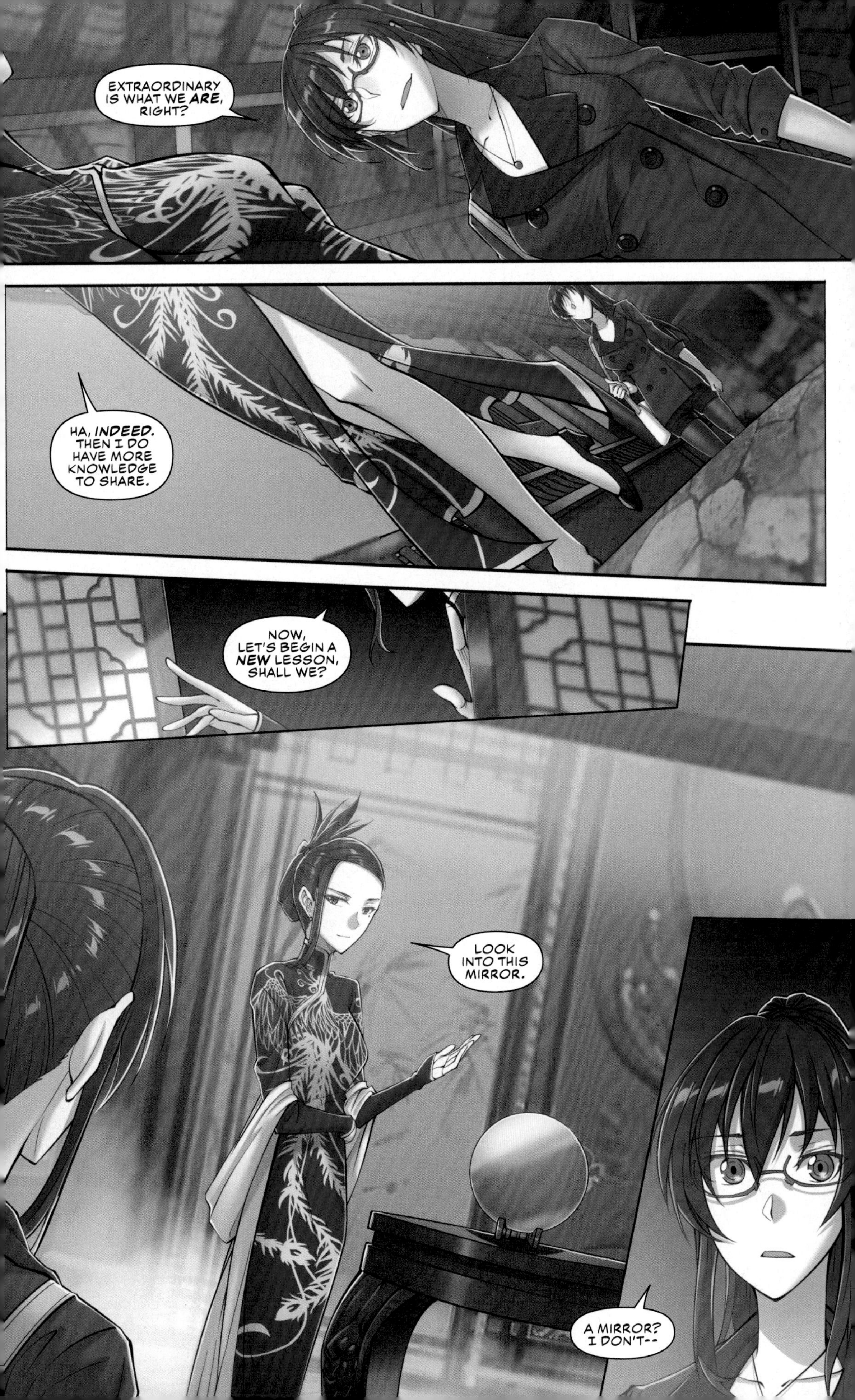
EXTRAORDINARY IS WHAT WE ARE, RIGHT?
HA, INDEED. THEN I DO HAVE MORE KNOWLEDGE TO SHARE.
NOW, LET'S BEGIN A NEW LESSON, SHALL WE?
LOOK INTO THIS MIRROR.
A MIRROR? I DON'T--

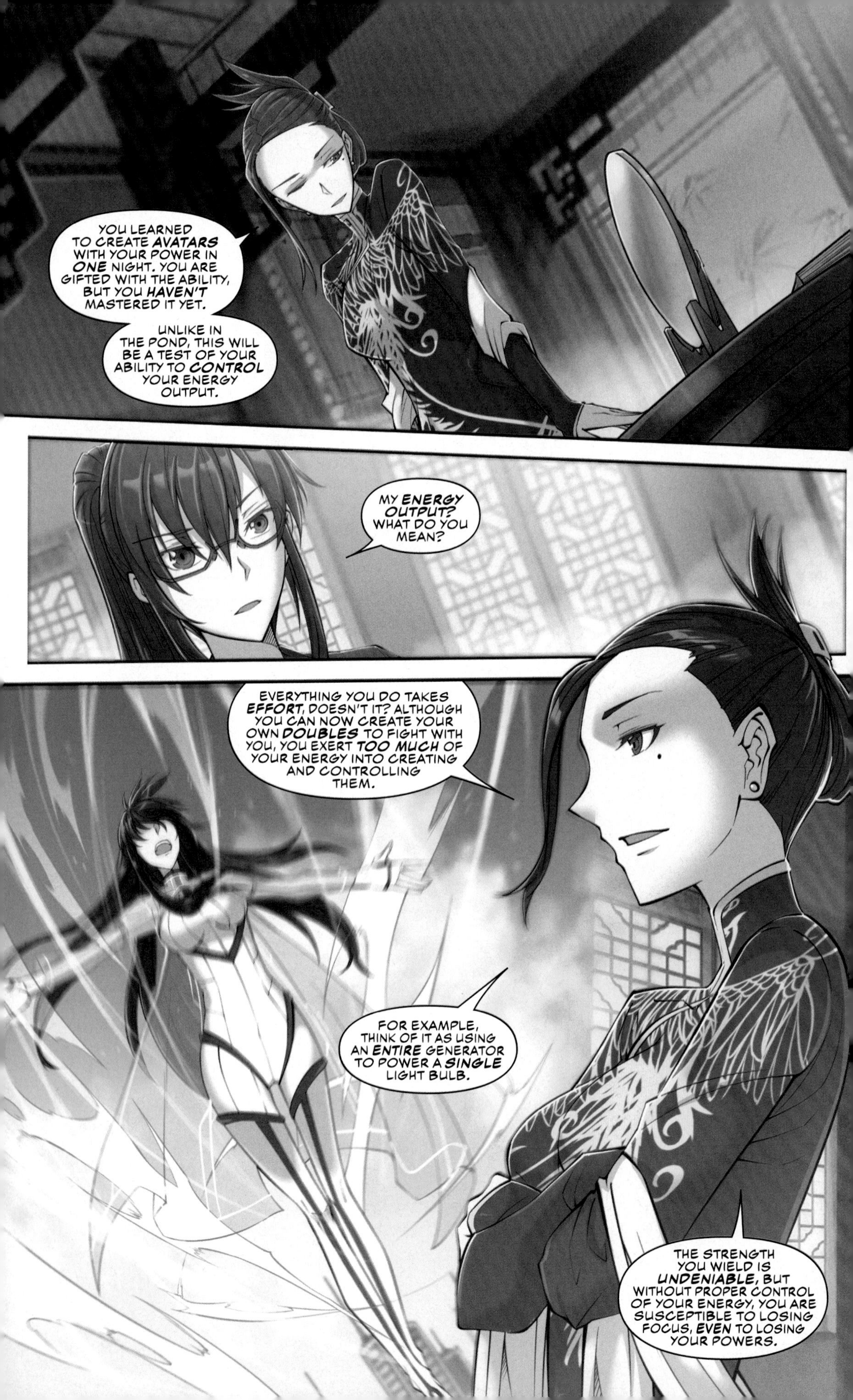

YOU LEARNED TO CREATE AVATARS WITH YOUR POWER IN ONE NIGHT. YOU ARE GIFTED WITH THE ABILITY, BUT YOU HAVEN'T MASTERED IT YET.
UNLIKE IN THE POND, THIS WILL BE A TEST OF YOUR ABILITY TO CONTROL YOUR ENERGY OUTPUT.
MY ENERGY OUTPUT? WHAT DO YOU MEAN?
EVERYTHING YOU DO TAKES EFFORT, DOESN'T IT? ALTHOUGH YOU CAN NOW CREATE YOUR OWN DOUBLES TO FIGHT WITH YOU, YOU EXERT TOO MUCH OF YOUR ENERGY INTO CREATING AND CONTROLLING THEM.
FOR EXAMPLE, THINK OF IT AS USING AN ENTIRE GENERATOR TO POWER A SINGLE LIGHT BULB.
THE STRENGTH YOU WIELD IS UNDENIABLE, BUT WITHOUT PROPER CONTROL OF YOUR ENERGY, YOU ARE SUSCEPTIBLE TO LOSING FOCUS, EVEN TO LOSING YOUR POWERS.

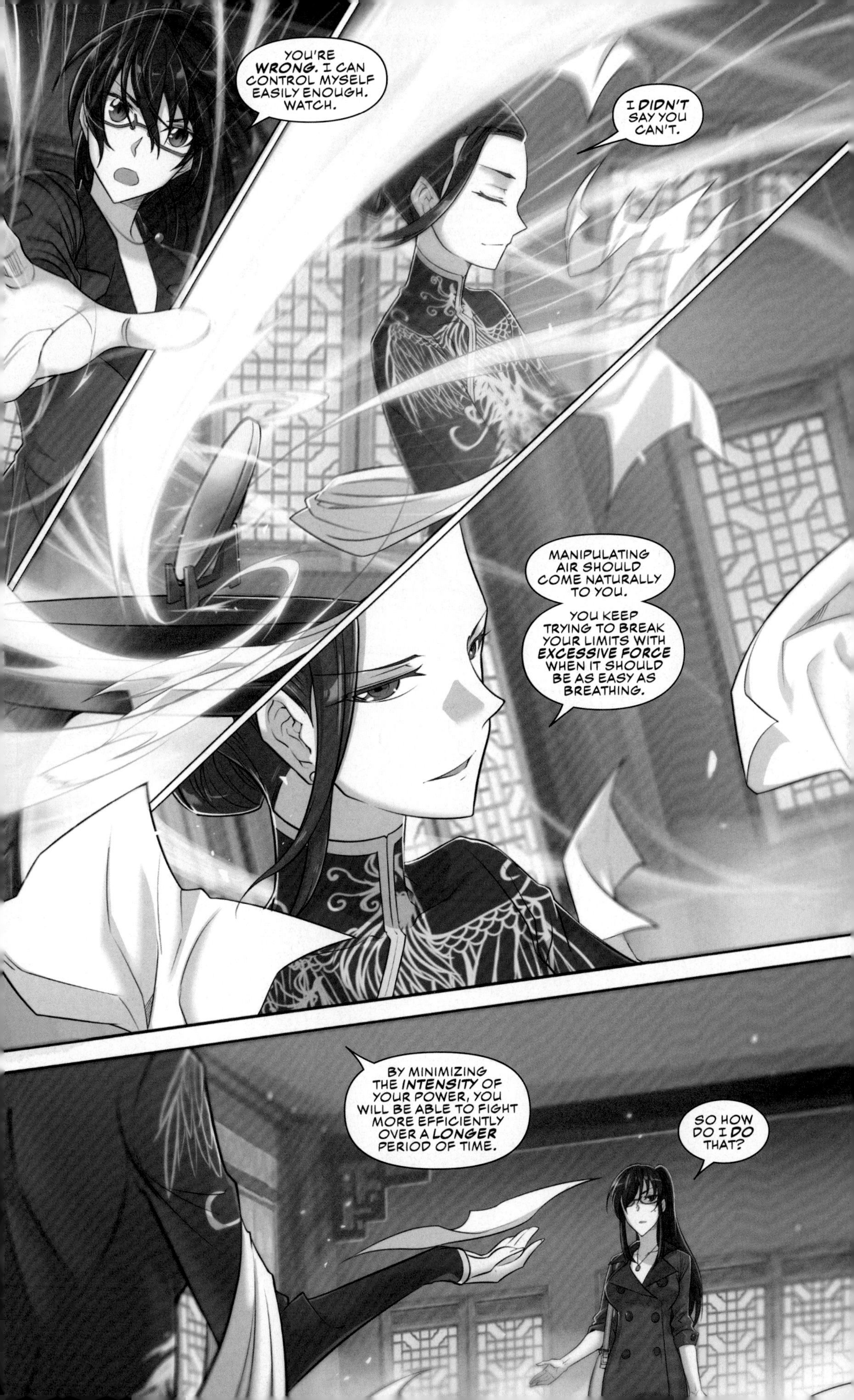
YOU'RE WRONG. I CAN CONTROL MYSELF EASILY ENOUGH. WATCH.
I DIDN'T SAY YOU CAN'T.
MANIPULATING AIR SHOULD COME NATURALLY TO YOU.
YOU KEEP TRYING TO BREAK YOUR LIMITS WITH EXCESSIVE FORCE WHEN IT SHOULD BE AS EASY AS BREATHING.
BY MINIMIZING THE INTENSITY OF YOUR POWER, YOU WILL BE ABLE TO FIGHT MORE EFFICIENTLY OVER A LONGER PERIOD OF TIME.
SO HOW DO I DO THAT?

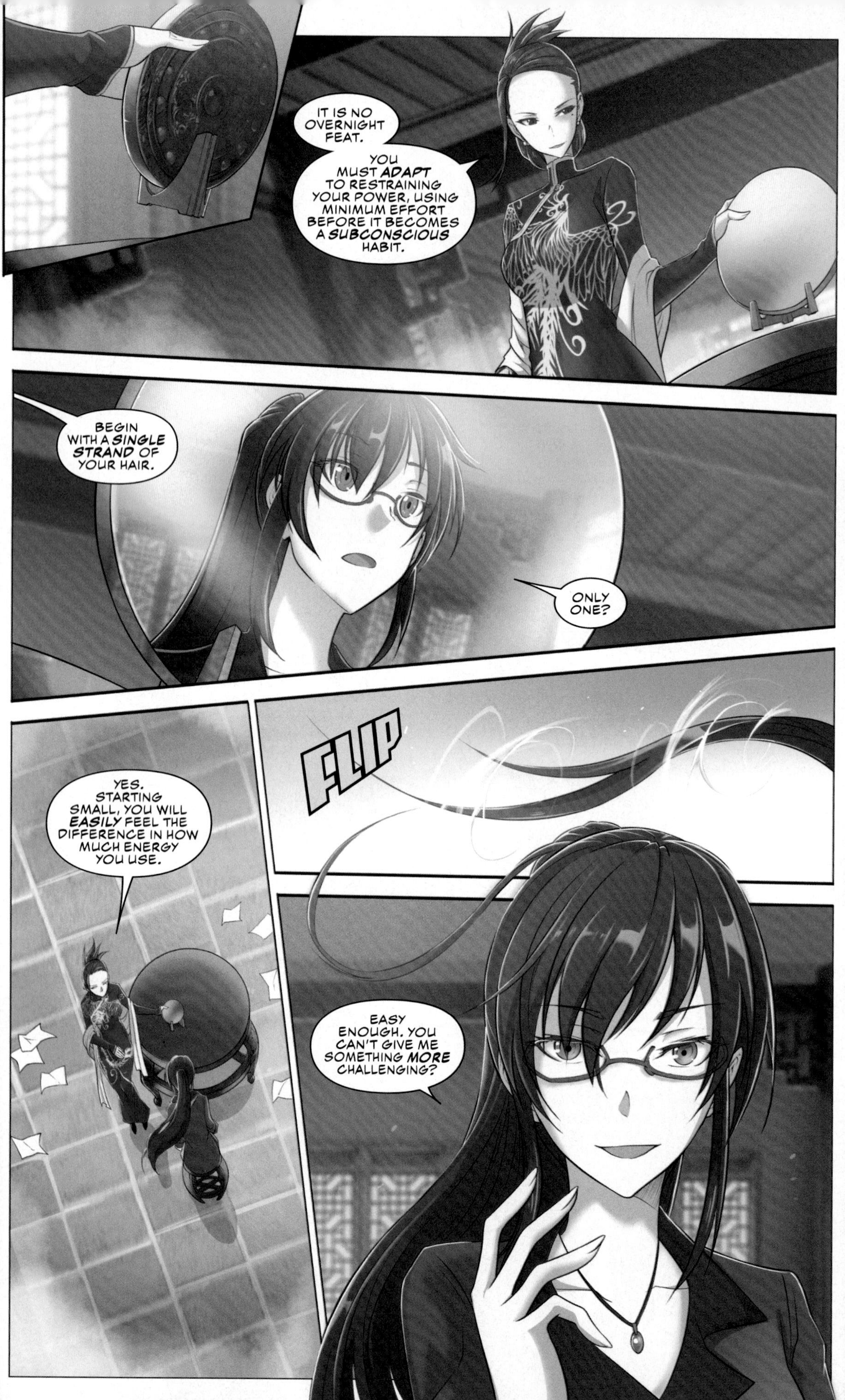
IT IS NO OVERNIGHT FEAT.
YOU MUST ADAPT TO RESTRAINING YOUR POWER, USING MINIMUM EFFORT BEFORE IT BECOMES A SUBCONSCIOUS HABIT.
BEGIN WITH A SINGLE STRAND OF YOUR HAIR.
ONLY ONE?
YES. STARTING SMALL, YOU WILL EASILY FEEL THE DIFFERENCE IN HOW MUCH ENERGY YOU USE.
FLIP
EASY ENOUGH. YOU CAN'T GIVE ME SOMETHING MORE CHALLENGING?

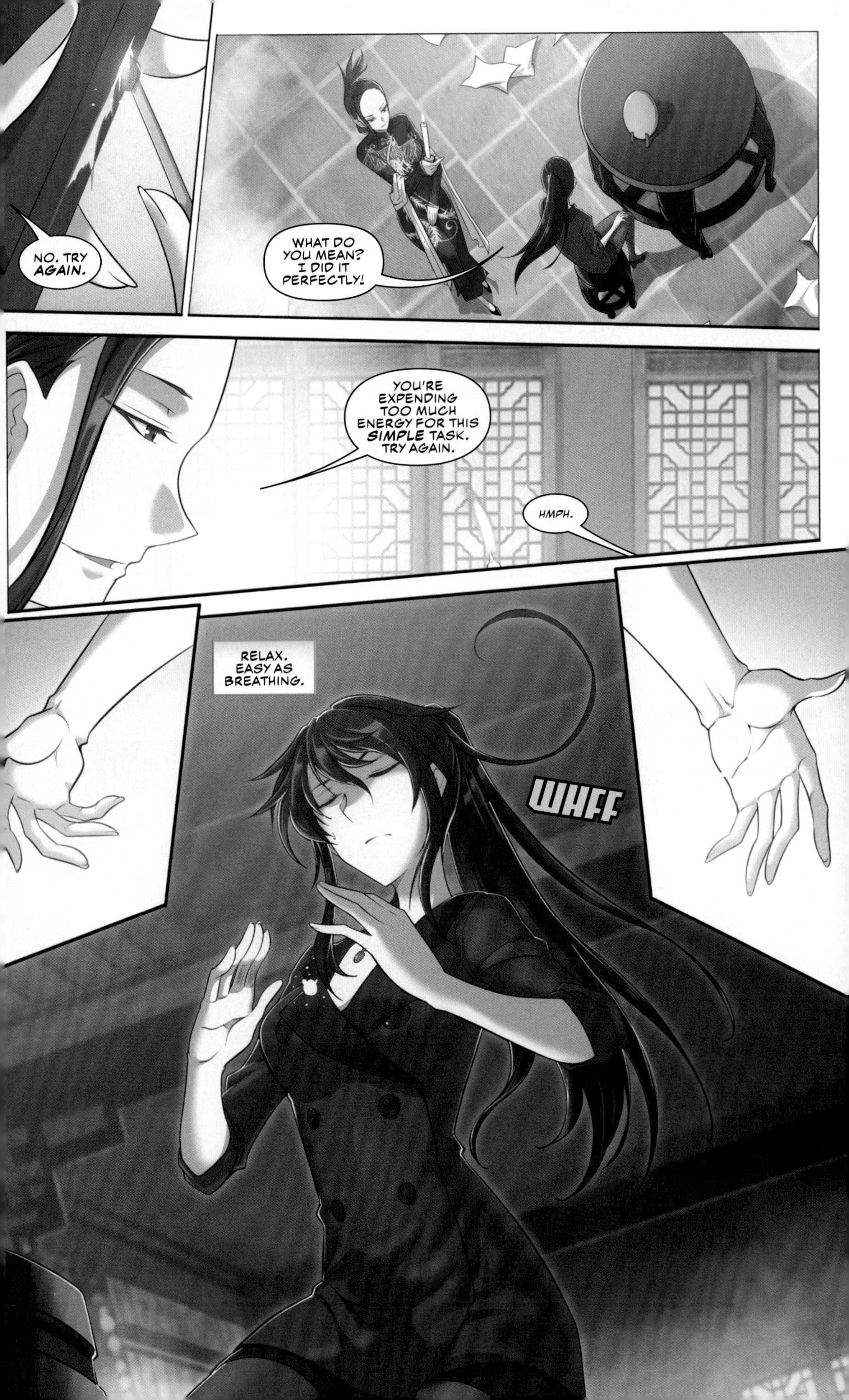
NO. TRY AGAIN.
WHAT DO YOU MEAN? I DID IT PERFECTLY!
YOU'RE EXPENDING TOO MUCH ENERGY FOR THIS SIMPLE TASK. TRY AGAIN.
HMPH.
RELAX. EASY AS BREATHING.
WHFF

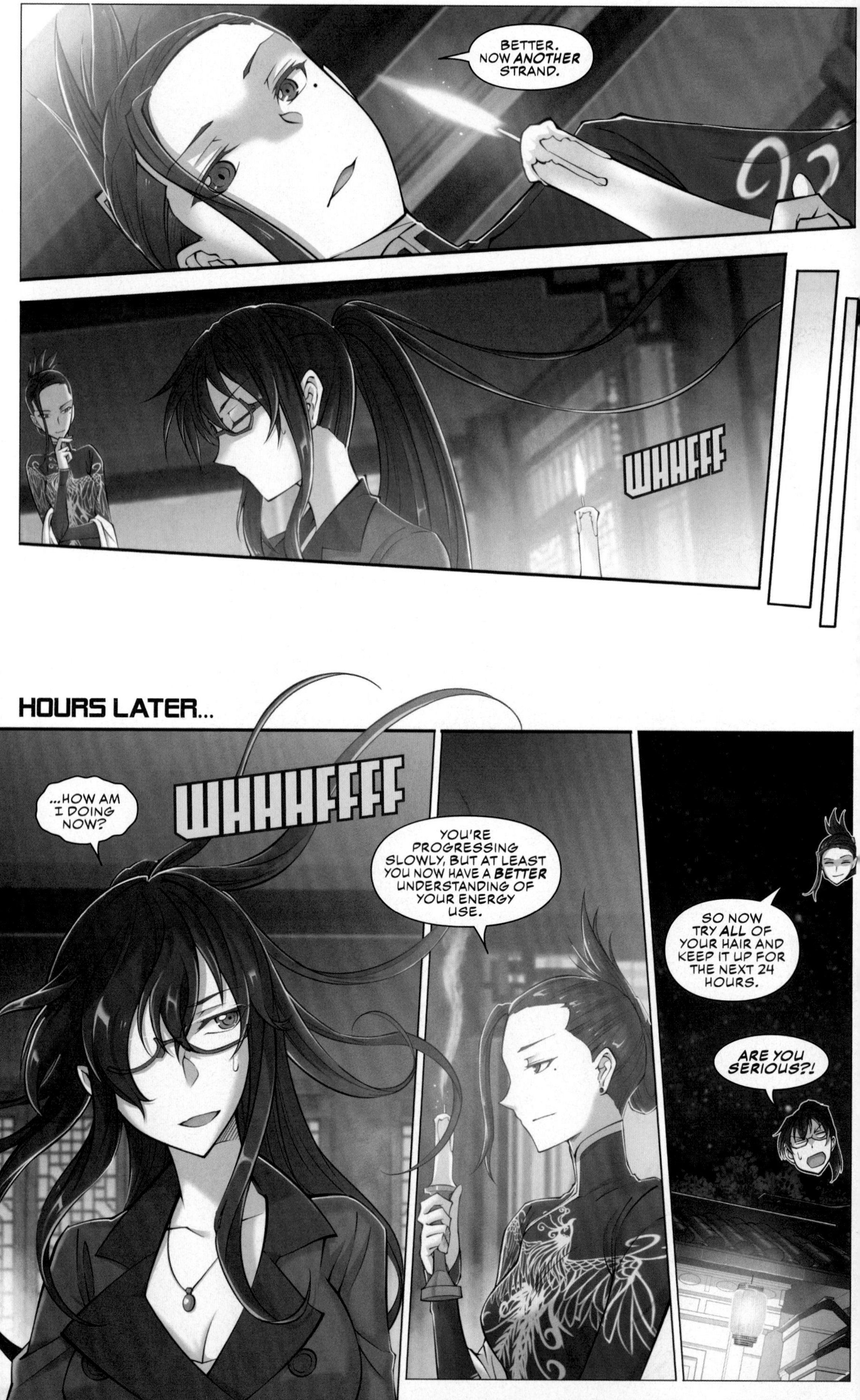
BETTER. NOW ANOTHER STRAND.
WHHFFF
HOURS LATER...
WHHHFFFF
...HOW AM I DOING NOW?
YOU'RE PROGRESSING SLOWLY, BUT AT LEAST YOU NOW HAVE A BETTER UNDERSTANDING OF YOUR ENERGY USE.
SO NOW TRY ALL OF YOUR HAIR AND KEEP IT UP FOR THE NEXT 24 HOURS.
ARE YOU SERIOUS?!

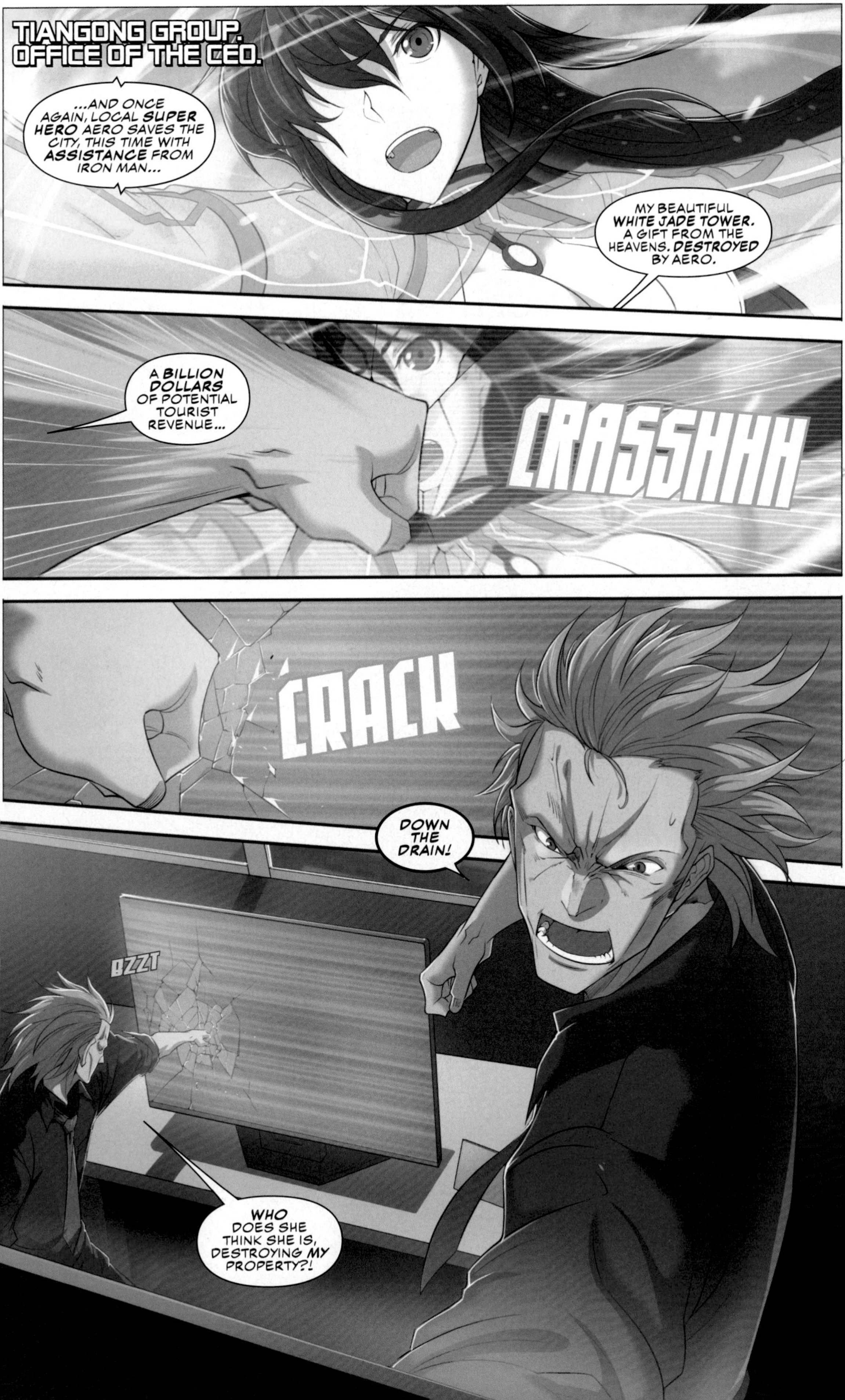
TIANGONG GROUP. OFFICE OF THE CEO.
...AND ONCE AGAIN, LOCAL SUPER HERO AERO SAVES THE CITY, THIS TIME WITH ASSISTANCE FROM IRON MAN...
MY BEAUTIFUL WHITE JADE TOWER. A GIFT FROM THE HEAVENS. DESTROYED BY AERO.
A BILLION DOLLARS OF POTENTIAL TOURIST REVENUE...
CRASSHHH
CRACK
DOWN THE DRAIN!
BZZT
WHO DOES SHE THINK SHE IS, DESTROYING MY PROPERTY?!

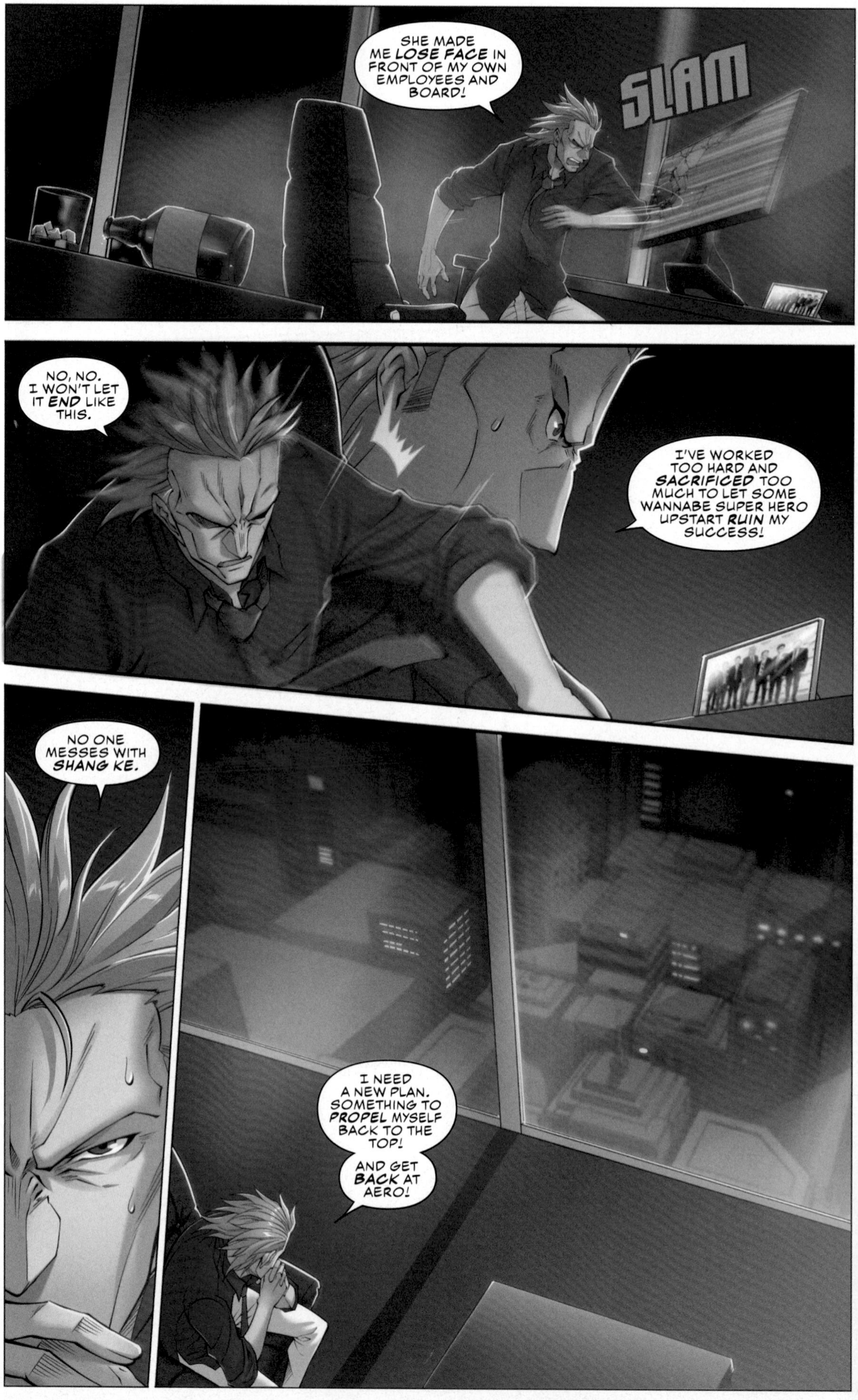
SHE MADE ME LOSE FACE IN FRONT OF MY OWN EMPLOYEES AND BOARD!
SLAM
NO, NO. I WON'T LET IT END LIKE THIS.
I'VE WORKED TOO HARD AND SACRIFICED TOO MUCH TO LET SOME WANNABE SUPER HERO UPSTART RUIN MY SUCCESS!
NO ONE MESSES WITH SHANG KE.
I NEED A NEW PLAN. SOMETHING TO PROPEL MYSELF BACK TO THE TOP!
AND GET BACK AT AERO!

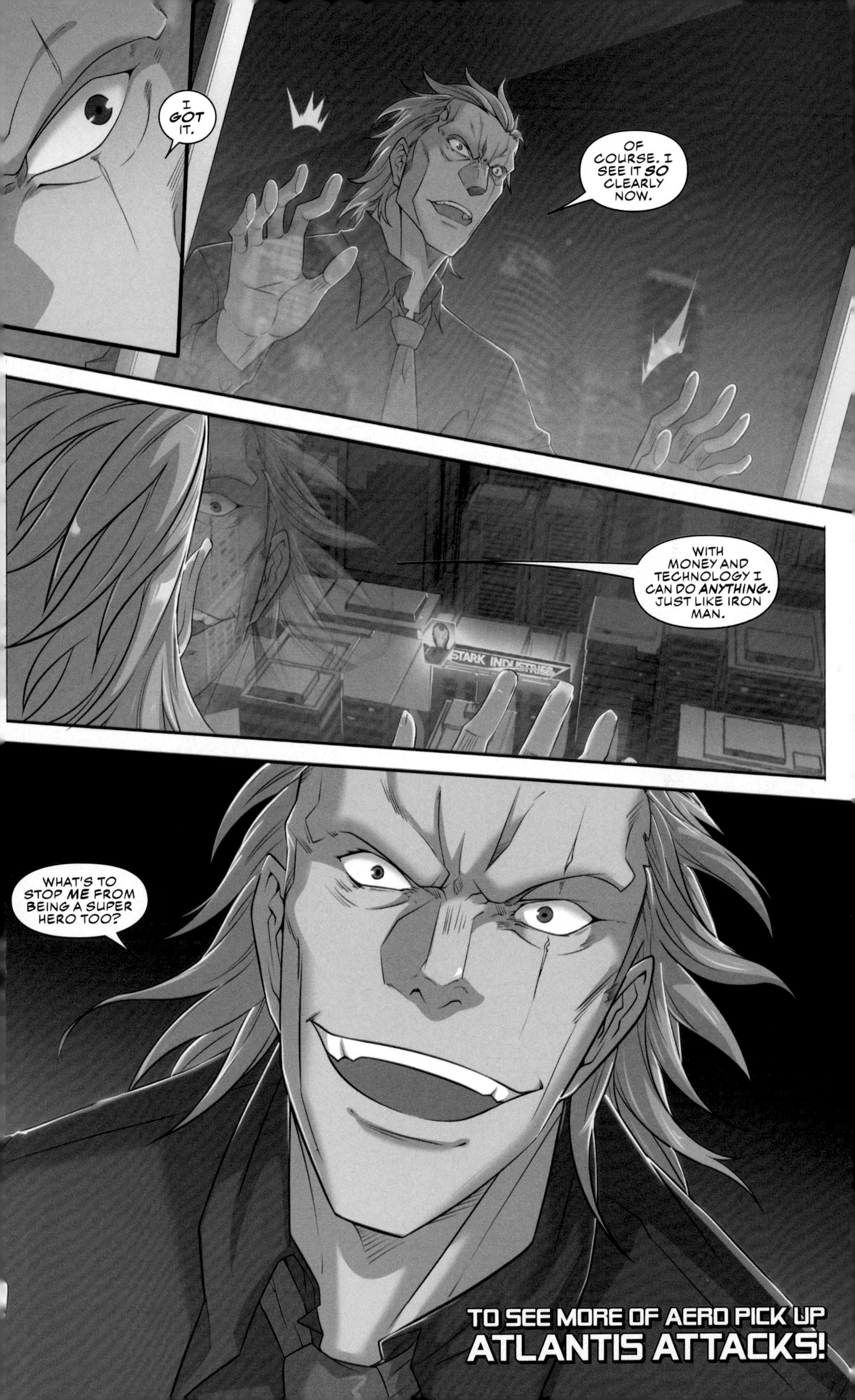
I GOT IT.
OF COURSE. I SEE IT SO CLEARLY NOW.
STARK INDUSTRIES
WITH MONEY AND TECHNOLOGY I CAN DO ANYTHING. JUST LIKE IRON MAN.
WHAT'S TO STOP ME FROM BEING A SUPER HERO TOO?
TO SEE MORE OF AERO PICK UP
ATLANTIS ATTACKS!

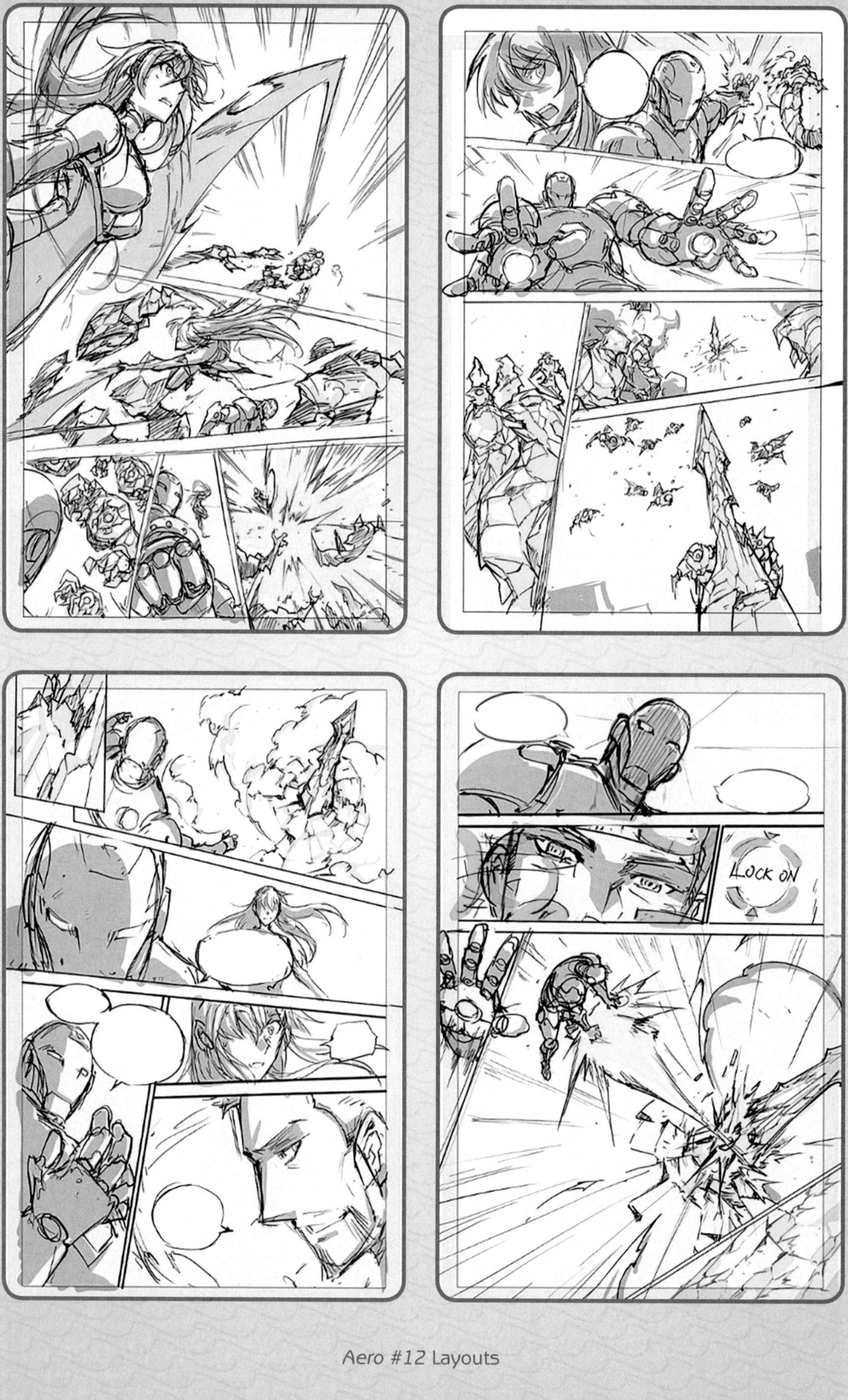
LOCK ON

Aero #12 Layouts

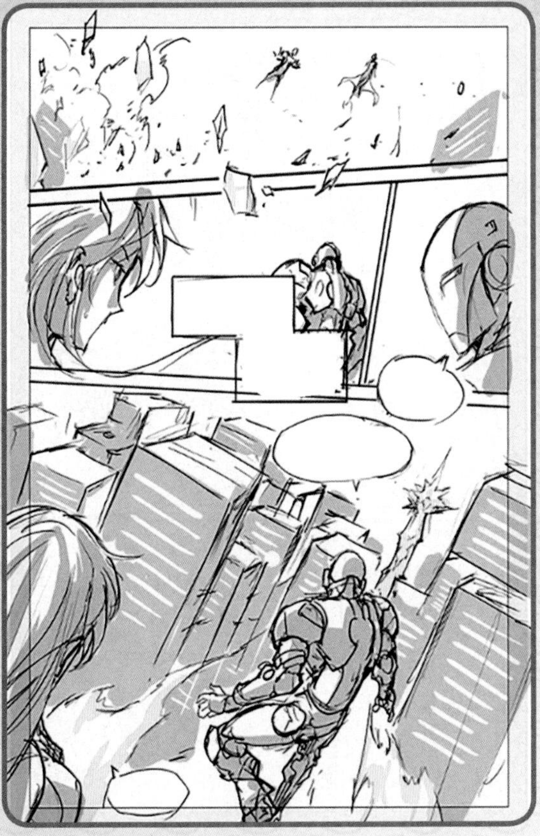
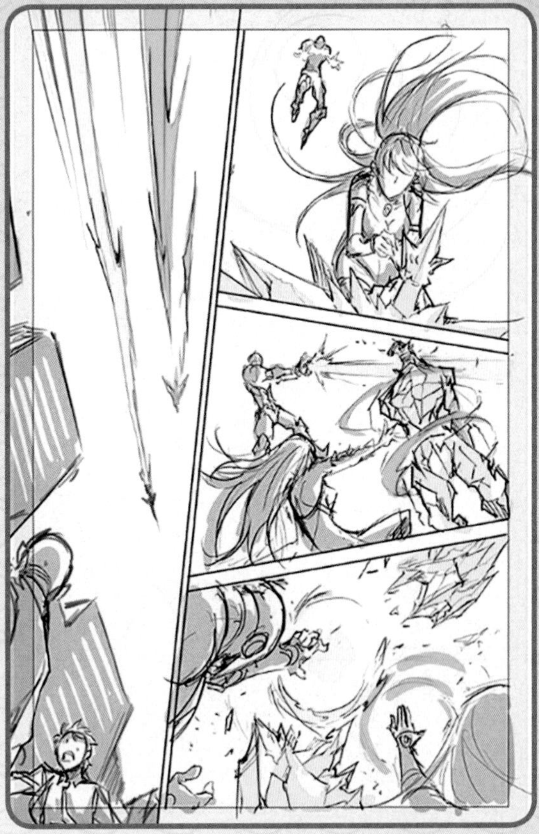
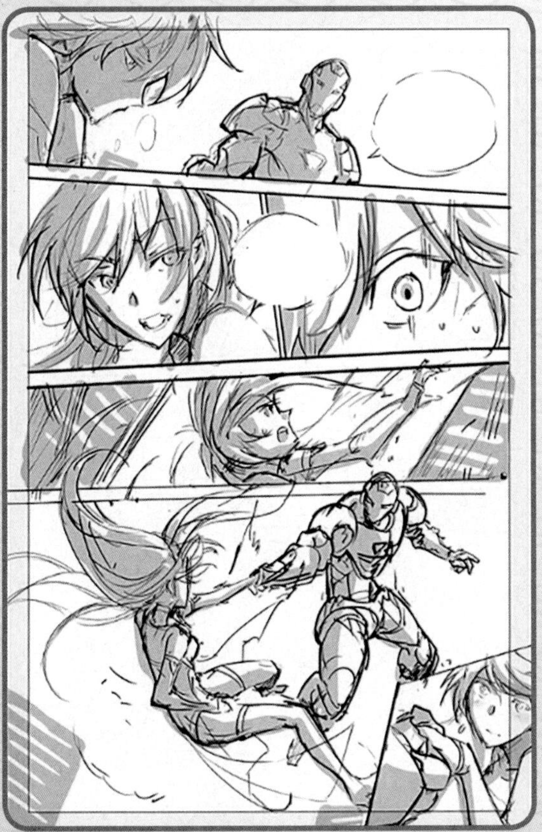
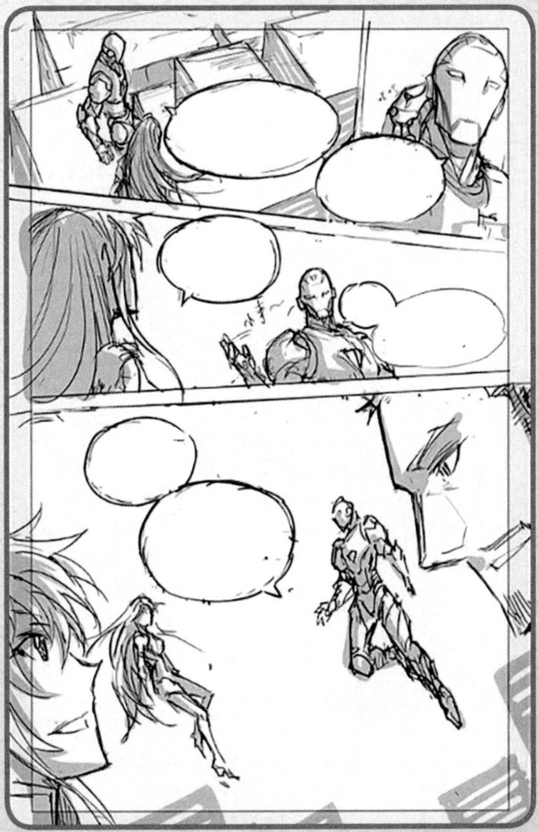

Aero #12 Layouts

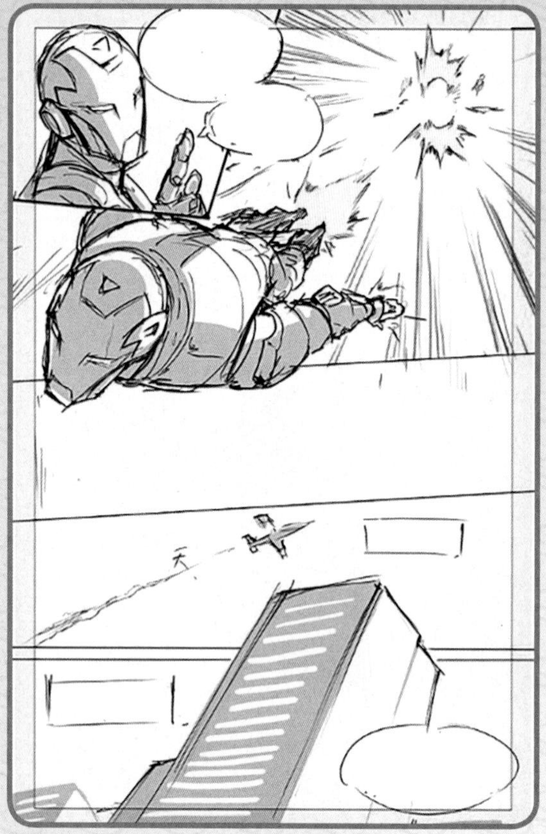
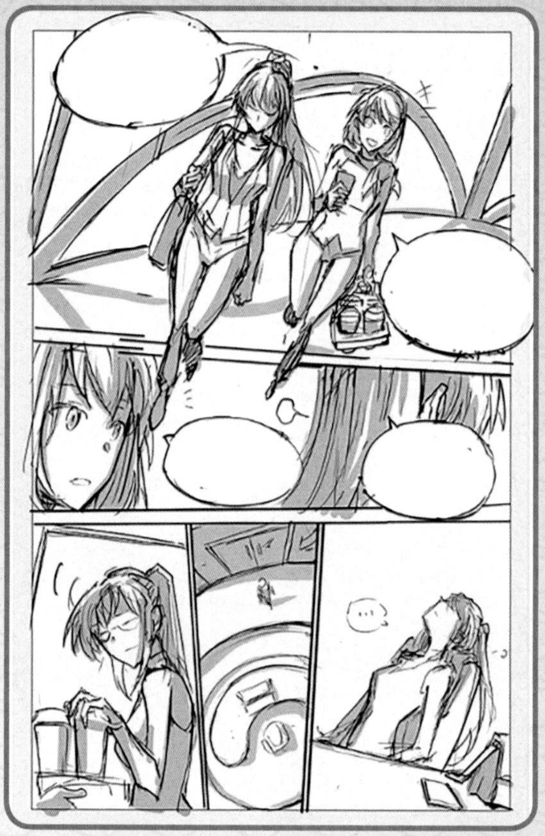
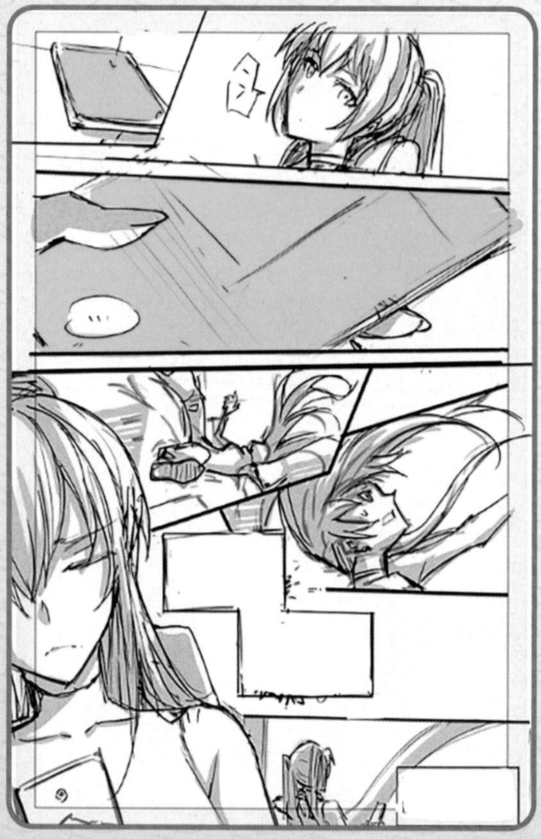
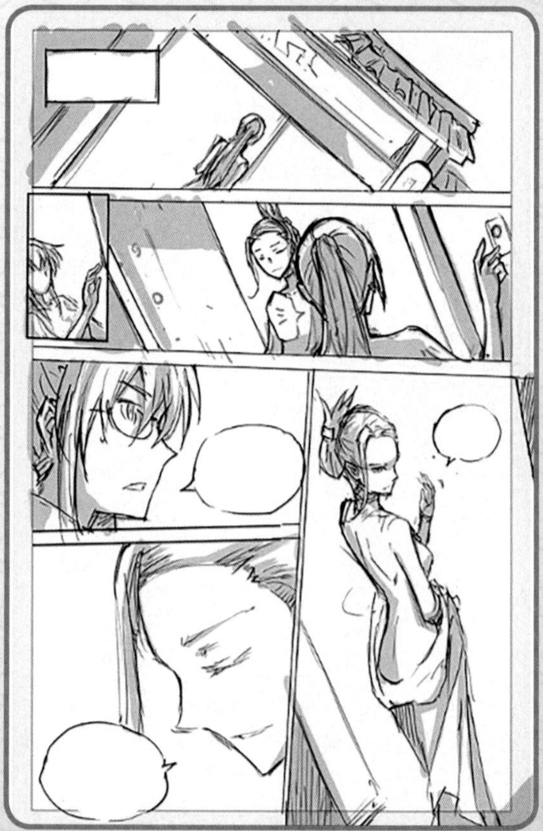

Aero #12 Layouts

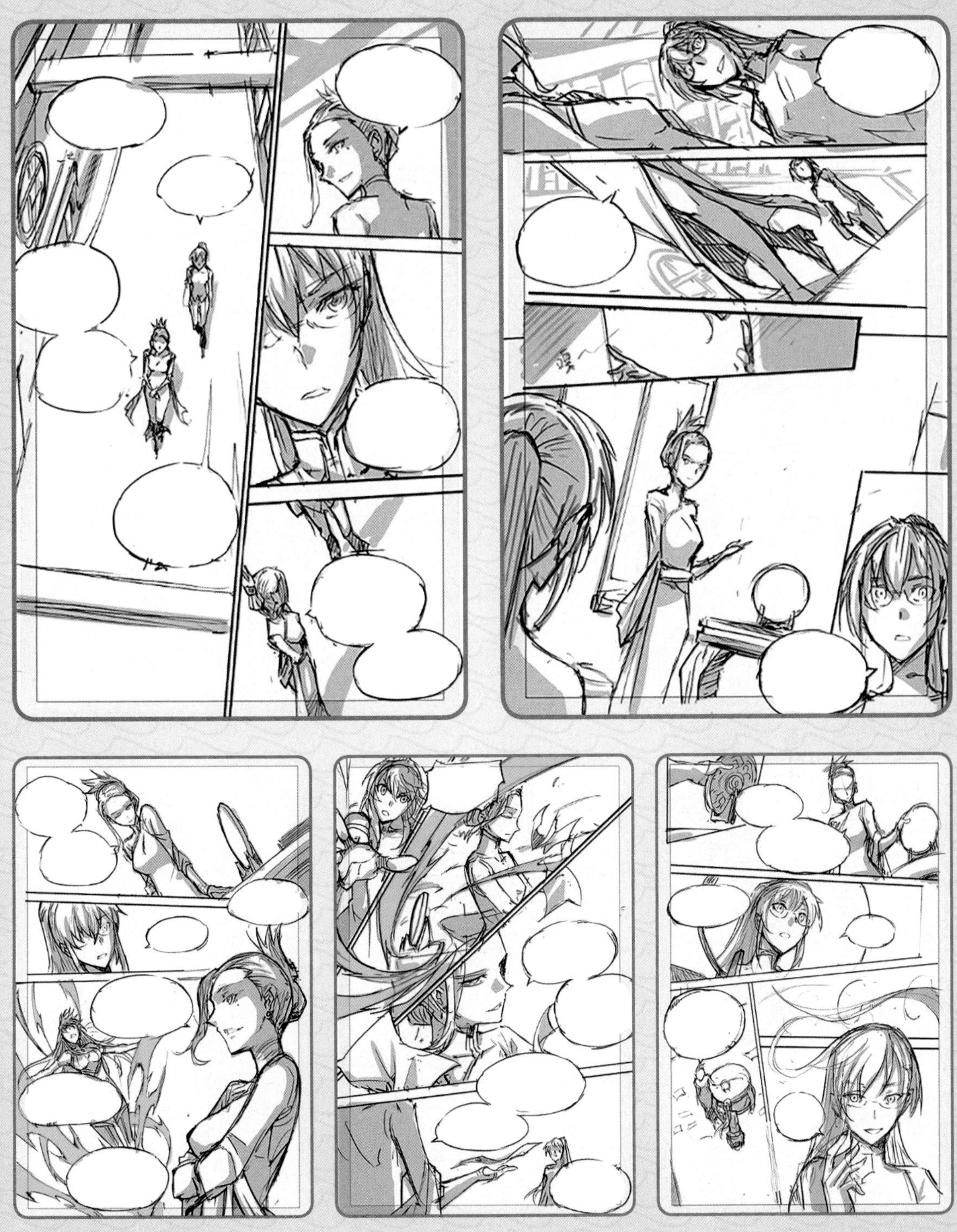

Aero #12 Layouts

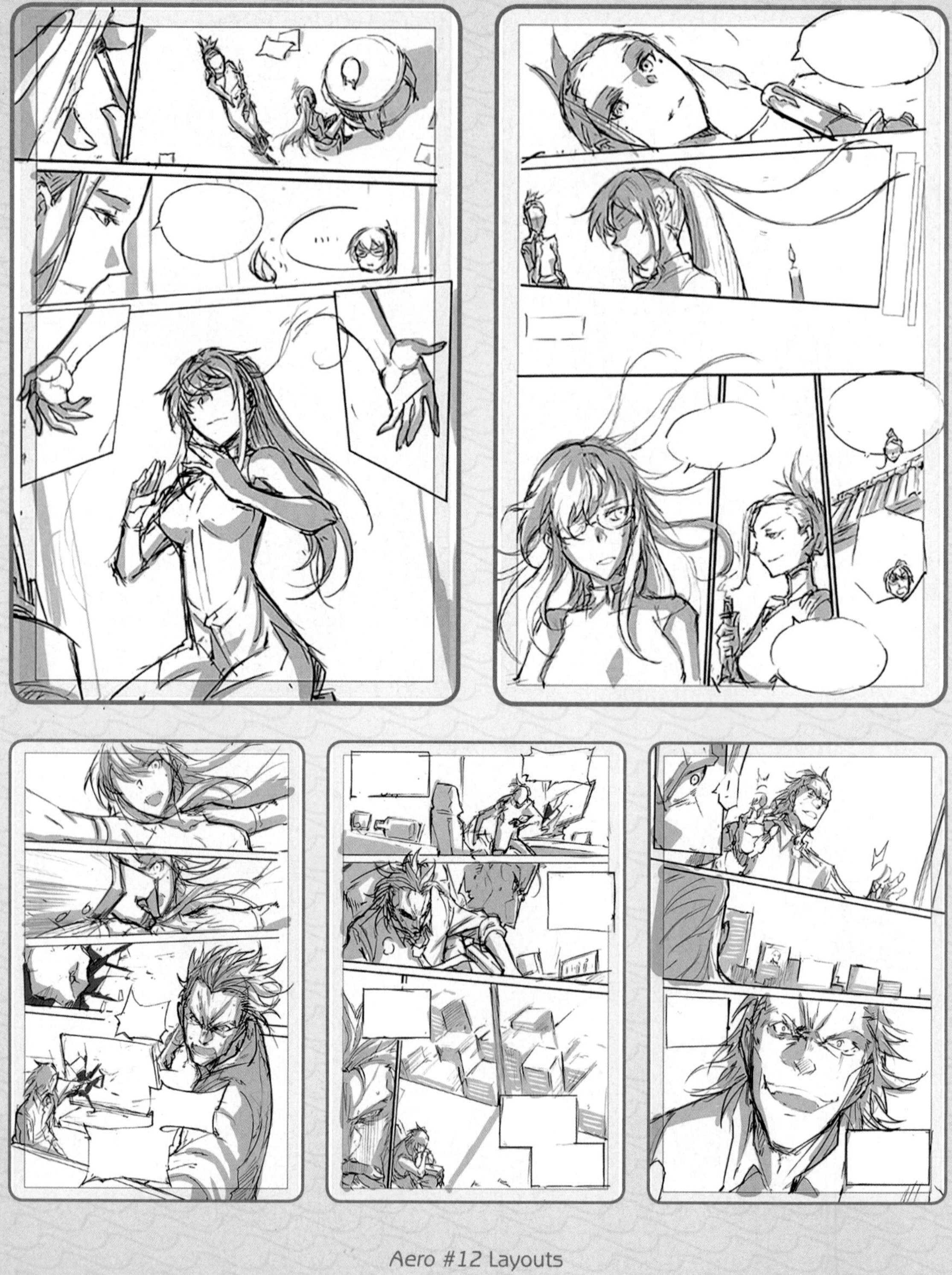

Aero #12 Layouts